The Principle of Protestantism

LANCASTER SERIES ON THE MERCERSBURG THEOLOGY

PHILIP SCHAFF

# The
# Principle of Protestantism

*Translated from the German*
*by* John W. Nevin, 1845

Bard Thompson and
George H. Bricker, *Editors*
LANCASTER SERIES ON THE MERCERSBURG THEOLOGY
VOLUME 1

United Church Press
Philadelphia          Boston

Library of Congress Catalog Card Number 64-14141

# Editors' Preface

THE SYNOD OF THE GERMAN REFORMED CHURCH convened at Allentown, Pennsylvania on October 17, 1844. At the opening of that solemn gathering, the sermon was delivered by the retiring president of the Synod,[1] Joseph F. Berg, distinguished minister of the Race Street Church in Philadelphia, who was widely celebrated as one of the grandees of the denomination. On October 25, having finished its routine business, the Synod retired directly to Reading—spiritual capital of this German Zion—to witness the inaugural ceremonies of Philip Schaff (Schaf),[2] who had been brought over from Germany in his twenty-fifth year, as professor of biblical literature and ecclesiastical history[3] in the Theological Seminary[4] at Mercersburg, Pennsylvania. Faultlessly turned out in black, the small, but robust, young scholar delivered a long German lecture entitled *Das Princip des Protestantismus*.

Even the most modest member of the Synod could readily decipher that the glorious Berg and the untried Schaff were scarcely striking the same themes. The differences between them were

---

[1] Editors' notes are numbered and appear on pages 235-253.

sparks in the fading autumn, which would ignite a major controversy in the year 1845.

In most respects the sermon by Berg[5] was a perfect reflection of
current denominational opinion. At the outset he struck a re-
sponsive chord by issuing an appeal for a new sense of Reformed
confessionalism:

> Among the difficulties which have had a tendency to retard the pros-
> perity of the German Reformed Church in this country, *the absence
> of a proper denominational spirit,* is worthy of notice. Party spirit
> is generally an evil. Sectarian bigotry is always a curse; like mildew
> it blasts the fruit of the field and converts food into poison. We are
> not pleading its cause when we contend that a certain *esprit du
> corps* [sic] is essential to our prosperity as a branch of the Christian
> Church. The partiality which we could wish to see more extensively
> cherished for the doctrines, order, and discipline of the Reformed
> Church is perfectly consistent with the largest charity and goodwill
> toward all who love the Lord Jesus Christ. We have no desire to
> add another stone to the walls which sectarian prejudice has built
> up between the portions of the Christian household. Heaven knows
> they are high enough and strong enough already; but we do wish to
> see our people entirely weaned from the propensity to forsake the
> landmarks which the ancients have set—to abandon all the peculi-
> arities which distinguish us as a people, and to adopt in their room,
> the so-called improvements of modern times.

These words, however, were not astonishing. Nearly every
right-thinking *Reformierter* was saying the same. Preaching to the
Synod of 1841, Bernard C. Wolff recalled with obvious distaste
the bygone era, when merger seemed to be the only solution to
the weakness of the German Reformed Church. But no longer!
The German Zion had come into prosperity—75,000 souls, 600
congregations (some noted to be "wealthy"), 184 ministers,[6] and
a fixture of learning at Mercersburg. "The time for . . . union
with any other denomination," said Wolff, "has forever passed
away." It is now imperative to regain our self-consciousness as a
denomination and exalt "all that distinguishes it from other denominations." The constitution of the Reformed Church, Wolff
concluded, is perfect in every part. "It wants no further Reformation."[7]

The new spirit acquired immediate and universal acclaim. It intoxicated John Williamson Nevin,[8] the wisp of a Scotch-Irishman who had recently been called to the chair of theology at Mercersburg, so that even he spoke teutonically: "The German Church must rise within herself. . . . She must adhere to her own standards. She must have her own ministry. . . . She should continue to cherish still her national sympathies and the hallowed associations of her own faith and worship."[9] At the Synod of 1844, J. H. A. Bomberger exclaimed to his brethren, "May we love our Zion more and more. Her peculiarities are not our own to throw away."[10]

Meanwhile, the Maryland Classis, by some doubtful dating, had launched a campaign to celebrate the centenary of the German Reformed Church in the United States. A centenary "Circular" was sanctioned by the Synod of 1840[11] and received wide distribution. Having paid its respects to "Zwinglius . . . that great Reformer of blessed memory" who gave the church her "distinctive features," the Circular proceeded to set the tone of the celebration:

Let the Centenary be an occasion for rallying around the standards of the church. . . . Let the idea be forever silenced that the interests of religion require the German Reformed Church in this country to merge itself in other denominations, or to lay aside its distinctive character as something obsolete.[12]

The curious thing about this "landmarkism" was that no one could quite spy the ancient landmarks. Except for Nevin, the *Ausländer,* there were few indeed who spoke or wrote about the Heidelberg Cathechism[13]; and the old Palatinate Liturgy (1563) was almost totally obscure to a church now devoted to free worship, extempore prayer, and a Zwinglian Eucharist[14] which was celebrated but twice a year.[15] The real issue of the day was how to deal responsibly with the revivalism which had increasingly shaped the life of the denomination since 1828.[16] This "landmarkism" was some sort of vague procedure to guide the church safely through the extremes of rationalistic formalism, on the one hand, and Finneyite revivalism, on the other hand—between "no-fire" and "wild-fire," as Bomberger said[17]—to that elusive ideal of a "true revival" in which nearly everyone believed.[18] The best that Berg could do with the "landmarks" was to argue (unconvincingly) that the old Palatinate Church Order really sanctioned certain features of New Measures revivalism:

> We are disposed to regard our own age as far transcending others in knowledge, zeal, and devotion to the cause of Christ, and to a certain extent it may be true, although very frequently more credit is claimed for the present century than belongs to it, or perhaps we should say, less account is made of the knowledge and piety of our ancestors than should be accorded to them. It is owing to this fact, for instance, that prayer meetings have been stigmatized as *New Measures;* just as if the men of God in former centuries had never known that there were special promises in God's word, addressed to those who agree as touching the things they shall ask. . . .
>
> The Book of Discipline of the Church of the Palatinate[19] made ample provision, in the sixteenth century, for the regular enjoyment of these means of grace, and it is worthy of remark that the large proportion of the original founders of the Reformed Church in America were emigrants from the Palatinate. By the regulations of their discipline, it was provided that, in addition to at least two services on the Sabbath, there should be preaching in every town and village, and in every country church, twice during the week. The evenings of Wednesday and Friday were to be spent in the house of God; and besides this, there was a short meeting for prayer every morning and evening, which was not to be protracted over half an hour. So far, then, from meetings during the week and special appointments for prayer deserving the epithet of innovations, they are as old as the Reformation.
>
> *They* are the innovators who have forsaken the good old way established by our fathers, and who, instead of seeking the things which make for the edification of the Body of Christ, are anxious to shut out every ray of light by which the carnal security of a sleeping church might be disturbed. *These* are the *New Measures men,* who teach customs which are unlawful!

If the Reformation itself was a landmark, Berg was not quite aware of it. Church history, as he saw it, was chiefly useful to support the idea of a perfect and changeless Reformed orthodoxy, which, being entirely untainted by the gross heresy of Romanism, traces back through the Medieval Waldensians, to apostolic times. Berg had already made it plain that "pure and undefiled religion is as unchanging as the holiness of God from which it emanates." And now he ventured to declare:

> When we say that a certain degree of denominational spirit is essential to our prosperity as a church, we would not encourage either bigotry or pharisaism, but we would foster a spirit of inquiry respecting the ancient doctrine, discipline, and history of the Reformed Church. If we had time, we might present no mean array of historical facts, establishing a claim to apostolic order and succession, if you will, which is based upon a foundation of acknowledged truth; but I must content myself with remarking that from the latter half of the second century to the present day, Christian churches have been in existence in the South of France and adjacent countries, and that from the Waldensian records which have been preserved, it is evident that the doctrines of the Reformation in their purity and strength were maintained from the days of the apostles until the age of Luther. It is to be regretted that the historical data of the period, extending from the fourth to the eleventh century are so few and meager, and yet even during these ages, we have the names and something of the history of apostolical men whom God raised up to feed the remnant of his scattered people.
>
> From the twelfth century, however, down to the present day, there is none of this uncertainty. The doctrine and discipline of Waldensian churches are contained in Mss. which have been preserved by Perrin[20] and printed in his history, and which date A.D. 1120, four hundred years prior to the great Reformation in Germany and Switzerland. To us, as a church, these documents are full of interest. The fathers of the Church of the Palatinate were Waldensian brethren, and the Church of the Palatinate is the mother of the Reformed interest in America. It is an error, though an exceedingly popular one, to regard Zwingli as the founder of the German Reformed Church. We are willing to pay all due respect to the memory of the great Reformer, who was an honored instrument in promoting a revival of Christianity in Switzerland—but we should be very sorry to expose our cause to the sneers of those who might justly point at us the finger of scorn, if we were to confess that our church is but of yesterday.
>
> When we can show that a constant and decided protest was maintained against the idolatry and strong delusions of both pagan and papal Rome, from the second to the twelfth century—when in every

century the names of faithful witnesses for God's truth are re-
corded, who in the midst of abounding heresy and iniquity lifted
up their voice like a trumpet and warned their fellowmen against
the errors of the times; when we trace the connection between the
churches of Lyons, Vienne, and others, which were scattered and
peeled in the second century by a bitter persecution, and the Waldensian brethren, and prove from unequivocal testimony the intimate relation between the Waldensian churches and the Church of
the Palatinate from which our fathers came to this country, we
have certainly presented no mean argument in favor of the apostolicity of the Reformed Church; for it must be remembered that
Irenaeus, who was bishop or pastor of the churches of Vienne and
Lyons, A.D. 177, was the disciple of Polycarp, bishop of the Church
of Smyrna, who suffered martyrdom, A.D. 160, and who is universally acknowledged to have been the contemporary and disciple of
the apostle John.

This is not a fanciful chain; no rope of sand. It will bear examining, and we believe that the Protestant churches have not done
justice to the cause of truth in overlooking this argument for apostolicity. The records of the Waldenses, moreover, present no trace
of diocesan episcopacy. Their Confession of Faith and Book [of]
Discipline, the Mss. copies of which bear the date, A.D. 1120 (though
they did not originate then, for the Christians of that age declared
that the doctrines which they contained, had been handed down in
their churches from time immemorial), contain not the slightest
allusion to any prelatical organization—but on the contrary, they
record three facts which to us as Presbyterians are of special interest:
the first is, that their churches were governed by elders chosen from
among the people; the second, that their ministers were all *ex officio*
equal; and the third, that they were accustomed to meet in an an-
nual synod.

These are great principles, and they settle important points.
The Waldenses were not Episcopalians; their government was not
diocesan, but presbyterian—it was not prelatical, for they insisted
on the parity of the ministry—neither was it congregational or independent, as their churches were under the supervision of a synod.
... The sum of our argument is this: not that we have a title to exclusive apostolicity—we are willing to share it with all whose doctrine
and order are scriptural and apostolical—but if others can claim
apostolic relation and succession, so can we; if others establish the
right to trace their descent from Waldensian witnesses, much more

we; if they may refer to annals of their fathers and glory in their
sufferings for Christ's sake, we have no reason to be ashamed of our
history, nor of the patience and zeal of our Christian ancestors. If
others may animate their churches with zeal to emulate the piety
and devotion of their fathers, all these resources are as abundantly
ours. Let us use them.

Not even Berg's hypothesis that the German Reformed Church
was neo-Waldensian came as a complete surprise to the fathers and
brethren assembled at Allentown. In the *Weekly Messenger* of
1842, correspondent "W" had unveiled the whole theory in his
"Origin and History of the German Reformed Church."[21] He
observed that Polycarp—disciple of John and bishop of Smyrna
—founded a mission at Lyons and Vienne in Gaul. During the
persecution of 177, refugees from those communities fled into
the Alps, where, in the sixteenth century, their descendants established the Reformed Church. "Others," he concluded, "may
boast of their connection with Rome. We are sprung from another quarter—from the Asiastic churches of the second century."
But "W's" theory involved a time lapse of some 1,300 years,
which Wolff and Berg wisely sought to overcome by relating the
refugees from Lyons to the Medieval Waldensians, and thus to
the Reformed theologians of the sixteenth century.

Zwingli, who had been greatly celebrated by the denomination,
owing, we suppose, to the congeniality of his eucharistic theology,[22] suffered a demise under this new theory of history. Berg,
as we have heard, was prepared to dismiss him outright. Wolff
was gentler: "Zwingli is commonly reputed to have been [our]
founder. We honor his name . . . but we carry our origin to a
remoter antiquity." Indeed, Wolff ventured to suggest that Lutheranism, by comparison, was a mere novelty. "We Reformed,"
he said, "are older stock."[23]

Underlying all these variations of the new "history" was the
idea of a static orthodoxy, brought down unchanged from apostolic times, completely uncontaminated by the Roman antichrist.
Berg, who was probably no more afflicted with the virus of anti-
Catholicism than many of his contemporaries,[24] had already delivered himself of two impassioned attacks against popery: *Lectures
on Romanism* (1840), which the unreconstructed Nevin found

adequate "to drag some of the most hideous features of the Romish system into the broad light of day,"[25] and *The Great Apostacy, Identical with Papal Rome; or an Exposition of the Mystery of Iniquity and the Marks and Doom of Antichrist* (1842). As far as Berg and his colleagues were concerned, it was an impossible thought that Protestantism had any connections with Medieval Catholicism, or that the Reformation must be seen as the Catholic Church Reformed. "If we admit," he warned, "that the Church of Rome has ever been the Church of Christ, you concede the entire ground."[26]

Against the background of Berg's sermon, the inaugural address of Philip Schaff is seen to be one of the most significant events in the history of the American church. The young professor who stood in the pulpit of the Reformed Church in Reading also stood against the inadequacies of American Christianity: its unhistorical character, its provincialism, its subjectivism and sectarianism. Schaff rejected Berg's "desperate" history as preposterous.[27] The Reformation, he argued, far from being a revolutionary disjuncture with Medieval Christianity, could only be understood as "the legitimate offspring" and "greatest act" of the Catholic Church—the unfolding of "the true catholic nature itself."[28] With that astonishing piece of intelligence, he introduced his colleagues to his theory of the historical development of the church.

Schaff proceeded to discover the Reformation in its full catholic dimensions. He analyzed the one-sided subjectivism which overcame post-Reformation Protestantism and manifested itself especially in rationalism and sectarianism. And he anticipated a new synthesis—an "evangelical catholicism"—and the advent of the ecumenical age.

The point at which modern readers are most likely to blanch at Schaff's inaugural address is its involvement with Hegel's philosophy of history, the implications of which have become quite critical in our own times. We should not assume, however, that Schaff was either naïve or uncritical in his relationship to the Hegelians. On the contrary, the ideas of Hegel were subject to *exploitation* for the sake of a genuinely "modern historiography," as Schaff himself explained in considerable detail in his subsequent work *What Is Church History?*[29] There he wrote:

We wish not to endorse Hegel's theology of development without qualification; but whatever may be thought of it, one thing is certain. It has left an impression on German science that can never be effaced and has contributed more than any other influence to diffuse a clear conception of the interior organism of history, as a richer evolution continually of the idea of humanity, as well as a proper respect for its universal and objective authority in opposition to the self-sufficient and arrogant individualism of the rationalistic school. The Hegelian method requires, moreover, that the historian should resign himself without prejudice to his subject, and thus suffer it to come to a living reproduction according to the law of its own nature. Hence it stands in direct contradiction to that subjective show of reason that is never satisfied with history as it stands, but must be always correcting it after the fashion of its own private fancies.

According to the whole standpoint of this philosophy, history is a self-evolution of the absolute spirit, and hence supremely rational throughout. Such is the sense of that celebrated, though often misunderstood, dictum of Hegel: All that is rational is real, and all that is real (or absolutely existent, substantial) is rational. Here, however, we come also on the fatal rock of this speculative method of history. While rationalism had scarcely the remotest conception of a divine presence in history, and resolved everything into free human activity, the philosophy before us falls over to the opposite extreme of pantheism and fatalism. The individual is regarded as the blind organ of the world spirit; evil is held to be a necessary medium for reaching the good; and thus the idea of guilt and moral accountability is necessarily lost.

We may say indeed that the Hegelian *method* rests on the supposition of the necessity of evil as the negative condition of moral progress. For sin in the sphere of morality is made to correspond exactly with contradiction in the sphere of logic; and this last, according to Hegel's dialectics, forms the impulsive force in the moving process of all thought. It results, moreover, from the pantheistic tendency just mentioned, that no sufficient account is made of the personal and individual. Such emphasis is laid upon the general, that life in the concrete dissolves into mere abstraction, the endlessly diversified fullness of history shrinks into a few logical forms, and living personalities are transformed into ideal shadows.

All these defects are found united in the modern Tübingen school, with Dr. Baur and Dr. Strauss at its head. These, preceded by Schwegler and Zeller, have handled particularly the history of primitive Christianity in the way of pretended dialectic construction, with a spirit altogether pantheistic and ruinous.

The Hegelian philosophy then is in itself no safe conductor through the halls of church history. Its logical forms of thinking are capable of being applied in the most opposite ways. While it has led the way for many to a historical and churchly spirit, and proved an admirable help toward the overthrow of the common rationalism, and a thorough speculative understanding and defense of orthodoxy; it has served, on the other hand, when sundered from the real life revelation of Christianity, to produce itself a new form of rationalism, very different from the first, more spiritual indeed, but for this reason also more dangerous, that from an opposite direction shows the most radical hostility to all concrete and individual historical life.[30]

In the following spring (1845), both of the contestants hastened to publish expanded versions of their pronouncements. Berg's sermon appeared under the improbable title *The Old Paths, or, A Sketch of the Order and Discipline of the Reformed Church Before the Reformation, as Maintained by the Waldenses Prior to That Epoch, and by the Church of the Palatinate in the 16th Century*. Schaff's inaugural address became a book of 194 pages, called *Das Princip des Protestantismus,* which Nevin turned into passable English under the title *The Principle of Protestantism as Related to the Present State of the Church.* The gist of Schaff's theory was explosive enough; but when it became entangled with Nevin's strong affirmation of Calvin's doctrine of the Lord's Supper—a doctrine generally conceded to be irrelevant to the American scene—it provoked an "examination" into the orthodoxy of Schaff's book by the Synod of York in 1845.[31] After four days of hearings, the Synod vindicated "the book" by an impressive vote of 40 to 3, one of the three votes being Berg's. Such was the start of the enduring controversy over the Mercersburg theology, which invigorated, if it disturbed, the German Reformed Church and had lasting repercussions in American Protestantism generally.

Interpretations of *The Principle of Protestantism* are to be found in the volumes numbered 98, 105, 115, 116, and 117 in the bibliography. We have reproduced Nevin's text exactly, being content to improve the translation here and there, to correct the Latin whenever the sources were available to us, to supply descriptive (not technical) notes, and to append a bibliography. Notable changes have been enclosed in brackets.

BARD THOMPSON
GEORGE H. BRICKER

Lancaster Theological Seminary
Lancaster, Pennsylvania

# Bibliographic Notes

## BELLARMINE

Works of Robert Bellarmine (1542-1621), Jesuit theologian and controversialist, are quoted extensively in *The Principle of Protestantism*. Schaff relied mainly on Bellarmine's *Disputationes de Controversiis Christianae Fidei adversus hujus temporis haereticos* (1586-89); and the reader should be aware that many of Schaff's citations refer to the principal "books" of that comprehensive work. Other writings by Bellarmine are listed in *The Catholic Encyclopedia* (New York: Appleton, 1905), II, 411 f.

## LUTHERAN AND REFORMED CONFESSIONS

Almost invariably Schaff quoted the Lutheran confessions as they are reproduced in Carolus Augustus Hase, *Libri Symbolici Ecclesiae Evangelicae sive Concordia* (2d ed.; Leipzig: Klinkhardt, 1837). Similarly he took his citations of the Reformed and Anglican confessions from H. A. Niemeyer, *Collectio Confessionum in Ecclesiis Reformatis publicatarum* (Leipzig: Klinkhardt, 1840). The page numbers which Schaff supplied in his footnotes refer respectively to these two books.

19

## MODERN HISTORIANS AND THEOLOGIANS

In the course of this book Schaff makes innumerable references to the historians and theologians of the eighteenth and nineteenth centuries. Supplementary notes, appended by the editors, will help the reader to identify these men. Yet the notes are no substitute for Schaff's own estimate of them, which he made chiefly in two collateral works: *History of the Apostolic Church* (New York: Scribner, 1853), pp. 1-134 ("General Introduction to Church History") ; and *Germany: Its Universities, Theology, and Religion,* with sketches of Neander, Tholuck, Olshausen, Hengstenberg, Twesten, Nitzsch, Mueller, Ullmann, Rothe, Dorner, Lange, Ebrard, Wichern, and other distinguished German divines of the age (Philadelphia: Lindsay & Blakiston, 1857) .

## ABBREVIATIONS USED BY SCHAFF

*Apol. Conf.*  *Apologia Confessionis,* the Apology of the Augsburg Confession, 1530-31.

*Art. Anglic.*  *Anglicana Confessio Fidei,* the Thirty-nine Articles of the Church of England, 1563.

*Artic. Smalc.*  *Articuli Smalcaldici,* the Smalcald Articles, 1537.

*Can. Syn. Dordr.*  *Canones Synodi Dordrechtanae,* the Canons of the Synod of Dort, 1619.

*Cat. Heidelb.*  *Catechesis Palatina s. Heidelbergensis,* the Heidelberg Catechism, 1563.

*Cat. Rom.*  *Catechismus Romanus,* the Roman Catechism, 1566.

*Conc. Trid.*  *Concilium Tridentinum,* the Canons and Decrees of the Council of Trent, 1545-63.

*Conf. Aug.*  *Confessio Augustana,* the Augsburg Confession, 1530.

*Conf. Belg.*  *Confessio Belgica,* the Belgic Confession, 1561.

*Conf. Gallic.*  *Confessio Fidei Gallicana,* the Gallican Confession, 1559.

*Conf. Helv. II*  *Confessio Helvetica posterior,* the Second Helvetic Confession, 1566.

*Conf. Scot. I*  *Confessio Scoticana I,* the First Scottish Confession, 1560.

| | |
|---|---|
| *Conf. Westmonast.* | *Confessio Fidei Westmonasteriensis sive Puritanae,* the Westminster Confession of Faith, 1646. |
| *Form. Conc.* | *Formula Concordiae,* the Formula of Concord, 1580. |
| *c.* or *cap.* | chapter. |
| *can.* | canon (s), usually in reference to the Council of Trent. |
| *decr.* | *decretum,* decree, usually in reference to the Council of Trent. |
| S. or *Sess.* | *Sessio,* session, usually in reference to the Council of Trent. |

# Contents

PART ONE

*The Principle of Protestantism
in Its Original Relation
to the Roman Catholic Church, 57*

THE

# PRINCIPLE OF PROTESTANTISM

AS RELATED TO THE

# PRESENT STATE OF THE CHURCH.

BY

**PHILIP SCHAF, Ph. D.**

Professor of Church History and Biblical Literature in the
Theological Seminary of the Ger. Ref. Church.

TRANSLATED FROM THE GERMAN

WITH AN

## INTRODUCTION

By JOHN W. NEVIN, D. D.

Chambersburg, Pa.
"PUBLICATION OFFICE" OF THE GERMAN REFORMED CHURCH.
1845.

# Introduction: John W. Nevin

THE WORK, of which a translation is here presented to the English public, has grown out of the author's Inaugural Address, delivered at Reading on the 25th of October, 1844, and still retains to some extent its original form. Only a part of the Address, however, as previously prepared was spoken at that time; and it has been since considerably changed and enlarged in the way of preparation for the press. It is now accordingly more like a book than a pamphlet. If this may be supposed to require any apology, it is found in the difficulty and importance of the subject and in the anxiety of the writer to have his views with regard to it fully understood, from the first, by the Church which has called him into her service. Both the difficulties and perils of the subject indeed were felt to be greater in the progress of the work than had been anticipated at the start; and hence it became necessary that the investigation, only to do justice to itself, should be extended in the same proportion.

It is trusted that the circumstances which have led to the publication will exonerate the author, in the view of all reasonable persons, from the charge of any improper presumption in venturing so soon before the American public with the discussion of so momentous a theme. He has himself felt sensibly the delicacy of his position in this respect; and would have been glad in the end to have kept back the work entirely, if circumstances had permitted, until he might have become more fully acquainted with the relations of the church in this country, that so no room might have been left for the semblance of impropriety even in his making them the subject of public remark. But the case has been one which he had no power, properly speaking, to control. His inauguration made it necessary that he should deliver an address; and he felt it to be due to the solemnity of the occasion that he should select a theme of central interest, belonging to the life of the age, and suited to reveal his own general position with regard to the church. The theme, as already mentioned, has controlled the character of the discussion. The publication of the whole in its present form has been in obedience simply to the law by which in the nature of the case every such address is required to appear also in print. The work besides has been prepared primarily and immediately for the use of the German Reformed Church in this country, and with an eye mainly upon the German community in general. As now translated, moreover, it is still a work intended directly of course for the German Church so far as this has become English; though it is expected that it will command in this form a still wider interest. In any view, however, the responsibility of the translation belongs not to the author.

In the circumstances described, it is not strange certainly that the work should be pervaded with a true transatlantic German tone from beginning to end. I have endeavored indeed to make the translation run smooth and free in English, so far as the mere language is concerned. But the method and argument and thought will be found to a great extent invincibly German still. How could it in fact be otherwise? The writer's entire nature and constitution are German. His whole *Entwickelung*[1] besides has proceeded from the first in the element of German thought and feeling, under the active power of a thoroughly German education, up to the moment, when without all previous expectation on his own part, he found himself as by a divine voice constrained to quit

Berlin for Mercersburg. In such a case, who would expect him to appear here in any different character? He is entitled to indulgence at least, as not yet having had time to become fully American.

But we may go further and say that no such renunciation of the German order of thinking, if it were even possible in such a case, would be either desirable or proper. He had no reason certainly to anticipate that, in coming to this country, he would be required to divest himself of his old life and become absolutely reconstructed, as a preliminary condition to all right activity in his new sphere. And the Church never intended certainly to insist on any such conditions. Why call a professor from Germany, if all that is German in the man is to be left behind, or as soon as possible forgotten? Is he to receive all from those to whom he comes and bring to them nothing of his own? Must he denationalize himself, lay aside his own nationality as barbarous and false; and not rather seek to make it available, as far as it may have value, for the improvement of the new life which has received him into its bosom? These questions it might seem hardly necessary to ask. And yet it is possible that some may be disposed after all to find fault with the present work as too German; just as if in the circumstances it either could have been, or should have been, in the fullest sense "Native American."*

---

* The case of Professor Schaff has been somewhat singular. No man could well be more thoroughly German in his whole constitution and character. Perhaps no one has ever come into the country with more zeal for the consecration and advancement of all properly German interests as such. And yet, strange to tell, no foreigner has ever before encountered among us, within the same time, such a tide of reproach from his own countrymen, on the charge of being untrue to the honor of his nation. Within three months from the time of his arrival upon our shores, a perfect whirlwind of excitement may be said to have been raised against him among the foreign German population, from one end of the land to the other; which has only of late begun to subside, in the way of sheer self-exhaustion; for even whirlwinds, if they are let alone, must in the end blow themselves to rest. The occasion of the uproar was a sermon preached by Professor Schaff,[2] in connection with his ordination at Elberfeld, in Prussia, just before he came to America; with reference particularly to the moral desolations of the field in which he was called to labor. In the nature of the case, the dark side of the subject was brought into view, especially as constituted by the character to some extent of the emigration itself from Germany to America; including, as it was known to do,

Some indeed seem to have the idea that whatever is characteristically German must be theologically bad. Especially the philosophy of Germany is regarded as almost universally either infidel
or absurd, and incapable altogether of being turned to any service-
able account in connection with religion. Now I would be sorry
to appear as the apologist of either German philosophy or German theology as a whole.[4] Few probably have been exercised with
more solemn fears than myself, in this very direction. One thing
however is most certain. The zeal affected by a large class of persons in this country against German thinking is not according
to knowledge. A judgment which is based, in any such case, on
the assumption that there is nothing defective or one-sided in the

---

in connection with much good, a large portion also of very different material.
Various classes in particular were described, who might be said to have left
their country for their country's good, carrying with them to the new world
dispositions and tendencies unfriendly to all right order in the state and all
true religion in the church. The sermon was afterward translated and published in this country. In this form, it fell under the eye of some, who immediately set themselves at work to turn it to mischief. A single paragraph was
retranslated into German, and sent thus to circulate through the political
German prints of the land, without the least regard to its original connections,
with such inflammatory comments as malignant passion was pleased to invent.
Various communications appeared at different points, intended to rouse, if
possible, general indignation. The author of the sermon, it was said, had
slandered and vilified the *whole* German emigration; betrayed his country;
sold himself to the service of the Native American party; and deserved properly to be tarred and feathered, or drummed out of the land, as not worthy to
enjoy its free air. The German mind is vastly excitable, and not particularly
noted for its moderation when under excitement. It was soon thrown accordingly into a perfect tempest of commotion, through the whole length and
breadth of the United States. The name of Dr. Schaff was at once made
famous in every direction. Within the course of a few weeks, as many perhaps
as thirty different papers were poured in upon him, to let him know how
heartily he was hated and cursed. Indignation meetings were held at a number
of places at which valorous speeches, and still more valorous resolutions, were
exploded in vindication of the German honor. All this on the part of a vast
body of people, not one of whom probably had ever seen the original sermon
of Professor Schaff, as published in Krummacher's *Palmblaetter;* not one in a
thousand of whom probably had ever seen the translation of it, as published
in the *Weekly Messenger*[3]*;* and of whose whole number, not one of a hundred perhaps could say when, where, or how the offense had occurred, with
which they were called to be so terribly displeased. In fact, however, the movement is to be referred to a much deeper ground. The whole occasion has
served, beyond any previous development, to reveal the true character of the
foreign German population in our country. This is reckoned to be now more

system of thought and life out of which it has itself sprung; especially if it proceed from such as show palpably that they have never been able to transcend that system in its traditional form at a single point, and who may be possibly altogether ignorant besides even of the language which includes the foreign mind they presume to charge with folly—a judgment so circumstanced, I say —can never be entitled to much respect. It is an immense mistake to assume that the Anglo-American order of religious life is all right and the German life in the same respect all wrong. Both forms of existence include qualities of the highest value, with corresponding defects and false tendencies. What is needed is a judicious union of both, in which the true and good on either

---

than a million, perhaps a million and a half strong, and is rapidly increasing every year. Beyond all doubt, it includes a large amount of virtuous and excellent character. At the same time, it has been equally certain all along that elements of an infidel, disorganizing order, have been comprehended in it to a serious extent. But no demonstration has before occurred so well suited as the one now in view, to set the matter in its true light, and to awaken apprehension in the direction here noticed. Because it has been abundantly evident to all who have been in a situation to understand the case, that the uproar which it has been contrived to create against Professor Schaff is attributable properly not to an honest zeal for the credit of the German name as such, but to a secret hostility to the religious views and principles of which he is considered a distinguished representative. At the bottom of the whole movement is to be traced distinctly the spirit of political libertinism and intolerant rationalistic fanaticism, answering too truly to a part of the sketch presented in the Elberfeld sermon, and lending it light and confirmation beyond all that could have been anticipated in the same form previously. The active part taken in the business by certain rationalist ministers serves only of course to establish this charge. The papers which have been making a noise in the case reveal their irreligious character in general with very little disguise, and the same thing may be said of the proceedings of the indignation meetings. In some instances the displays of rationalism have been carried to the point of downright blasphemy. One sheet in New York has shown itself particularly vile and abominable in this way. Altogether the movement has been carried forward in the most low and ribald style. It has however served one important purpose in the case of Professor Schaff, besides revealing more than had been revealed before of the spirit of this section of our foreign population. It has shown clearly in how little sympathy he stands with the rationalism and radicalism with which we are so unfortunately invaded from abroad. From no quarter has he been so immediately and violently repelled, as with an instinctive consciousness of irreconcilable opposition. This in the circumstances must be counted a high advantage—one of the greatest recommendations, in fact, under which a learned German divine could make his appearance in our **country.**

side shall find its proper supplement in the true and good of the
other, and one-sided extremes stand mutually corrected and re-
ciprocally restrained. Realism and idealism, practice and theory,
are both, separately taken, unsound and untrue. Their truth
holds, can hold, only in their union.

We are a practical people preeminently and are entitled to
great credit on this account. But it is in vain to expect that in
this character simply we shall be able to do our duty to the
world or to the Church of Christ. All great epochs in the world's
development, after all, owe their presence primarily to theory and
speculation. Our religious life and practice can be sound and
strong only in connection with a living, vigorous theology. But
to be thus living and vigorous, our theology must be more than
traditional. It must keep pace with the onward course of human
thought, subduing it always with renewed victory to its own
power. Not by ignoring the power of error, or fulminating upon
it blind ecclesiastical anathemas, can theology be saved from
death; but only by meeting and overcoming it in the strength of
the Lord. Now this requires, in our day, a legitimate regard in
this form to the errors of Germany in particular. For it is preposterous to suppose that in the most speculative portion of the
whole Christian world these errors stand in no connection with the
general movement of the world's mind, or that they do not *need*
to be surmounted by a fresh advance on the part of truth, as being
only the dead repetition of previously vanquished falsehood.

In immediate contact with the evil, the friends of religion in
Germany itself know the case to be different. There it is felt that
theology *must* advance so as fairly to conquer or die. *We* may not
feel the pressure of the same necessity. But this is no evidence
that we stand on higher or surer ground. In the end our theology,
to be worth anything as a science, must be carried over this limitation. It may not devolve on us possibly to achieve the work for
ourselves. We may trust rather that this precisely is the special
commission of the church in Germany itself, the land of Luther
and the glorious Reformation. Certainly at this very time the
struggle with error may be regarded as most auspicious and full
of promise. And if there be one country in the whole compass
of the church, where at this moment orthodox theology is not

dead, but full of life and spirit and power, that country is Germany. We may hope then it will be found sufficient for its own work. This however when accomplished must be viewed as a work properly for the whole Christian world; and we owe it to ourselves at least, to be willing to take advantage of it in its progress, and to employ it for the improvement of our own position, if it can be so used.

This much I have thought it proper to say on this point, merely to counteract, if possible, the poor prejudice that some may feel toward the present work, simply because of its German source and German complexion; as if all must needs be either rationalistic or transcendental, that breathes a thought in common with Hegel, or owns a feeling in sympathy with the gifted, noble Schleiermacher.

But after all, the work stands in no special need of apology in this direction. It is more likely to be met with distrust, in certain quarters, under a different view. It may seem to occupy suspicious ground with regard to the church question. With the argument for Protestantism, in the first part, in its positive, separate character, even the most rigid in their zeal for this interest can hardly fail to be generally satisfied. But some may not like the relations in which it is made to stand, nor the consequences it is made to involve. And then they are still less likely of course to be pleased with the formal development of these consequences in the part that follows. They may think that too much is surrendered in the controversy with Oxford and Rome. They may not be willing to endure that the nakedness of Protestantism, in its modern position, should be so freely exposed. It is always difficult in the case of earnest, violent controversy to have an eye for anything less than extremes. All must be right in one direction, and all must be wrong in the other; although in fact, no great controversy in the church is ever precisely of this character. So at this time, the excitement which prevails on the subject of popery and Puseyism, and for which undoubtedly there is good reason, must naturally render it hard for many to exercise any moderate judgment upon questions that lie in this direction. In such circumstances then particularly, there is some danger that this book may not escape censure in the view already mentioned.

This much however is certain at the same time. The work will not be regarded by Puseyites and papists as a plea in their favor. Rather, if I am not much mistaken, it will be felt by them, so far as it may come under their observation, to be one of the most weighty and effective arguments they have yet been called to encounter in this country in opposition to their cause. For it is not to be disguised that a great deal of the war which is now carried on in this direction is as little adapted to make any impression on the enemy as a battery of popguns in continual fire. Instead of being alarmed or troubled on its account, the enemy is no doubt pleased with it at heart. Nothing can be more vain than to imagine that a blind and indiscriminate warfare here can lead to any true and lasting advantage. Not with circumstances and accidents simply must the controversy grapple, but with principles in their inmost life, to reach any result. The present argument accordingly, in throwing itself back upon the true principle of Protestantism, with a full acknowledgment of the difficulties that surround it, while proper pains are taken to put them out of the way, may be said to occupy the only ground on which any effectual stand can be made against the claims of Rome.

To contend successfully with any error, it is all-important that we should understand properly and acknowledge fairly the truth in which it finds its life. The polemic, who assails such a system as popery or Puseyism with the assumption that its pretensions are built upon sheer wind, shows himself utterly unfit for his work and must necessarily betray more or less the cause he has undertaken to defend. All error of this sort involves truth, apprehended in a one-sided and extreme way, with the sacrifice of truth in the opposite direction. Hence a purely negative opposition to it, bent simply on the destruction of the system as a whole, must itself also become inevitably one-sided and false, and can only serve so far to justify and sustain what it labors to overthrow. Romanism includes generally some vast truth in every one of its vast errors; and no one is prepared to make war upon the error, who has not felt, in his inmost soul, the authority of its imprisoned truth, and who is not concerned to rescue and save this, while the prison itself is torn to the ground.

In this view, no respect is due to an infidel or godless zeal, when it may happen to be turned in this direction; and that must be counted always a spurious religious zeal, which can suffer itself to be drawn into communion with such an irreligious element simply because for the moment it has become excited against Rome. It is greatly to be feared that the spirit into which some are betrayed in this way is unhallowed and profane, even where they take to themselves the credit of the most active zeal for the glory of God. So with regard to Puseyism. Nothing can well be more shallow than the convenient imagination that the system is simply a religious monstrosity, engrafted on the body of the church from without, and calling only for a wholesale amputation to effect a cure. Such a supposition is contradicted, to every intelligent mind, by the history of the system itself. No new phase of religion could so spread and prevail as this has done, within so short a period of time, if it did not embody in itself, along with all its errors, the moving force of some mighty truth, whose rights needed to be asserted, and the want of which had come to be felt in the living consciousness of the church, vastly further than it was clearly understood. If the evils against which the system protests were purely imaginary, it could never have acquired so solid a character itself, as it has done in fact. Most assuredly the case is one that calls for something more than a merely negative and destructive opposition. Only by acknowledging and honoring that which is true and good in the movement is it possible to come to any right issue with it so far as it is false. The truth which it includes must be reconciled with the truth it rejects, in a position more advanced than its own, before it can be said to be fairly overcome.

In this view, it is not saying too much to affirm that a large part of the controversy directed against it thus far has been of very little force. It has been too blind and undiscriminating, as one-sidedly false in its own direction at times, as the error it has opposed in the other. Our newspapers and reviews and pamphlets and books show too often that the question is only half understood by those who undertake to settle its merits. While they valiantly defend the citadel of Protestantism at one point, they leave it miserably exposed to the attacks of its enemies at another. With many it might seem to be the easiest thing in the world to demolish the pretensions of this High Church system. Its theory of the church is taken to be a sheer figment; its idea of the sacraments, a baseless absurdity; its reverence for forms, a senseless superstition. The possibility of going wrong in the opposite direction is not apprehended at all. Such a posture however, with regard to the subject, is itself *prima facie* evidence that those who occupy it are not competent to do justice to the case.

Some have told us that the controversy comes simply to this: whether we shall have a religion of forms or a religion of the spirit. They claim accordingly to be the friends of inward, living, practical piety, and charge upon the opposite tendency a secret disaffection to this great interest, as exalting the letter above the life, and substituting for the fact its mere sign. But the issue in this form is false. Religion is the union of soul and body, spirit and matter. To resolve it into naked forms is indeed to part with the substance for mere show; but it is just as vain to think of holding the substance, where forms are treated with contempt. The man who takes the issue in the way now stated shows himself to be disqualified for the controversy. Because it is not a question with him then simply as to the quality or quantity of forms, whence they shall come and how far they shall reach; but a question as to the right that forms have to be included in the idea of religion at all; in the case of which he shows clearly that his own conception of the true nature of religion is one-sided and false. He will be a spiritualist only, and not a formalist. Why not then become at once a Quaker? In its own nature, the issue is false. No such alternative as it supposes has any place in the idea of religion. It separates what God has joined together. Not soul *or* body, but soul *and* body, is the formula that represents humanity, as truly after its union with Christ as before. The issue is false, monstrously false; and the champion who takes ground upon it, is not fit to be entrusted with the interests of truth, in opposition to Oxford or in any other direction.

Again we are told the controversy has for its object the question whether salvation be an individual concern or something that comes wholly by the church—the fruit of a private, separate transaction of the subject with God's word and Spirit, or the product of a more comprehensive, inexplicable force, residing in

the mystical body of Christ, and showing itself particularly in
and through the sacraments. But here again the issue is false and
those who plant themselves upon it only betray their own incom-
petency for intermeddling with the subject. Ecclesiasticism, as
held by Rome and also by Oxford, is indeed a terrible error; but it
does not follow that the mere negation of ecclesiasticism is the
truth. The error itself includes a truth—a vast, great, precious,
glorious truth—and if our negation annihilate this along with
the error, it has become itself an error as false as the other. The
position that religion is an individual interest, a strictly personal
concern, a question between a man singly and his Maker, is one
which it would be treason to the gospel to reject. He that believeth shall be saved; he that believeth not shall be damned. Every
tree that beareth not good fruit is hewn down and cast into the
fire. Here is a vast, vital truth. But if it be so held as to exclude
the dependence of the individual spiritual life on the general
life of the church, it becomes necessarily one-sided and false. Individualism without the church is as little to be trusted as ecclesiasticism without individual experience. Both separately taken
are false, or the truth only in a one-sided way; and the falsehood, sooner or later, must make itself practically felt. The full
truth is the union of the two. Every issue then which puts them
apart must be counted an untrue issue; and as before said, the
very fact that any man should make it, in contending with popery
or Puseyism, proves him unfit for the task he has been pleased
to assume.

So again when the controversy is made to lie between the liberty
of private judgment and the authority of the church, the issue
is equally false. And the matter is not mended at all, but only
made worse, when the alternative is exhibited as holding between the Bible and the church. It is indeed an abominable
usurpation, when the church claims to be the source of truth
for the single Christian separately from the Bible, or the absolutely infallible interpreter of the sense of the Bible itself, and
so requires him to yield his judgment blindly to her authority
and tradition. But it is a presumption equally abominable for a
single individual to cast off all respect for church authority and
church life, and pretend to draw his faith immediately from the

Bible, only and wholly through the narrow pipestem of his own
private judgment. No one does so in fact.

Our most bald, abstract sects even, show themselves here as
much under authority almost as papists themselves. Where shall
we find a greater traditionist than the Scottish Seceder?[5] Who less
free ordinarily in the exercise of what he calls his private judgment, upon the sense of scripture? His ecclesiastico-theological
system, as handed down by his church, or fraction of a church,
sways his interpretation at every point. Such a thing as an absolutely abstract private judgment we meet with in no denomination, party, or sect. But if we had it, what would it be worth?
Or so far as we find anything like an approximation to it, to what
honor or confidence is it entitled? For at the last, what sort of
comparison can there be between the naked judgment of a single
individual and the general voice of the church? The argument
from prescription here is one which no spiritually sane mind can
despise. We employ it with overwhelming force against the anti-
Trinitarian, the antipedobaptist, the antisacramental Quaker, and
the whole host of fanatical upstarts who modestly undertake to
make the world believe that the City of God has been buried for
eighteen centuries like Herculaneum and Pompeii, and is now
to be dug out of the Scriptures for the first time by such as themselves. Even the theories of a learned man are deservedly borne
down by the weight of this authority; clothed in such a form, for
instance, as it carries in opposition to the fancy of Professor Bush,[6]
when he tries to persuade us that the resurrection of believers
takes place at their death. The private judgment of a Grotius,
*as such,* is a small thing as compared with the judgment of the
church.

But we are told, the issue is properly not between a Grotius or a
George Fox and the church, but between the Bible and the
church, evangelism and ecclesiasticism. As if the Bible could interpret itself, without the intervention of a human judgment,
either public or private! There is gross sophistry in the alternative, as thus presented. In any true statement of the case, neither
the judgment of the church nor that of the individual is to be
exhibited as a professedly separate *source* of truth. Romanism and
nationalism, in this view, fall here in opposite directions under

the same condemnation. The only fair alternative lies between the Bible as apprehended by the church, and the same Bible as apprehended by an individual, or by some party or sect to which he may happen to belong. Shall the church interpret the Bible for the single believer, or shall he interpret it for himself? The question comes at last to this. But the issue in such a form is false. Neither side of the alternative separately taken is true, and yet neither is absolutely untrue. The church may err; and every man is bound to exercise his own reason in things pertaining to his salvation. But still the church is the pillar and ground of the truth. The Bible lives and has power as God's word, only in and by the church, the Body of Christ.

It is most certain then that private judgment, extrinsical to all felt communion with the life of the church, as a continuation through all centuries of the life of Jesus Christ, is entitled to no confidence whatever. Private judgment, or if anyone please, the use of the Bible in this form, is a sacred right, to be parted with for no price by those whom the truth has made free; but it can hold only in the element of true church authority. In proportion precisely as the sense of that general life, which has constituted the unity of the church from the beginning, is found to be wanting in any individual; in proportion precisely as it is possible for him to abjure all respect for the organic whole, in virtue of which only he can have any life as a part; in proportion precisely as he is ruled by the feeling that the Bible is to be interpreted as a revelation just fallen from heaven, without any regard to the development of its contents, the stream of its living waters, as carried forward in the faith of Christendom from the beginning down to the present time—in the same proportion, I say, precisely—must such an individual, be his qualifications and resources in other respects what they may, be counted an unsafe expounder of God's word, either for himself or for others. The Bible mirrored from his mere private judgment, as thus sundered from all proper church consciousness, is likely to reveal but little of the mind of the Spirit. The issue then as made between the Bible and the church is false and sophistical; and the polemic who takes ground upon it as though it were of any real force, only shows himself again unequal to the wants of this great controversy.

The case requires a reconciliation of these unhappily divided interests, in such form that the truth which each includes may be saved in the union of both. This of course is not to be reached by yielding to Rome. The very nature of the papacy is that it sacrifices the rights of the individual wholly to the authority of the church, which so far at the same time becomes itself false and dead. Puseyism is but a return toward the same error. We need not this. But as little may we feel ourselves abidingly satisfied with the mere contrary. What is to be reached after, as the true normal form of the Christian life, is such an inward marriage of the two general tendencies, as shall be sufficient to make them one. There is no reason at all why zeal for experimental godliness and zeal for the idea of the church should not go hand in hand together. The single case of Paul, to say nothing of Augustine and Anselm and Luther and many others that might be named, may furnish full proof to the contrary. Who more zealous for all that is comprehended in the personal piety and personal freedom of the single believer? And yet who more carried away and ruled continually by the idea of the church, as the Body of Christ, and the organic whole in which and by which alone all individual Christian vitality must be upheld and carried forward to its proper perfection? This is the only form in which religion can deserve to be considered complete. This is to be regarded as the true consummation of the church, in which the life of the whole body and the life of all its parts may be expected to proceed harmoniously and vigorously together. Toward the full and final accomplishment of this glorious result, should be directed the prayers and efforts of all who love the prosperity of Zion or seek the salvation of the world.

Or will it be seriously pretended by any competent to discern the signs of the time that the state of the church at present involves no necessity for looking or reaching after any such new position? Is all that is wanted for the great ends of the gospel, that is, for the actualization in full of the idea of the kingdom of God in the world, the simple annihilation of all the elements and tendencies embraced in the objective church system as such, and the undisputed supremacy of the opposite subjective interest, in the form in which it now prevails in the Protestant world? Can we say of

Protestantism that, as it now stands, it forms the true, complete, symmetrical, and ultimate state of Christianity; or that this requires at most, only that its existing tendencies should be carried out still further in the same direction? They must be dull of vision truly, who can impose upon themselves so far as this. Vast evils, and tendencies that must, if carried out, inevitably defeat the whole movement, are palpably incorporated at this time with its very constitution. These must be acknowledged and put away before it can be expected to prevail.

Taking the present state of Protestantism as ultimate and complete, we must despair of its being able to stand against its enemies. Our faith in its divine mission can be intelligent, only as we confidently trust that it will yet in due time surmount its own present position, and stand forth redeemed, and disenthralled from the evils that now oppress it, to complete the Reformation so auspiciously begun in the sixteenth century. The necessity of some such new order of things is coming to be more and more sensibly felt, and may we not trust that the way for it is fast being prepared—though to our narrow view, chaotically still and without light—in the everdeepening and extending agitation with which men's minds are beginning to be moved, as it might seem all the world over, in this direction. The feeling that we are on the eve of some vast religious revolution, by which a new epoch shall be constituted in the development of the history of the church as a whole, has taken strong possession of many of the first minds in Europe. And it is quite evident that in this country, too, a sentiment of the same general sort is steadily gaining ground. Men feel that they have no right to be satisfied with the actual state of the church, and they are not satisfied with it in fact.

That there is reason in these circumstances for looking with apprehension toward popery, particularly in these United States, is not to be doubted. Both the author and the translator of the present work, participate in this apprehension, to a greater extent probably than most of those who may be ready to exclaim against it as treasonable to the Protestant interest. The danger however is of a much deeper kind than is often imagined. It lies principally in the fact that we have come to such a crisis in the history of religion as has just been mentioned; involving for the moment at

least a reaction in the direction of Rome, and making it necessary
for the Protestant interest to advance to a new position in order
to save itself; while at the same time those who stand forth in its
defense show themselves too generally ignorant of the true posture
of the case, and not unfrequently by their blind misguided zeal
only help on in fact the cause they oppose. Meantime Romanism,
with an instinctive sense of the importance and critical opportunity of the time, is putting forth vast policy and immense effort for the purpose of securing the land. The system is growing
rapidly. It is beginning to assume a bold and confident tone. All
its works are on a large scale and all its enterprises are crowned
with success. No religious body is advancing at the same rate.
Then it is a united, well-organized phalanx, from one end of the
land to the other. Protestantism, alas, is a divided interest.

Most assuredly the danger that threatens us on the side of
popery is real and great. But for this very reason it is not to be
turned aside by superficial declamation, hard names, or blind
opprobrious epithets; especially if with all this no corresponding
zeal be shown to build up and clothe with strength the positive
life of Protestantism itself. Still we will hope that the end of all
these things is destined to be different from what might seem to
be their tendency at this time. It belongs to the crisis of the age
that, along with this new impulse imparted to popery in the way
of life, the same system is itself made to tremble at other points
with infirmities and disorders that threaten its very existence. All
this is included in the chaotic struggle by which the way is to be
opened for that new epoch which seems to be at hand; and which,
it may be with good assurance expected, will be, not a retrogression of the church to papal bondage, but an advance by the grace
of God to the true standpoint of Protestant Catholicism.

The present state of Protestantism is only interimistic. It can
save itself only by passing beyond itself. In this country particularly, our sect system is an evil that may be said to prey upon
the very vitals of the church. The evil itself however is but the index of a false element, incorporated with the life of Protestantism
itself. The case then is not to be remedied by any merely external change. We are not called to a crusade against sects as they
stand, as though by storming them to the ground we could do for

Christianity all that is needed in this direction. Only as the sect principle can be reached and cured in the inward habit of the church, may any such revolution (in connection with the openings and orderings of God's providence) be expected to take place, as the existing crisis demands. Not by might, nor by power, but by my Spirit, saith the Lord. We are not to run before God, nor to take his work rashly and violently into our own hands. All true redemption and salvation, in the case of the church, must come in the way of historical development, self-mediated under God, and in a certain sense self-produced. Still it may not be said that on this account we are at liberty to sit absolutely still, inwardly as well as outwardly, passively content with the present, in the midst of the onward flow of the counsels of the Almighty.

If our present position be unsound, it is right that we should feel it, and lay it solemnly to heart; that we may not cling to the old superstitiously, like the papists in the age of the Reformation, when the fullness of time is come for the new. Though we may not be able to see at once how our sect leprosy is to be healed, it must be a great evil still to justify it as something compatible with good health, or to acquiesce in it patiently as merely a necessary inconvenience. What is first of all and most of all needed in the circumstances, as a preliminary to the coming of a more glorious church epoch, is that the Protestant Christian mind generally should be brought to see more and more the actual wants of the time, and thus be engaged to sigh and reach after the deliverance, which in that case might be supposed to be at hand.

Some, I know, have no faith in this idea of church progress. Rather they regard it as derogatory to the perfect character of the gospel, and false to the true unity of the Christian life. The subject is one of great importance, and very liable to be misapprehended; and as the light particularly in which it has lately been exhibited by Professor Bush in his *Anastasis*[7] or theory of the resurrection cannot be regarded perhaps as exactly the most fortunate, it seems proper to bestow upon it here some additional consideration.

The knowledge of revelation, Mr. Bush tells us, is progressive. But the progress he seems to have in his mind, may be said to be more of an outward than inward sort. The knowledge of the truth is expected to grow only by accretion, accumulating new material in an external, mechanical way. A certain number of truths are taken to be at hand for all, clear and complete from the beginning. But along with these are many dark things in the Bible, which come to be understood gradually by dint of study and helps of science, improved hermeneutical apparatus, and new external facilities and opportunities generally. The discoveries thus made are to be added from age to age to the knowledge previously collected, so that the quantity of it may be continually increased; and this is what we are to understand by the law of progress and gradual development in the sphere of religion.

Now it is certainly true that the case does include the conception of such enlargement simply from without, although it is clear that the form in which this conception is presented by Professor Bush is perilous as rationalism itself. For if all foreign science as such have a right to require that its discoveries, so far as they may seem to be related to religion, shall be allowed to assist in shaping its structure and making out the sum of its contents in a merely external, mechanical way, the independent life of Christianity may be considered gone at the same time.

But in opposition to this we say, with Schleiermacher, that Christianity is a new living creation in itself that can be enlarged properly speaking only from within, and not at all from without. Not by mechanical accumulation or accretion can it be said to grow, but only in the way of organic development. These conceptions are entirely different, and it is of the first importance that the difference should be understood and felt in the present case. The outward gain that may be secured for the interpretation of the Bible, or that may be found in the actual results of such interpretation, can become important only as it is taken up by the inward life of Christianity itself, and is made subservient to its progress in this view.

Christianity, we say, is organic. This implies, in the nature of the case, development, evolution, progress. The law of its life moreover in this form includes its whole life. It is not as though the knowledge of some truths had been absolutely complete, and so stationary from the beginning, while the knowledge of other truths has been numerically added to it from time to time. But the whole, in all its parts, is comprehended more or less in the same law; since no truth can be absolutely complete separately from the rest, though the general process may require that some should be developed to a certain point at least, as it might seem, in advance of others. In this view Christianity has an inward history, vastly more important than that which is simply outward; and all its leading doctrines have a history, too, and cannot be understood, it may be added, apart from their history. The idea of such a development does not imply of course any change in the nature of Christianity itself. It implies just the contrary. It assumes that the system is complete in its own nature from the beginning, and that the whole of it too is comprehended in the life of the church, at all points of its history. But the contents of this life need to be unfolded, theoretically and practically, in the consciousness of the church. What it includes potentially and in principle or idea, requires to be actualized or made real in humanity as a new creation in Christ Jesus. All this is something very different from such a *Fortbildung des Christenthums,* as has been commended to us by the rationalist Ammon.[8]

Christianity can never transcend itself. It can never become absolutely more than it has been from the beginning, in the person of Christ and in the truth of the gospel. It belongs to its very nature, however, that it should not remain in the person of Christ or the letter of the gospel, but pass over into the life of the church. This implies development. In its very constitution the church involves a process, which will be complete only when the "new heavens" shall reflect in full image the "new earth wherein dwelleth righteousness." And still all this will be nothing more than the full evolution of the life that was in Christ from the beginning, and the full power of which has been always present in the church, struggling through all ages toward this last glorious "manifestation of the sons of God."

I am not able to see how any intelligent person, with a distinct understanding of what is meant in the case and any tolerable knowledge of history, can refuse to admit this view at least to some extent. Can any such person seriously imagine that the consciousness of the church at the beginning of the second century, in the days of Ignatius and Polycarp, included all that properly belonged to it in the century following, or all that it reveals in the sixteenth century through the persons of Luther, Melanchthon, Calvin, and the Reformers in general? Was the new spiritual creation in Christ Jesus exhibited from the start as a finished system, clearly bounded and defined at every point; or was it not rather the power of a divine life that was expected to subdue the surrounding elements to its own law, and organize itself continuously from within? No one surely can read the masterly church history of Neander,[9] without being compelled to yield his mind in some measure to the force of this idea; and for one who has at all entered into the spirit of the work, the impression is never likely to be erased. Without this idea indeed, church history may be said to be shorn of all its interest and meaning. It is no longer entitled to the name of history, and for all practical ends must be counted the most barren and useless of all studies; while in fact in its true form, it is a river of instruction—deep, broad and full —conveying life to every other department of theology and religion. No man who rejects this idea entirely can penetrate the spirit of any of the early centuries, or do justice to the character of a single church father.

But has not the church in fact gone backward at times, instead of forward? Have not doctrines been obscured? Has not Christianity been vastly corrupted? And what shall we say of the law of progress, in view of such facts? Does the great Roman apostasy constitute part of the development of Christ's Body? Is the tenth century to be held in advance of the third?

To one who has any right sense of history, questions like these will not be particularly confounding. Assuredly those who hold the idea of historical progress, with any proper knowledge, do not conceive of it as a continuous movement, under the same form, in the same direction. They mean by it only a movement, whose general, ultimate tendency is forward and not backward; and which, though it may seem at times to be differently turned, is still found in the end steadily recovering and pursuing its original course; as a stream of water carried aside, or pressed back upon itself, by some obstruction, does but force for itself a more circuitous way, or only gather strength to burst or overflow the barrier, that so it may roll onward as before. Truth can be said to advance, only as error is surmounted and thrown to the rear. But this requires that the error should always, in the first place, make itself known and felt. A position in which the elements of a still latent error are included is of course less advanced than a position which has been gained by overcoming the same error after it has come to light; and as this can be reached only through the manifestation of the error, we may say that the intermediate stage itself in which such manifestation takes place, though it may seem to be a falling away as compared with the period before, is nevertheless also an onward movement in fact. In certain circumstances it may be absolutely necessary that false tendencies should work themselves out through a long, vast experiment of disastrous consequences, before they can be so brought home to the consciousness of the church in their root and principle, as to admit a radical cure. Whole centuries even may be comprehended in the circuit of such a process.

With this explanation then, we need not shrink from saying that the course of the church has always been onward, in periods of apostasy as well as at other times; onward in such sense that the position gained in surmounting such apostasy has never been just the same ground that was occupied before, but an actual advance upon it that could not have been made in any other way. The proposition of course holds good, only of the proper central stream in which the one life of the church is organically comprehended and carried forward; without regard to separate, particular movements that may refuse to go along with this in its general course. In this view the Middle Ages form, properly speaking, no retrogression for Christianity. They are to be regarded rather as the womb in which was formed the life of the Reformation itself. For it is perfectly unhistorical to imagine that this might have connected itself directly with the life of the fourth century, or third, or second, in the way of simple continuation in the same direction, and under the same form. Palpably the tendencies, which at last produced the papal system as a whole, were all in operation as early as the end of the second century. The Middle Ages then as the resolution of the latent mystery of iniquity, in connection with the life of the church, stood nearer the redemption that followed, not only in time, but also in constitution, than

the period that went before. The tenth century, with all its darkness, must be considered in advance of the third.

And so too, according to the view presented in the present work,
it is our privilege to believe that the course of Protestantism—
comprehending since the Reformation the main, central stream
of the history of the church—involves in the same way a true
onward movement of Christianity; although manifestly it has included from the start certain false tendencies, which are working
themselves out interimistically in great and sore evils. If it should
prove inadequate in the end to rise superior to these, it must stand
convicted of falsehood. Our faith is however that it will in due
time surmount them, and thus throw to the rear the epoch of
the sixteenth century itself, by taking a position in which the elements of such aberration shall no longer be found; which in such
case must be regarded of course as the end toward which, through
all seeming retrogression in the way of heresy and division, the
church of the Reformation has been steadily tending from the beginning.

Such a view of church progress is certainly much more full of
encouragement than any theory in which the idea is rejected. What
a depressing imagination, if only it were properly laid to heart,
is that by which the papacy is taken to have been for eight long
centuries the grave of all true Christianity; and the honor of the
Reformation is supposed to require that the whole life of the
Middle Ages should be relinquished to Rome, as part and parcel
of the great apostasy, instead of being claimed as the catholic heri-
tage of the Reformation itself. If Protestantism be not derived by
true and legitimate succession from the church life of the Middle
Ages, it will be found perfectly vain to think of connecting it
genealogically with the life of the church at any earlier point. For
if it might even be imagined possible to effect a junction—say with
the fifth century, or the fourth, or the third—by means of the
small sect of the Waldenses[10] and other such "witnesses of the
truth" (than which no dream can well be more visionary), still,
who that has the least true knowledge of history can feel that the
Reformation was in fact the continuation simply of the life of
the church as it stood in either of these centuries, secretly carried
forward to the age of Luther in any such way?

The life of the church in the fifth, fourth, and third centuries,
looks indeed toward the age of Luther; but not immediately or
directly. It looks toward it only *through* the Middle Period that
was to come between; the entire constitution of which it may be
said to have carried in its womb. If the Reformation has indeed
sprung directly from the life of the third century, it must have
been something widely different from what we find it to have
been in fact: a birth that could only have repeated, in its subsequent development, the general course of the Roman apostasy
itself, as we may see exemplified to some extent in the tendencies
of Puseyism as borrowed from this distant antiquity. That Protestantism in its true character has been something immeasurably
better, is owing altogether to the fact that it did *not* spring in the
way of direct historical continuation from the fourth century, or
the third, or the second; but strictly and fully from the more advanced life of the Middle Ages, by means of which only the way
was prepared for it to surmount, as it has done, the gigantic errors
that have been left behind.

As regards too the present state of the church, there can be no
comparison again between the two theories, that which admits
and that which rejects the idea of progress, in the same general
view. Only as we can believe that Protestantism is itself a process,
which three hundred years have not yet conducted to its issue,
and that its very diseases, monstrous as they may seem, are only
helping it onward to a triumphant resolution of its appointed
problem, does it appear possible to be intelligently satisfied with
the present posture of the great experiment.

Thus much it has been thought proper to say on this subject
of the progressive development of Christianity, as it is one which
is very liable, in certain quarters, to be misunderstood and misrepresented. The difficulty which is made with regard to it comes
partly from this, that no proper distinction is made between Christianity itself in its ideal character, and the same Christianity as
actually apprehended and realized in the life of the church; and
partly also from the fact that so far as some notion of such a distinction may prevail, the relation between the two is still con-
templated as outward and mechanical, rather than inward and
organic. In any true view of the case, however, Christianity must

be regarded as the only proper idea of humanity itself. It is not to be joined with its other modes of existence externally to make them complete, but it is to penetrate all modes of existence alike with its own life and take them up organically into its own constitution. Till this be done, humanity must remain imperfect, and the idea of Christianity cannot be said to be fully evolved in the world. And yet who will dare to say that the history of the church has not this evolution for its object, which however is only to say, in other words, that it is such a process as has now been represented.

In the case of the individual believer, something of the kind is generally admitted. His religion is expected to pervade his entire nature, not at once, but gradually and progressively, like leaven; till in the end the whole man, soul and body, shall appear transfused and transfigured with the power of it at every point. Here is a process, beginning at regeneration and ending in the resurrection; and yet at the last it cannot be said properly to include more than it has included from the first; only that which existed at first in principle merely, or potentially, in a state of involution, is fully actualized or evolved in the end in the perfect life of its subject. But such a process in the case of single Christians separately considered, can never fully represent the relation of Christianity to our nature. The life of man, in any view, is not something single and separate. To a great extent, it holds in the order and constitution of his nature as a whole. Humanity is not an aggregation merely of men, but an organic unity rather in which all men are one. And so Christianity also as the perfect conception of humanity, must take possession of it not by separate individuals simply, separately taken, but generically. It must penetrate and transform into its own image the life, the whole life of the race, as such; and not till this shall have been done, can it be said to have fulfilled its mission, or actualized its idea, or accomplished its full development in the consciousness of the world.

Thus we have in the church as a whole necessarily, the same progressive, leavenlike action of the Christian life, which we have just seen to hold in the history of the single believer. The kingdom of heaven here also is like leaven, not simply as diffusing itself extensively through the world, but in a still more important sense as transfusing itself intensively into the life of humanity itself, as an organic whole. We do not yet see the life of humanity in this view thus transfigured—just as little as we see the single saint made perfect in holiness and glory. Science and art and government and social life are by no means yet taken up organically into the living constitution of the church. How then can it be imagined that the life of the church involves in its totality no process? And does it not lie clearly in the nature of the case that this process must actualize or evolve from the idea of Christianity, age after age, what was not apprehended in the consciousness of the church before, till it shall become complete finally in the new heavens and the new earth? Only indeed as it is comprehended in this general process, can the particular process by which the salvation of the single Christian is accomplished, from the new birth to the morning of the resurrection, be carried successfully forward. He is saved in the church—the mystical body of Christ —and can become complete only as the whole is made complete of which he is a part. His resurrection accordingly, the last result of the organific power of his new nature, will be reached only in connection with the consummation of the life of the church as a whole, when, in the fullest and most glorious sense, old things shall have passed away and all things become new.

The great question of the age undoubtedly is that concerning the church. It is evidently drawing to itself all minds of the more earnest order, more and more, in all parts of the world. Where it comes to be apprehended in its true character, it can hardly fail to be of absorbing interest; nor is it possible perhaps for one who has become thus interested in it to dismiss it again from his thoughts. Its connections are found to reach in the end, through the entire range of the Christian life. Its issues are of the most momentous nature, and solemn as eternity itself. No question can be less of merely curious or speculative interest. It is in some respects just now of all practical questions decidedly the most practical. In these circumstances it calls for attention, earnest, and prayerful, and profound. At the same time the subject is clearly one of great difficulty and hazard, as we may see from the strange confusion and contradiction in which the controversy with regard to it has come already to be involved. A subject manifestly that is not to be disposed of in any way satisfactorily in such flippant wholesale style as with some might seem to be considered sufficient for the purpose.

Both the solemnity and difficulty of it have been deeply felt in the preparation of the present work. It is the fruit of painfully severe thought, baptized it is trusted in the element of prayer. Not without true spiritual conflict does it make its appearance in the world. And not without prayerful anxiety is its course followed, now that it is launched from the press, as the first fruit of the author's labors in this form, in the new hemisphere. Should the views it offers be disapproved in any direction, it is desired only that it may be in the same spirit of earnestness in which they are presented. If anyone can show them to be wrong, not by declamation or positive assertion, but with deeper and more thorough exposition of the question itself, it will be not only respectfully but thankfully received. For the theme is one that calls for light; and if the publication should only indirectly serve this end, by leading to the exhibition of some higher and better view, in which its own position shall be fairly and truly surmounted, it will be felt that it has not appeared in vain. The author however *does* deprecate all hasty and superficial judgment in which ignorance and presumption may prevail more than a heartfelt reverence for truth. Especially he protests solemnly beforehand against all false or partial statement of his views—an evil, to which from the nature of the subject and the posture of the times with regard to it, he cannot help feeling that he is particularly exposed.

JOHN WILLIAMSON NEVIN

Mercersburg, Pennsylvania
March 4, 1845

# Introduction: Philip Schaff

BRETHREN BELOVED AND HONORED IN THE LORD:

Guarded and led by the almighty hand, which rules the winds and the waves, I find myself standing at length in your midst, on the threshold of my new sphere of labor. But little more than a year ago I had not the most distant idea of ever visiting the new world, while to *you* all my very existence was unknown. You had sent two worthy representatives of your church to the mother country to secure for your theological seminary a man, whose name simply, carrying with it such a charm as it does for the friends of the gospel on both sides of the Atlantic, was sufficient to clothe the institution with new importance and credit; for whose sake alone you were led to embark in so bold and weighty a movement. In the hands of Him who so often frustrates the prayers and plans of his people in one form, to establish them contrary to their shortsighted wisdom in another, this distinguished servant of God became the medium by which you were conducted to myself. In no turn of my life have I ever held myself more passive, than in this removal to America; in none, at the same time, have I endeavored more conscientiously and steadily to surrender myself entirely to the guidance of the Lord.

Strong indeed was the temptation, I confess, to remain in the world-renowned metropolis of German science, where my academic career had just begun under favorable auspices, in the society of so many cultivated, profound, and noble minds, well-fitted to enlarge and invigorate my inexperienced powers, and under the fostering care of a pious and highly gifted monarch, who has rendered his name immortal also in the annals of *your* church, by the magnanimous interest he has shown in its welfare; there, along with the German Evangelical Church and theology, though only as one of the least in her service, to fall or conquer in the deadly war, that now rages with fire and sword in the spiritual life of the old world. But the voice of nature became dumb when the most competent judges in Germany, honored instructors and beloved friends, men long conspicuous in the religious history of the age, with strange unanimity joined in recommending me as one specially qualified for the vacant post at Mercersburg; and when your Synod subsequently, after the most earnest and mature deliberation, saluted me, as from the mouth of a single man, with the solemn call: "Come over and help us!"

And thus I stand here today with the consoling consciousness, by which all darkness is made light, that in forsaking literary connections, country, kindred, and friends, as a missionary of science, I have not pursued a road cast up by my own hands. How could I do otherwise than I have done? Israel's pillar of cloud and fire has gone before me, in clear unbroken vision, from the palaces of Berlin to the foot of the Blue Mountains; so that I almost tremble in view of the vast perspective that is made to open upon me through such foretokenings, and under an unfeigned sense of my own weakness am ready to ask misgivingly, of one greater than myself, "Who am I, Lord, that thou shouldst send me!"

Yes, I speak it plainly in your presence, when I consider the vast expectations that rest upon me, and the unmerited marks of honor which attended my reception on the 12th of August, before all service on my own part, I should be cast down utterly, were it not for the stay I find in God's encouraging word: "I will be with thy mouth, and will teach thee what thou shalt do. Fear thou not; for I am with thee; be not dismayed, for I am thy God. I will strengthen thee; yea, I will help thee, I will uphold thee with the right hand of my righteousness. Behold, I give power to the faint, and increase strength to them that have no might. Even the youths shall faint, and be weary, and the young men shall utterly fall; but they that wait upon the Lord shall renew their strength; they shall mount up with wings as eagles; they shall run and not be weary, and they shall walk and not faint."

Whether now I shall close my earthly career in the western world, or find myself called to the temporary service simply of scattering some germs that may be watered afterward and brought to perfection by more competent hands; then to return to my original home, enriched with such observation and experience touching the church, as are to be gathered from a land, mirroring like this her youthful infirmities and the fresh practical zeal of her first love, in one picture; this, I say, is a question that is not for me, nor for anyone else, at this time, to decide. God's thoughts are not our thoughts, neither are his ways our ways; and the man is to be counted happy, who by humble renunciation of his own counsels, and passive surrender of his course to the conduct of his heavenly Father, provides against painful disappointments; planting his feet on the firm ground of the actual present, and devoting his entire strength to its claims, free of all useless cares or empty dreams for the future. Now at least I am *here,* to serve your church, and in and through this the *Church Universal* of Jesus Christ.

At present no field is before me save that to which I have been called in America, and I have no ear for any call besides, cheerfully resigned to any issue that may follow. "Whether we live, we live unto the Lord," it matters not where, in the old world or in the new; "and whether we die, we die unto the Lord. Whether we live therefore or die, we are the Lord's."

In such frame of mind I proceed, according to ancient, venerable custom, before entering formally on my appointed work, to lay down in your presence, as representing here the German Reformed Church in this country, a sort of scientific religious confession, that may serve to explain distinctly the ground on which I expect to stand in your midst. I find myself at no loss, in these circumstances, in choosing my theme. On the practical relations of the service to which I am called, I have already spoken, in my ordination sermon, at another place. Here we have to do with its theoretic side; in such method however as to hold in full view at the same time the connection of this with the other interest, and the end toward which it should continually reach in the life of the church.

I may say then comprehensively that the foundation on which I stand, since by the grace of God I have come to any clear consciousness of religion and theology, is no other than the orthodox Protestant, or what in my view is the same, the Reformed Catholic faith; as it was preached loudly and powerfully by the Reformers of the sixteenth century, or rather by the Spirit of God in their persons, at once purifying the church from the springs of its primitive life, and raising it besides into a new and higher form. Upon this ancient, venerable rock accordingly, against whose front so many hostile waves have already been broken, I propose to build, with divine help, in my present vocation; making due account at the same time of the past history of our church as a medium of instruction, and having constant respect also to the special wants of our own country and our own age.

Allow me then to speak of *the Principle of Protestantism, and its relation to the present posture of the church, particularly in the United States.*

---
PART ONE
---

# The Principle of Protestantism
# in Its Original Relation
# to the Roman Catholic Church

To BE TRUE to its own idea, a *reformation* must hold its course midway, or through the deep rather, between two extremes. In opposition on the one side to *revolution,* or the radical and violent overthrow of an existing system, it must attach itself organically to what is already at hand, and grow forth thus from the trunk of history, in regular living union with its previous development. In opposition to simple *restoration,* on the other side, or a mere repetition of the old, it must produce from the womb of this the birth of something new.

Christianity was such a reformation, not simply of Judaism, but of humanity as a whole. With what gentle and loving accommodation the Savior and his apostles applied themselves to meet the general wants of the human heart, and those particularly of their own time! Toward the institutions of the old dispensation, disfigured though they were with arbitrary human additions, and toward its official ministers also, however poorly for the most part their personal character comported with their office, they exhibited all becoming respect. No iconoclastic zeal distinguished their steps; no revolutionary whirlwind gave token of their presence. Christ must *fulfill all righteousness* himself, and charged his hearers to observe and do what was commanded by those *who sat in Moses' seat.*

Paul, as he informs us himself, became to the Jew a Jew, to the Gentile a Gentile, and in one word *all things to all men,* that he might if possible gain all to Christ. John was ready to allow the gift of prophecy to Caiaphas in his character of high priest; and found no difficulty in admitting that the everlasting light of the divine *Logos* had *shined in darkness* through all ages, gradually preparing the way for its personal manifestation. And yet the watchword both of himself and his fellow apostles, openly and broadly proclaimed upon their common banner, was the Lord's declaration: "Behold, I make all things *new!*" And what was the result of their mission? In the end these humble, unlettered fishermen of Galilee caused both the Jewish and pagan systems to fall to the ground together, and turned the history of the world into a different channel altogether.

The same twofold character belongs to the vast ecclesiastico-religious movement of the sixteenth century. This, too, carries upon its standard the sacred field motto: "I am not come to destroy, but to fulfill!" And thus neither the unhistorical radical on the one hand, nor the motionless slave of the past on the other, can find in the true representatives of the Reformation either precedent or pattern.

The case requires to be surveyed under both aspects, in order that the principle of our church may be fully comprehended, and its position turned to right account for the purposes of God's kingdom.

# . 1 .

## The Retrospective Aspect of the Reformation; or Its Catholic Union with the Previous History of the Church

IN THE FIRST PLACE, we contemplate the Reformation in its strictly *historical conditions,* its *catholic union with the past.* This is a vastly important point, which thousands in our day appear to overlook entirely. They see in the 31st of October, 1517, it is true, the birthday of the Evangelical Church, and find her certificate of baptism in the ninety-five theses of Luther; but at the same time cast a deep stain upon the legitimacy of this birth itself, by separating it from all right relation to the time that went before. In this way all interest is renounced in the spiritual wealth of the Middle Ages, which however belongs to us of right as fully at least as it does to the Church of Rome. And what is worse still, the lie is given practically to the Lord's promise itself: "Lo, I am with you always, even unto the end of the world."

No work so vast as the Reformation could be the product of a single man or a single day. When Luther uttered the bold word which called it into being, the sound was at once echoed back again, as in obedience to an enchanter's wand, not only from every quarter of Germany, but from England also, and France and Italy and Spain. He gave utterance to what was already darkly present to the general consciousness of his age, and brought out into full view that which thousands before him, and in his own time, had already been struggling in various ways to reach.

Genuine Protestantism is no such sudden growth, springing up like a mushroom of the night, as the papist, and certain narrow-minded Ultra-Protestants, would fain have us believe. Its roots reach back to the day of Pentecost. In all periods of the church, in connection with the gradual progress of Romish corruption, it has had its witnesses, though not always fully conscious of their own vocation. And it was only when it had become fully prepared, in all parts of the Christian world, both negatively and positively, to stand forth in full separate, objective manifestation, that the Lord of the church in the end, from an obscure corner of Germany, called into life the herald, whose word was to solve the oppressive riddle with which all Christendom had been so long burdened—the spiritual Columbus, that should open the way into the territory, still unknown though long at hand, of evangelical freedom.

As the several departments of human life are bound together by an inward organic union, like the members of the same body; while religion in particular, which takes hold upon the entire man, in the inmost ground of his personality, must exert a modifying influence in every other direction; the case requires that we should take account of the tendencies which led the way to the Reformation in the spheres of politics and science, as well as in that of the church strictly taken.

As regards the first, it is clear that both Romanism and Protestantism rest constitutionally upon a national basis. Christianity, in its eternal and everlasting character, is raised indeed above every distinction of nation or race. It is a religion for the whole world. Still, on its first publication, it found on all sides a given historical development, a settled system of society, already at hand. This, of course, it did not seek to demolish and reconstruct, but simply to transfuse with the power of its own divine life. In this way it became possible for the old order of existence to break into view again, with all its characteristic faults and virtues in the bosom of the church itself, reflecting the Christian religion under its own peculiar image.

Where previously the eagle of the war god spread forth his powerful talons, and the earnest, manly spirit of pagan Rome was enabled to organize and hold together, by the force of one gigantic and yet minutely specific system of law, the entire world lying submissive at her feet; there, now, a new empire appeared, Rome restored in the church; built up in part by the same agencies as before, invigorated only by the presence of a higher principle; subduing the most barbarous nations, under the banner of the cross, and binding the most distant to a common center; but at the same time repeating the lightnings of the Capitol in the thunders of the Vatican, directed against every motion of freedom, and in its conflict with the world gradually taking up all the elements of the world's corruption into its own constitution.

In both cases we meet essentially the same features of character: immovable resolution, iron constancy, a restless grasping after universal dominion, and confidence of perpetual stability; but in connection with all this, an artful, cunning policy, disguised beneath a show of urbanity, the Jesuitic maxim of the end sanctifying the means, and a heartless disregard to both national and individual rights, in the midst of vast pretensions to liberality and broad-hearted pliant toleration. *The papacy is a Christian universal monarchy, erected on the popular spirit of ancient Rome.* And as it is necessary that authority should go before independence, the general before the particular and single; which implies that barbarous tribes require the force of a heavy disciplinary institute, in the first instance, to bring them to a full, free knowledge of themselves; no unprejudiced historian will dispute the merits of the Romish system, as eminently fitted for this service. Nay, in view of such countries as Italy, Spain, and Ireland, which have not yet outgrown their political minority, must we not allow a relative necessity for it, even in our own day?

Protestantism springs, as all know, from the *German* life, which may be considered constitutionally its proper womb and cradle; as we find prophetically indicated by many voices of the Middle Period even, like that of Mechtildis,[1] with her *remansurum pauperem et afflictum coetum in Germania, qui pie ac pure*

*Deum colat.** It was not a matter of mere chance therefore, or
something indifferent in its nature, that the father of the Reformation, surpassing all his followers both at home and abroad,
should have borne upon him the impress of this particular nationality, in its purest, most perfect form; and that his German
translation of the Bible became the recruiting call to so many
thousands, to rally around the standard of the new, or rather,
renovated faith.

In Luther all the essential traits of the German nationality are
found collected as it were into a single focus: indomitable energy,
earnest childlike integrity and simplicity, unaffected humility,
and a predominant tendency toward the world of thought and
feeling; to which must be added, it is true, a blunt carriage,
running not unfrequently into downright rudeness, and a certain
undervaluation of the outward costume of life, not to be approved
in any case. Such a nationality is fitted constitutionally for a deep,
inward apprehension of the Christian system; while the Roman
and Romanist spirit, as naturally, was led to embrace it prevailingly in more outward way, as a body of mere rules and statutes.

Those forms of character which have distinguished the German
nature from the beginning, its love and truth, its geniality and
depth, should be regarded as a prophetical preparation for
Christianity. They were so, more emphatically even than the
penitential discipline of the Hindus, or the earnest idealistic
longings of the Platonic philosophy; the latter, as is well known,
served the purpose of a bridge, to conduct so many of the early
fathers to Christ.

These two opposite orders of life, which might have seemed to
be forever disjoined by inward, ineradicable, mutual hatred, no
less than by the heaven-climbing mountains of snow that separated them outwardly, found the middle wall of partition between
them broken down notwithstanding by the power of Christianity,
as the religion of the world. But now in proportion as the German

---

*"Only the inwardness of the German nation," says Hegel (*Philosophie
der Geschichte,* Works, 1st ed., Vol. IX, p. 417), "was the soil of the Reformation; only from such simple, straightforward character, could the great work
proceed. While other nations were wholly taken up with worldly dominion,
conquests and discoveries, a plain monk toiled after perfection in his spirit
and brought it to pass."

tribes, under the motherly supervision of Rome, began to wake to self-consciousness, the old struggle of Arminius[2] also, which may be said to have foreshadowed the disruption of the papal yoke by Christian Germany, was gradually renewed.

The entire Middle Period is full of the conflicts of the imperial power in Germany with the papal authority at Rome. German blood was poured out like water on the battlegrounds of Italy. As far back as the time of the Hohenstaufen, a sect in Swabia declared the pope a heretic; and it was long a popular tradition in Germany that Frederick II would one day return, or an eagle spring from his blood, to overthrow the Romish Church. The conflict grew always more violent and fierce in proportion as the papacy surrendered itself more and more to the Machiavellian policy of employing mere worldly influences for the accomplishment of its ends, and laid itself out, under cover of the church, to advance the private interests simply of the popes and their courtiers, directing the sword of St. Peter against every liberal movement that came in their way.

Such foul prostitution of things sacred and divine to mere secular ends, carried to the most shameless climax at last in the traffic in indulgences as conducted by Tetzel, together with such hierarchal despotism intolerant of all right and all freedom, could not fail to shock the moral earnestness of the German spirit in the most serious manner. How could it be otherwise in the case of a people, that in its purest representatives has ever subordinated national, political, simply egoistic interests to the world-embracing claims of the spirit, as embodied in the church; and that in the sixteenth century, in particular, when almost every other nation either remained altogether in communion with Rome or stood forth simply on general Protestant ground, chose to be torn in pieces of its own children, and to see its fields laid waste and its fair territory divided, rather than to give up eternal truth for a political advantage, the momentous issue which divided the two Confessions, to save the unity of the nation.

The long-cherished opposition just mentioned passed over toward the close of the Middle Ages into the most distinguished popular productions of the German national literature, particularly in its epic, dramatic, and satiristic forms. It is sufficient to remind those who are acquainted with the subject, of the *Eulenspiegel,* the German version of *Reineke Fuchs,* and the *Fastnachtspiele* of Hans Rosenblut. All these compositions served to bring continually nearer to the consciousness of the people, the faults of the time, and especially the corruption of the clergy and the pernicious consequences of transalpine influence. In the end the tendency of the popular national literature found its most eloquent expounders, simultaneously with the appearance of Luther, in the persons of Ulrich von Hutten[3] and the celebrated Hans Sachs.[4]

But with all the importance of this political and literary opposition to Italy, it is by no means sufficient of itself to explain the Reformation. To suppose this would be superficial in the extreme; as is shown at once by the fact that a large part of Germany still continues, though in a more inward and free way than other nations, to do homage to the see of Rome. It would have been a calamity rather if the political tendency had drawn the direction of the Reformation into its own hands. Luther found no pleasure in the later enterprises of Hutten and Sickingen[5]; taking the ground against them, that the church was not to be revived by means of outward, carnal weapons, but only by means of the divine word from which it had its life in the beginning. The war of the peasants, which rose like a dark column of smoke in connection with the pure flame of the Reformation, was repudiated by him as a miserable caricature of his work; and just as little respect did he show for the Anabaptists and their wild dreams of liberty and equality.

The way of the Reformation was prepared in like manner in the smaller circle of the learned by the *revival of the sciences;* and it is a circumstance accordingly not to be overlooked that the representatives of the movement, in particular Melanchthon, Calvin and Beza, surpassed in thorough humanistic culture, almost all their contemporaries. The emigration of learned Greeks to the West, which took place after the destruction of Constantinople, and the fruitful labors of Petrarch, had contributed to extend still more and more the study of the ancient languages; the darkness of ignorance and superstition was coming gradually to disperse; **the spiritual horizon of the nations had begun to grow clear.**

In Italy the ancient life, through living contemplation of the monuments of classic art, stood forth in fresh reproductions, revolutionizing on a large scale the entire literature, and indeed the whole order of thinking. Almost all the philosophical systems of Greece and Rome were honored again with living adherents and advocates. Platonism once more, as in the first ages of the church, excited a longing for something higher and better than all that was offered by the present. We see this particularly in Marsiglio Ficino,[6] who may be taken as the representative of a widely extended feeling, and who especially in his latter years—a sort of Christian Plutarch—endeavored to reconcile the culture of the age with Christianity.

The knowledge of the Hebrew and Greek languages, promoted with untiring zeal by Reuchlin and Erasmus, furnished the key to the understanding of the Old and New Testaments, and enabled the Reformers (indispensable for the purpose) to translate them into the vernacular tongues, and so to open the way for them into the life of the people. It deserves notice particularly that the two first editions of the Greek New Testament, that of Erasmus in the year 1516 and that of the Complutensian Polyglot in the year 1520, appeared simultaneously with the commencement of the Reformation; and under protection too of the papal authority, which dreamed not yet of the powerful assault that was to be made upon it soon from this book. The edition of Erasmus was repeated in a short time, over and over again, and thus by means of the art of printing, not long before discovered, found its way into thousands of hands.

It shows strikingly how very general the feeling of opposition to the superstition and immorality of the clergy had become, that this same small, cowardly and cautious Erasmus was enabled to occupy so successfully, as he did, the apparently bold and perilous position in which he stood. No one attacked the vices of the clergy so sharply with the same cutting wit and inexhaustible humor. His hatred for the monks seemed to be constitutional. He made it his great business to draw theological study off from the reigning scholastic method and back to the fathers of the church and the New Testament, and to this last, not as exhibited in the Vulgate, which he was bold enough to convict of an immense mass of errors, but as found in the original text. And still this man stood in the most honorable correspondence with the leading men of his time. Presents and marks of respect were showered upon him from all sides. Wreaths of fame adorned his person. His presence was courted, with special invitation, in all parts of the world. And his *Encomium Moriae,* the most severe of all his works against the clergy, passed during his lifetime through twenty-seven editions, and made its appearance in every cultivated language of the age.

But still these scientific and humanistic tendencies again, are not sufficient to account for the Reformation. Many, by the study of the ancient languages and philosophy, were led, in Italy particularly, into the most decided infidelity, which is worse of course than superstition itself. Erasmus himself, it is known, drew back in his latter years always more and more from the work of the Reformation. We cannot pronounce him void of all regard for evangelical truth; but altogether his influence was mainly of the negative sort, and was just as likely, but for the intervention of the Reformation in its true form, to have called forth a false and perilous action, in the freethinking, liberalistic style, as it was to serve the cause in question. "He knew well," as Luther tells us, who saw through him completely, "how to expose errors, but not how to teach the truth." Indeed if science and art could have produced the Reformation, Leo X, in whom they found so zealous a patron, must have been one of the best reformers. The learning and cultivation of the age were primarily of the nature of a mere instrument, which, as it came to be associated either with piety or with the spirit of the world, might be made subservient to exactly opposite ends.

Leaving behind now the outer court of politics, popular literature and profane science, as thus far surveyed, we approach nearer to the proper sanctuary of the Reformation, and fix our attention on the movements by which its way was prepared in the sphere of theology and the church. Here however we must distinguish carefully between simply negative action, so directed against error as to make war upon the truth more or less at the same time, and that of a positive character, springing from the life of the church itself.

The first we find exemplified, in general, by the sects of the Albigenses, the Beghards and Beguines, the Bogomiles, and Catharists[7]; and by such men moreover as Arnold of Brescia,[8] Amalrich of Bena,[9] David of Dinanto,[10] and others, who without any proper church feeling, and under the influence of hyperspiritualistic, and not unfrequently Manichean and pantheistic views, set themselves in opposition to truth and error promiscuously. The Catholic Church regarded all these properly as heretics, but employed carnal weapons, instead of the sword of the Spirit, to put them down and in this way rendered them only so much the more dangerous.

Of much greater account, of course, is the positive tendency of the theology and church of the Middle Ages toward the Reformation. Here we meet whole *communities,* and also *single* voices. Among the first, a principal place belongs to the Waldenses, who accompany us, in spite of the fierce persecutions of the papacy, like a lamp in the night, from the middle of the twelfth century down to the time of Luther; and whose life of simplicity and strict virtue is still perpetuated indeed, even in our own time, amidst surrounding Romish superstition, in the valleys of Piedmont, near Turin. They based their opposition to the reigning church upon the holy Scriptures, which many of their members knew almost entirely by heart; so that, in some instances, they were called in even by the Romish ecclesiastics themselves to assist them in their disputations with heretics.

Wickliffe in Oxford, and Huss in Prague, though apparently overwhelmed by the ruling hierarchy, had not labored in vain in contending against abuses and false doctrine, and in calling men's minds away from externals to inward godliness, and from human traditions to the word of God as the only fountain of true theology. We find a large number of Wickliffites in England; and from the Hussites arose by degrees the Bohemian and Moravian Brethren, who made it their object to restore the simplicity, spirituality, and strict discipline of the apostolic age. They had already as many as two hundred churches and houses for prayer, in the beginning of the sixteenth century.

The Society of the *Fratres communis vitae*,[11] instituted by Gerhard Groot, toward the close of the fourteenth century, also must not be forgotten. It proposed to preserve what was true and good in the conventual system of the age, without its excrescences. Thus for instance it allowed no monastic vows, but only free resolutions in dependence on God's grace. From this association proceeded many distinguished men, with Thomas à Kempis at their head; who preached the word of God in the vernacular tongue; devoted themselves earnestly to the instruction of the young; insisted in a style very different from the Pharisaic formality of the times on deep, inward, practical piety; and in opposition to the prevalent dry learning of the schools, acknowledged no wisdom, but such as carried with it at the same time a sanctifying power.

Attention is due further to an association that rose in Italy and formed an interesting analogy of German Protestantism, though for reasons easily understood it fell far short of it in its development. An *Oratory of Divine Love* was established in the Church at St. Sylvester and Dorothea, across the Tiber at Rome, where in the time of Leo X as many as fifty or sixty distinguished men, including such names as Contarini, Sadolet, Giberto, Caraffa, and Lippomano,[12] were accustomed to meet statedly for mutual religious edification. These men, some of whom afterward struck into a very different path when they came to be adorned with the cardinal's cap, had come to the very threshold of the evangelical doctrine of justification!

Contarini composed a treatise on the subject, which led Pole to say, in writing to him: "You have brought into the light a precious jewel, which was before half concealed in the keeping of the church." Another member of this association, M. A. Flaminio, writes in his letter to Theodorina Sauli: "The gospel is nothing else than the glad tidings, that the only-begotten Son of God, clothed in our flesh, has rendered satisfaction to the righteousness of the eternal Father on our account. *He who believes this* enters into the kingdom of God, finds universal forgiveness, is changed from a carnal to a spiritual nature, from a child of wrath to a child of grace, and leads a life of sweet peace in his conscience."*

But among all the movements and connections in which a reformatory element may be discovered to have been at work before the time of Luther, none is more worthy of being noticed than

---

* For more on the subject of this interesting tendency, the influence of which extended even to the gay, pleasure-seeking Naples, the reader is referred to Leop. von Ranke's *Die roemischen Paepste im 16ten und 17ten Jahrhundert* (2d ed.), Vol. I, p. 134.

the interest of mysticism. Its influence was felt indeed by several of the associations to which we have already referred, particularly by the Brethren of the Common Life. But we find it besides running in various forms, with more full development, throughout the Middle Ages; and the influence of it, in this view, on Luther himself, is not to be mistaken. He was the affectionate disciple of John von Staupitz, in whom a profound, Augustinian, mystical tendency strongly prevailed; and he was the publisher and eulogist of the old treatise entitled *The German Theology*,[13] which may be regarded as the flower of the ascetico-speculative spirit in this form.

The reformatory bearing of the mystical system appeared in this, that it drew attention away from mere externals, in which the idea of religion and the church had become well-nigh lost, to the exercises of the heart; and breaking through the barriers, which had been interposed between man and his Maker by the hierarchical framework of the papacy, and in defiance at the same time of the dialectics of the schools, threw itself directly into the stream of the divine life itself. In its view, religion was to be apprehended not as a system of forms, but as the inmost life of its subject. It thirsted after direct communion with God.

Mysticism however had no power of itself to produce a reformation. It is deficient in practical energy. Predominantly subjective in its nature, and resting too exclusively in mere feeling, it has no capacity to overcome the world. Its life proceeds accordingly in lonely retirement, without action, like the mysterious flower that unfolds its petals in the stillness of the night, but gathers them in again with shrinking sensitiveness as soon as they are touched by a hand.

Not less significant however than these collective tendencies, are the *separate* strivings toward the Reformation to be considered, which show themselves in particular individuals with growing frequency, in the course of the fifteenth century and with the opening of that which followed. These sprang partly from a practical religious interest, and partly from an interest in theology as a science, and in both forms wrought powerfully, in the way of controversy and in the way of quiet positive teaching, to prepare the way for the new era that was at hand.

The celebrated Councils of Constance and Basel, which had insisted on a reformation of the church in its head and members, though with their self-contradictory constitution they could not accomplish the work; and the deep-toned lamentations of Nicolas of Clamenge (de Clemangis)[14] Pierre d'Ailly,[15] John of Gerson,* and others, over the reigning corruption, had served to disseminate a longing desire for a better state of religion through all sections of Europe. This feeling found its organs in such men as the Dominican Savonarola of San Marco in Florence, who preached with prophetic indignation, in the boldest style, not without a hurtful mixture indeed of political zeal, against the licentiousness that had come to abound in the church, and sealed his testimony with his blood in the year 1498. Such also were John von Wesel (de Wesalia), professor of theology at Erfurth (d. 1482), John von Goch, a native of Cleves (d. 1475), and the Frieslander, John Wessel (d. 1489).[16]

These all insisted more or less clearly on the Augustinian doctrine of grace, in opposition to the prevailing Jewish idea of righteousness by works and bondage to the law, and appealed to the

---

* In the way of example I present a single passage from the most conspicuous of these, John of Gerson [Jean Charlier de Gerson], Chancellor of the University of Paris (d. 1429). "The apostle says indeed, Let every soul be subject to the higher powers. But this must be understood with the provision that such obedience shall not run into blasphemy against God Almighty, or dishonor to Christ and his gospel. Certainly however there can be no greater blasphemy against God Almighty than when our superiors without distinction expose the church to sale publicly as merchandise, and for gold deliver her like a strumpet into the hands of murderers, adulterers, malefactors of every sort; the church, which is the glorious bride, the elected virgin of Christ, that he has purchased of his mere mercy by his precious blood, his sufferings, his reproach, the accursed death of the cross itself. Judas sold Christ *once* for thirty pieces of silver; these sell him continually a *hundred times* over. In many cases they sell to one, and when they have the money take his purchase from him again, to offer it the next hour for more money to another. I conclude then that obedience to superiors ceases to be a duty, where their works are openly bad and a source of scandal to the whole church; where the shepherds are shearers; not sheep, but wolves; not sober, but drunken; not prelates that give their lives for the sheep, but Pilates that serve the lusts of others; casting forth their net, not to catch souls, but money." (*De reformatione ecclesiae in concilio universali*, c. 24.) "The church of the present day is not apostolic, but apostate; not a place to stay in, but to flee from rather to the greatest distance." (*Ibid.*, c. 25.)

sacred Scriptures as the only sure ground and source of Christian doctrine. This was carried so far indeed in the case of John Wessel, who went beyond all others before the Reformation in his apprehension of the Protestant doctrine of justification, that Luther, [although he undervalued his own merits], did not hesitate to say, "If I had read Wessel previously, my adversaries might have supposed that Luther had borrowed all from Wessel, so well do our views agree." In none of these men however was there found such a union of all the powers that are needed for a reformation, as was possessed by Luther and Calvin, for whom it was reserved accordingly to accomplish so great a work.

Enough has been said already to vindicate an absolute historical necessity to the Reformation, and to expose in its utter emptiness and nakedness the reproach, cast upon it by its enemies, as an uncalled for innovation. We go further, however, and affirm that *the entire Catholic Church as such, so far as it might be considered the legitimate bearer of the Christian faith and life,* pressed with inward necessary impulse toward Protestantism, just as Judaism—not in its character of Pharisaism and Sadduceeism indeed, but as a divinely appointed preparatory institute, and viewed in its true historical import—rolled with steady powerful stream, in its interior legal, symbolical and prophetical principle, directly toward Christianity, as the fulfillment of the law, the prototype of all its symbols, and the accomplishment of all its prophecies. The Councils of Constance and Basel alone furnish proof that the call for a reformation had its ground, not simply in the sects, and in single individuals more or less estranged from the objective life of the church, but in the heart of the church itself, and in the persons of those who were most fully penetrated with its life. This affirmation, as well as the appeal to the case of Judaism, may require some additional illustration.

The Catholic Church of the Middle Ages, as already intimated, was a church of law and authority; well-fitted, by means of its vast disciplinary system, turning on a single living center and perfectly complete in all its parts, to exercise a wardship over the nations, still in their childhood, till such time as they might be ripe for a fuller appropriation of the evangelical principle, and the use of an independent, manly freedom. In saying this we do not question the presence of the gospel in the communion of the Roman Catholic Church, any more than we doubt the comfort of the promise that went hand in hand with the development of the Old Testament law. Still, the *predominant* spirit, in both cases, was legal; as might easily be proved, in minute detail, if this were the proper place.*

Now it belongs always to the nature of the law to excite in man a feeling that reaches beyond itself and refuses to be satisfied by its means, a feeling that craves reconciliation with the lawgiver and the full possession of that righteousness which he requires. More definitely expressed, the law is a schoolmaster to bring men to Christ, who has fulfilled its requisitions in their largest extent and makes over to us the benefit of this obedience, as a free unmerited gift, by the power of his Spirit. Thus the Jewish dispensation looked always toward the gospel; and in like manner the discipline of the Roman Church involved an inward struggle that became satisfied at last only in the evangelical emancipation of Protestantism.

It is only from this point of view we come to understand fully the personal life of Luther, in which the genesis of our church itself is reflected with the most clear and graphic representation. It was no political, national, scientific, or theological interest even, that impelled him to his work. The immediate, original ground of it, is to be sought in the very center of the religious life of the Catholic Church itself, as it stood at the time. This church he was proud at one time to call his mother; and his separation from her visible head cost him a struggle, a self-immolation, of which, now that the great rupture is past, it is hard for us to form any clear

---

* This legal character of the Middle Ages was clearly perceived by many of the forerunners of the Reformation themselves. Specially worthy of notice in this respect is an uncommonly striking description of Cornelius Graphaeus, of Flanders (b. 1482), which is to be found in the classic work of my much esteemed friend Ullmann, entitled *Reformatoren vor der Reformation*,[17] Vol. I, pp. 153 ff. All who wish to become acquainted with the forerunners of the Reformation in Germany and the Netherlands, may find all they need for the purpose in this thoroughly learned and well-written work presented in the most entertaining form. May the learned author soon add to the two volumes which have already appeared, a further continuation on what still remains of his general subject, at least so far as the philological and humanistic precursors of the Reformation are concerned.

conception. The most faithful and conscientious of monks, he subjected himself intellectually to the logical discipline of the schools,
and bore practically the prescribed penances and other legal bur-
dens of the Catholic Church, as those of Judaism had been borne
by Paul. To become righteous before God, to appear as a saint in
his presence, was the object for which he wrestled without inter-
mission.

But the longer he continued in this hard school, [the more he
became aware] of his own weakness, and of his immeasurable distance from the ideal he was laboring to reach, and in the same
proportion was brought to long for a redeemer from the body of
such death, and the terrible conflict between the law in his members and the law of the Spirit; till in the end, like his great apostolical pattern, he beheld the Crucified in his spiritual glory, and
by faith in him received at once, in all its fullness, as a free gift,
all that he had been vainly endeavoring to secure by his own
strength before. Of a truth, we may say, the pains endured in the
mortification of the flesh and in legal wrestlings after righteousness with God, by the noblest spirits of the Middle Ages, the mystics in particular, with the anxiously religious Augustinian monk
at their head, are to be regarded as the true birth pangs of our
Protestant Church.*

As the result then of this whole representation, we reach the
following [proposition which is vastly important and even indispensable for the vindication of Protestantism]: *The Reformation
is the legitimate offspring, the greatest act of the Catholic Church;
and on this account of true catholic nature itself, in its genuine
conception: whereas the Church of Rome, instead of following*

---

* We may observe in Calvin also, and to a greater extent indeed than in
Luther, the traces in every direction of the severe legal discipline, intellectual
and practical, which the Catholic Church, in spite of all her corruptions, still
continued to exercise at least over minds of the more serious order. It would
be wholly beyond the capacity of our own age to produce such an amount of
resolute, vigorous, large-proportioned character, as is presented to us in the
Reformers. We have lost almost entirely the consciousness of the power of the
law, as it is felt always in the earlier stages of life. Along with our scientific
seminaries, we stand in great want of institutions expressly for the cultivation
of character; and in this particular we might, and should, learn much from
the Romish Church, the schools especially of the Jesuits.

*the divine conduct of history has continued to stick in the old law of commandments, the garb of childhood, like the Jewish hierarchy in the time of Christ, and thus by its fixation as Romanism has parted with the character of catholicity in exchange for that of particularity.**

* Compare, on the difference between Catholicism and Romanism, my articles in the *Literar. Zeitung* of Berlin, 1843, No. 87 and No. 100.

# . 2 .

## The Prospective Aspect of the Reformation, or the Protestant Principle in Its Positive Force

WITH THIS PROPOSITION we have already touched upon the *second* essential constituent of the Reformation, according to which it is to be viewed as a *historical advance* on the part of the church; and in the closest connection with the pressure of previous, long-accumulating want, a *new birth* from the womb of its life in the old form. The subject however in this aspect, calls now for closer elucidation, in a direct way.

It must be remarked, in the first place, that when we speak of advance or progress here, we do so with reference only to the previous *apprehension* of Christianity in the *church,* and not to Christianity itself, as exhibited in its original and for all times absolutely normal character in the writings of the New Testament. Our comparison of the relation of the Evangelical Church to the Roman Catholic, with the relation of Christianity to Judaism, must be taken therefore with a material limitation. Christianity stands related to Judaism, not simply as fulfillment to presentiment, enlargement to compression, substance to shadow; but is at the same time specifically a new creation. No expansion simply of the idea of the Old Testament, as such, was sufficient for its production. This could take place only by the creative act of God, in his incarnation, his life, sufferings, death, and resurrection, as God and man in one person, and in the real and full communication of the Holy Spirit, which had irradiated the human consciousness before only in a transient and sporadic way.

Beyond Christianity itself however, as thus introduced into the world, there can be no similar advance. Our faith must be subverted in its very ground, if now that Christ has appeared, "the fullness of the Godhead bodily," and given his Spirit to the apostles to "lead them into all truth," we should allow ourselves to expect, like the Jews, a still higher revelation. In its own nature, as a new order of life, Christianity has been complete from the beginning; and there is no room to conceive that any more perfect order can ever take its place, or that it may be so improved as in the end to outgrow entirely its own original sphere.

But notwithstanding this, we are authorized to speak of advance or progress in the case of the church itself, and on the part of the Christianized world; and of this not merely as extensive, in the spread of the gospel among pagans, [Muslims], and Jews; but as intensive also in the continually growing cultivation and improvement of those four great interests of the church: doctrine, life, constitution, and worship.

The church, not less than every one of its members, has its periods of infancy, youth, manhood, and old age. This involves no contradiction to the absolute character of Christianity; for the progress of the church, outward or inward, is never in the strict sense creative, but in the way only of reception, organic assimilation, and expansion. In other words, all historical development in the church, theoretical and practical, consists in *an apprehension always more and more profound of the life and doctrine of Christ and his apostles—an appropriation, more full and transforming always of their distinctive spirit, both as to its contents and its form.*

Only so far as a doctrine or ordinance of the church bears this character, may it be allowed to have normative and enduring force. If it could be clearly shown, for instance, that the doctrines of the Trinity and the two natures in Christ, as dogmatically developed and symbolically established in opposition to heretical errors in the fourth and fifth centuries, are not contained so far as substance is concerned in the New Testament, but contradict it rather, their authority must fall before the culture of the age to make room for a different view in consonance with the Scriptures.

In this sense then the Reformation is an advance, not of Christianity itself, but of its tenure at least upon the consciousness of the Christian world. We may bring forward indeed many passages from the writings of Augustine, Anselm, Bernard of Clairvaux, and other men occupying a position near to the Reformers, which seem to teach the cardinal doctrine of justification by grace; and it may be affirmed with truth that all real Christians from the beginning had lived upon this doctrine at bottom, unconsciously to themselves. But still their piety, in its general character, must be admitted to carry with it more or less of a legal complexion. Only in single, exalted moments of their existence at best, were they enabled to lay hold of the freedom, the assurance of salvation, and full triumphant faith, to which we have been raised by the Reformation. This merit at least belongs to the Reformers, that they have brought into clear consciousness what existed only darkly before in the soul, and have made that to be common property in the church which had belonged previously only to single and highly gifted individuals.

On the other hand, when we bring the soteriological ground principle of the Reformation into the light of the New Testament, particularly the letters of Paul, we find it ratified here with such clear and distinct enunciation that we are ready to wonder why the church should not have come to the knowledge of it a great while sooner. But to penetrate from the surface into the depth, from the shell to the kernel, is something far more difficult than it seems; a work belonging to God's chosen instruments, the architects of the world's history, the wakers of slumbering centuries.

The new vital principle of the Reformation, as compared with the form in which Christianity had been held previously, is not to be sought in the sphere of the objective, more theoretic doctrines, such for instance as the Trinity, the incarnation, or the relation of the divine and human natures in the person of Christ. These it incorporated into itself rather, as they had been previously perfected by the great ecumenical councils, asserting and maintaining thus its catholic interest in the true spiritual acquisitions of the ancient church.

On the contrary, the sixteenth century was the classic period for the full exposition of the Christian soteriology, as standing in the subjective appropriation of the work of redemption. The reappearance of Unitarian and Arian errors at the time[18] must be considered a mere accidental excrescence, such as we find attending every great historical occasion. The essential, fundamental doctrines of the Reformation then fall within a sphere, which had not previously been occupied by the decision of any general council, as in the case of the Trinity and the constitution of Christ's person, and where accordingly it was possible to advance new scriptural statements, without contradicting the true Catholic Church. The movement in this view was not an effort to overthrow and reconstruct the work of this church in the case of its great cardinal doctrines as already positively defined by the general councils, but to carry forward and complete that work rather by going on to define and settle what had not yet been made the subject of action, in the same positive style.

As little may we say that the Reformation stood essentially in an effort to subvert the papacy and hierarchy, although this is often affirmed. Those who regard it in this light do not consider that Luther had already uttered his positive life principle, before he thought of a breach with the pope; and that much later even Melanchthon, in subscribing the Articles of Smalcald, professed himself willing to accept the pope, as *de jure humano* head of the church. Such a principle besides would give no distinction between the Protestant Church and the Greek, or common sects even, which all agree in rejecting the primacy of Rome to the same extent. The great point was to eradicate popedom from the heart itself, which is too prone, away from all connection with Rome, to make an idol of mere human authority, in forms that may appear more plausible perhaps, but are often more intolerably tyrannic on this very account.

Still more prevalent is the view by which the essence of the Reformation is placed in the emancipation of the human mind subjectively considered, that is, in the triumphant assertion of the liberty of faith and conscience, as well as of unlimited scientific inquiry. Rightly understood this, to be sure, has its truth; but as commonly represented, it is a sheer caricature of history. It is made to mean very often, for instance, a full liberation of the subject from every sort of restraint, the overthrow of all authority as such. But of such escape from discipline and rule, the Reformers had no thought. Their object was rather to bind man to the grace of God, and to lead his conscience captive to God's word.

In every view, the act of protesting is not the first and main constituent in the Reformation, but the result only of a positive affirmation going before. This last accordingly is the great point from which alone its true importance springs. Only in connection with such an original *positive* life principle, and as flowing from it, can deliverance from the papacy and the restitution of private judgment to its rights find any right sense, any religious value. Apart from this connection, they fall over to the province of infidelity, with which the Reformation has nothing to do.

Such a positive religious principle now, is the doctrine of the exclusive authority of the sacred Scriptures as a rule of faith; and it is a very current idea, particularly in the *Reformed* Church, that this doctrine forms the proper center and root of Protestantism. But this also we cannot admit, although the Christian life of the Reformers was shaped from the beginning by the Scriptures. For this principle is formal only, and so secondary, presupposing the presence of a definite substance which it must include. In order that the Scriptures may be taken as the exclusive source and measure of Christian truth, it is necessary that the faith in Christ of which they testify should be already at hand, that their contents should have been made to live in the heart by the power of the Holy Spirit accompanying the word and the church. And so all turns upon the particular constitution of this faith. The Socinians, Swedenborgians, later Unitarians, and other sects, made the same strenuous appeal to the Scriptures as their only authority, but they stood quite off from the true living ground of the Reformation notwithstanding, and gave accordingly a wholly different sense to the Bible in the most weighty points.

### THE MATERIAL PRINCIPLE OF THE REFORMATION

That we may come to the furthest source then, we must inquire
after the *material* or *life principle* (*principium essendi*) of the
Reformation. This, according to history, is no other than the
great doctrine, which is presented by Paul especially as the entire
sum of the gospel—the doctrine of the *justification of the sinner
before God by the merit of Christ alone through faith.* This doctrine was the fruit of Luther's earnest spiritual conflicts already
noticed; and it formed the proper soul, the polar star and center
of his life from the commencement of his reformatory career on
to his last breath.* The Romish Church may be said to urge
precisely her most earnest and pious members always toward this
point; as we see in the case of the Jansenists, condemned indeed
by the pope, and in our own day in such men as Sailer, Veith,
Gossner, Boos, and others.[19] For all earnest legal wrestling after
righteousness and holiness leads naturally at last to the abandon-
ment of every fleshly confidence, and a reliance on God's grace
alone.

[By virtue of this doctrine, the Reformers first discovered the

---

* Hence he says himself in the Articles of Smalcald, p. 305 (Edition of the
Symb. Books by Hase): De hoc articulo cedere aut aliquid contra illum lar-
giri aut permittere nemo piorum potest, etiamsi coelum et terra ac omnia
corruant. Non enim est aliud nomen hominibus datum, per quod salvari pos-
simus (inquit Petrus, Act. 4:12), et per vulnera ejus sanati sumus (Esaj. 53:5).
Et *in hoc articulo sita sunt et consistunt* omnia, quae contra Papam, diabolum,
et universum mundum, in vita nostra docemus, testamur et agimus. Quare
oportet nos de hac doctrina esse certos et minime dubitare, *alioquin actum est
prorsus,* et Papa et diabolus et omnia adversa jus et victoriam contra nos obti-
nent. Comp. *Form. Conc.,* p. 683, and Melanchthon, *Locus de grat. et justif.,*
where he says of the doctrine of justification: Hic locus continet summam
evangelii. When the younger Bengel (*Archiv fuer die Theol.,* Bd. 1., St. 2.,
S. 469) and the celebrated historian Planck (*Worte des Friedens an die kath.
Kirche,* 1809, pp. 47 f.) represent the whole controversy between the Protestants and Romanists on the doctrine of justification as of no vital account, a
mere logomachy in fact, the thing finds its explanation in the dogmatic indifferentism of the age to which these men belonged. But it is incomprehen-
sible how at the present time, when the difference of the Confessions has come
to be more clearly felt again in a recurrence to its foundations, the latest Protestant expositor of the Catholic system, Koellner (in his otherwise very accu-
rate and learned *Symbolik der heil. apost. kath. roemischen Kirche,* Preface,
p. xix), should affirm the same thing, and find on the contrary the main difference in the outward relations, constitution, and worship of the two churches.

scripture to be what they claimed it to be]; and Luther, it is known, employed this doctrine as a measure for the sacred canon itself, not allowing it to include as God's normative word anything that might carry an opposite sense. His harsh censures on certain portions of the established church canon, the Epistle of James, the Epistle to the Hebrews, and the Revelation to John, we do not of course defend, but reject them rather as one-sided and rash; [but we would recite them as facts for the position which we assign to the doctrine of justification by faith]. Pressed as he was by his Romish adversaries, with whom James especially was always a favorite authority, Luther's unfavorable judgment of the books just named arose altogether from his not being able to find in them his cardinal truth, justification by faith only.*

It devolves upon us now to go into a somewhat closer examination of this material principle of the Reformation; and for this purpose it is necessary to direct our view first, in brief, to the opposite tenet of the Romish Church. The Christian salvation rests upon the primary truth that Jesus Christ, the absolute God-man, is the only Redeemer and Mediator between man as a sinner and his offended Maker. It is a long time, however, before man is brought to take up this doctrine in its full import into his consciousness, and to part radically with the Judaism that is in him from his birth. So we find it in the experience of the individual child of God at all times; and so it has been with the life of the church as a whole, from the beginning.

In the Church of Rome, we find the doctrine, according to the

---

* From this it appears, with how much wrong, the modern negative criticism makes its appeal to Luther's example. *He,* standing in the element of God's unwritten word, and animated by the one all-regulating principle of justification, uttered his judgment against certain parts of the canon handed down by the church, because they seemed to him to be in conflict with that word, as the essence of the gospel itself. Luther's criticism in one word was the action of faith in the free grace of God in Christ against all human distortion of the truth. The modern criticism of a David Friedrich Strauss or Bruno Bauer[20] however, in full reverse, starts from unbelief in this grace, and is aimed destructively against the positive ground of the gospel itself. (Comp. my articles on true and false criticism in the *Literar. Zeitung* of Berlin, 1843, No. 40 and No. 61.) Let anyone read Luther's judgment upon the Epistle of James continuously in Walch, Vol. XIV, pp. 148 f., and he will be fully satisfied of the truth of our representation.

Council of Trent, acknowledged objectively and *in thesi,* but always laid under restriction, as soon as it comes to a particular explanation of the way in which the atonement is carried over into the life of its subject, and made available for his salvation. In opposition, not only to Pelagianism, but to Semi-Pelagianism also (which may be charged indeed upon the papal bull, "Unigenitus," A.D. 1711,[21] and the whole practice of the church, but not on the Council of Trent), she teaches, it is true, that the grace of God, as *gratia praeveniens,* commences the work of conversion in man, by calling him to the salvation which is in Christ.*

In her view, however, the natural condition of man is not as with us, a state of positive corruption, but holds simply in the absence of *supernatural endowments,* as *defectus justitiae originalis,* on the one hand, and a mere *debilitation* of the *natural* powers of reason and freedom on the other†; and so the natural man is made to take part also in the work of his own conversion and justification. When the power toward good, which is still in him though debilitated by original sin, is again set free and invigorated in his gracious calling, he *disposes* himself, we are told, to the acquisition of justification; so that God's grace *(gratia operans)* and the human will *(voluntas humana cooperans)* work now in conjunction, the first in the way of illumination, and the other freely consenting and moving toward God.‡

---

* *Conc. Trid.,* S. VI, c. 5—6.

† S. VI, Decr. I, c. 1, and can. 4, 5, 7. Bellarmine consequently *(Disputt.,* etc., de gratia primi hominis, I, 1) states the doctrine of his church correctly, when he says: Docent enim (catholici Doctores), per Adae peccatum totum hominem vere deteriorem esse factum, et tamen *nec liberum arbitrium neque alia naturalia dona,* sed solum supernaturalia perdidisse. And what he remarks, de gratia primi hom., c. 5., agrees with this fully: Quare non magis differt status hominis post lapsum Adae a statu ejusdem in puris naturalibus, quam differt *spoliatus a nudo;* neque deterior est humana natura, si culpam originalem detrahas, neque magis ignorantia et infirmitate laborat, quam esset et laboraret in puris naturalibus condita. Proinde corruptio naturae non ex alicujus doni naturalis carentia, neque ex alicujus malae qualitatis accessu, sed ex sola doni supernaturalis ob Adae peccatum amissione profluxit.

‡ *Conc. Trid.,* S. VI, can. 4: Si quis dixerit, liberum hominis arbitrium a Deo motum et excitatum nihil *cooperari* assentiendo Deo excitanti, atque vocanti quo *ad obtinendam justificationis gratiam se disponat ac praeparet,* neque posse dissentire, si velit, sed veluti inanime quoddam nihil omnino agere, mereque passive se habere; anathema sit. In the 5th and 6th cap. of the same session, this is made the subject of further positive explication.

As the result of this twofold action justification in due time takes place, not suddenly however, but gradually, partly by faith, and partly by works of love. For justification here, agreeably to the etymology of the word indeed, but against both classical and biblical use, is taken to mean *making righteous* in the proper sense; whence it is made the same substantially with *sanctification,* and regarded as a property residing in the man personally, *justitia inhaerens* or *infusa.*\*

The objective ground of justification, according to the Council of Trent, is in every view the propitiatory death of Christ; but the apprehension of it is not by faith alone. This has justifying power only so far as it is the beginning of salvation, the root of justification, *humanae salutis initium, fundamentum et radix omnis justificationis.*† Full justification, however, it cannot effect, if it were only for the reason that in the Romish view of it, differing from the evangelical, it is exhibited prevailingly as simple historical assent.‡ The grace becomes complete only by means of good works flowing from faith; and has different degrees accordingly answerable to the character and number of these works.§

---

\* S. VI, cap. 7: Hanc dispositionem seu praeparationem justificatio ipsa consequitur, quae non est sola peccatorum remissio, sed *et santificatio et renovatio* interioris hominis per voluntariam susceptionem gratiae et donorum, unde homo *ex injusto fit justus* et ex inimico amicus, ut sit heres secundum spem vitae aeternae. Comp. can. 16.

† S. VI, cap. 8. Comp. can. 9, 11, and 12. In the 9th can. it is said: Si quis dixerit, sola fide impium justificari, ita ut intelligat nihil aliud requiri, quod *ad justificationis gratiam consequendam cooperetur* et nulla ex parte necesse esse eum suae voluntatis motu praeparari atque disponi; anathema sit.

‡ S. VI, cap. 6: credentes vera esse, quae divinitus revelata at promissa sunt. Comp. *Cat. Rom.* I, 1, 1: [Sed quoniam in divinis literis multiplex est fidei significatio, hic] de ea fide loquimur, cujus vi omnino assentimur, iis, quae tradita sunt divinitus. Bellarmine, *de justific.,* I, 4: Catholici fidem in *intellectus* sedem habere docent.

§ S. VI, cap. 10: Sic ergo justificati et amici Dei ac domestici facti, euntes de virtute in virtutem, renovantur, ut Apostolus inquit, de die in diem; h.e., mortificando membra carnis suae et exhibendo ea arma justitiae in sanctificationem, per observationem mandatorum Dei et ecclesiae, in ipsa justitia per Christi gratiam accepta, cooperante fide, bonis operibus crescunt atque *magis justificantur.* Comp. can. 13, 14, and 24. In the last it is said: Si quis dixerit, justitiam acceptam non conservari atque etiam non *augeri* coram Deo *per bona opera,* sed opera ipsa fructus solummodo et signa esse justificationis adeptae, non autem *ipsius augendae* causam; anathema sit.

In this way a proper merit is held to belong to such works; *a meritum de congruo,* as they speak, to those which precede justification and a *meritum de condigno* to those which follow.*

Practically however this coordination simply of faith and works, as producing justification, cannot be preserved; but the chief weight must be given to the last; since they can be multiplied indefinitely, coming thus under the category of number and quantity, while faith is one act properly flowing over into a continuous state. The Romish Church accordingly has carried her estimate of human virtue so far that she not only holds a *perfect* fulfillment of the law to be possible†; but in broad opposition to that scripture, *When ye have done all, say, We are unprofitable servants,* has to tell even of a surplus meritoriousness of good works, her so-called *opera supererogationis,* in which a man may do more than his duty, and raise himself to the character of a saint. Such supermeritorious works are deposited in the treasury or fund of the church, which has the right to dispose of the trust at pleasure, and may employ it to cover the sins of less advanced Christians, or of souls even that have already passed into purgatory.‡

---

* Comp. the way in which this doctrine was carried out by the scholastics with the notices furnished in Koellner's *Symbolik der heil. apost. kath. roemischen Kirche* (Hamburg, 1844), pp. 325 ff.

† Conc. Trid., S. VI, cap. 16.

‡ The *Conc. Trid.* indeed does not utter itself clearly on this point (comp., however, S. VI, cap. 11, can. 18 and 32; S. XXI, de reform, c. 9); and it is remarkable that the *Cat. Rom.* has not a word on the subject. But the doctrine had already become complete with the scholastics, particularly Thomas Aquinas; and the Council informs us, S. XXV, *decr. de indulg.,* that it was to be held agreeably to the authorities, and only the practical abuses of it to be put away. The Roman Catholic divines accordingly bring it forward without reserve. Comp. Bellarmine, *de indulg.,* I, 2: Extat in Ecclesia thesaurus satisfactionum ex Christi passionibus infinitus, qui numquam exhauriri poterit.— *Ad hunc thesaurum superfluentium satisfactionum pertinent etiam passiones b. Mariae virginis et omnium aliorum sanctorum, qui plus passi sunt, quam eorum peccata requirerent.*—Cap. 14. Res autem certissima est et apud catholicos indubitata, indulgentiis juvari posse animas, quae in purgatorio poenas luunt. Theologians of more evangelical views in the Romish Church, such as Hirscher,[22] regard indulgences, to be sure, as the regular continuation simply of the early penitential discipline, a remnant of the old church punishments. But the whole practice of the church serves to confirm the other view.

Hence sprang the traffic in indulgences, the abomination that gave the first shock to the moral sensibilities of Luther. In this scandalous trade, that which forms the inmost sanctuary of man's life—the pardon of sin and holiness—was put to sale for the most paltry and outward of all interests, money. The profits thus made were applied to the building of St. Peter's Church, to gratify the ambition of the popes. But the completion of this dome, whose Sistine chapel Michelangelo had decorated with the scene of the Last Judgment, might be said to have brought with it at the same time the *last judgment* for the Romish Church itself, thus fallen into the arms of the world.

Where full justification is thus made to depend on the fluctuating subjective ground of human works and merit, it is impossible, on the other side, for a Christian, however honest and humble, to attain to any certainty of his salvation; and all such assurance is expressly condemned accordingly by the Council of Trent, unless as it may be the product of a special revelation.* Thus it happens very generally that the piety of precisely the most excellent and earnest members of this church carries with it a legal, fettered, anxious character, that never allows them to come to the full joy of faith, the glorious liberty of the children of God. The further the man advances, the more he sees and feels what is still wanting; while such as *can* be satisfied with themselves, only show the absence of all right judgment and feeling by this fact. Such self-righteousness no doubt is much more common in the Roman Catholic Church than rigid self-probation or self-knowledge.

The Tridentine view then of this most momentous dogma, in which all subjective Christianity is comprehended, is fairly chargeable with the following serious defects: (1) a very superficial knowledge of human sinfulness, in affirming a *dispositio*, *praeparatio* and *cooperatio,* on the part of man, as necessarily preceding and making way for justification; (2) a confounding of *justificatio* with *sanctificatio* in the conception of the central idea itself; (3) a most insufficient representation of the nature of faith; (4) an overvaluation of good works after conversion, invest-

---

* Sess. VI, cap. 9 and 12, and can. 13-16.

ing the whole Christian life with a Pelagianistic complexion; and (5) an entire want of evangelical freedom and assurance.

Now in all these points, which are inseparably connected with the doctrine of justification itself, the Protestant system, both as Lutheran and orthodox Reformed, exhibits a greater depth of Christian consciousness, and an advance consequently upon the soteriology of the Middle Ages. The doctrine as it stands in this system presupposes necessarily a much more thorough knowledge of sin, the guilt of which is to be taken away by justification. The natural state of man, or his original depravity, is viewed not simply as a debilitation of the moral powers, *egestas naturalis, justitiae debitae nuditas,* as Thomas Aquinas expresses it; but as a real corruption of these powers, of such sort, that before the introduction of a new life-giving principle into his person, so far as a *justitia spiritualis* is concerned on which all turns in the case, he is unable to produce from himself anything that is good. After the will has once made choice of evil, it is no longer free, no longer an undecided *liberum arbitrium;* but on the contrary, it is filled with the contents of evil, sold under its power, and thus an object of divine wrath.*

The only disposition then which Protestantism can require, and in fact does require,† as a prerequisite to justification, is the consciousness of guilt awakened by the judicial function of the law—that "schoolmaster to Christ"—and grounded on this the felt need of redemption, which is still included in our nature in spite of its corruption, and without which indeed redemption

---

* That the tract may not be unduly extended, we must limit ourselves mostly to mere references, leaving the reader to consult the proof passages for himself, as every Protestant divine at any rate should have them within reach. We cite the Lutheran symbols, from the edition of Hase (*Libri Symbolici,* 1837); the Reformed, as published by Niemeyer (*Collectio Confessionum in Ecclesiis Reformatis publicatarum,* 1840). On original sin, and the whole state of the unregenerate, see *Confessio Augustana,* Art. 2, pp. 9 f.; *Apologia Confessionis,* Art. 1, de peccato origin, pp. 50 ff.; *Articuli Smalcaldici,* III, 1, pp. 317 f.; on the Reformed side: *Confessio Helvetica* II, c. 8—9, pp. 477 ff.; *Catechismus Heidelbergensis,* quaest. 7-8, p. 431. *Articuli Anglicani,* Art. 9, p. 603; *Confessio Fidei Gallicana,* Art. 10-11, p. 332; *Confessio Belgica,* Art. 15, p. 370; *Confessio Scoticana* I, Art. 3, p. 342; *Canones Synodi Dordrechtanae,* cap. 3, Art. 1-3, pp. 708 f.; *Confessio Fidei Westmonasteriensis sive Puritanae,* c. 6, § 1—6; c. 9, § 1—5.

† Comp., for example, *Formula Concordiae* V, de lege et evangelio, p. 711.

could have no place. This repentance and desire however are so little operative and meritorious as regards justification, that they form rather the sense of complete unworthiness, the feeling of absolute emptiness and want, resembling bodily hunger, which craves food, but has no power to satisfy its own call.

The renovation of the sinner can proceed only from the creative grace of God. If the divine goodness, in the first creation, formed for itself its own object, this is necessary much more in redemption, where its object is in the first place its opposite also and enemy (Romans 5:10). Not the love we bear to God, but the love with which he has loved us in Christ, is the ground of our salvation (1 John 4:10). This love accordingly has prevented [gone before] us; it has borne all sin and expiated all guilt in our stead, but fulfilled at the same time all righteousness, as required by the law, that is the published will of God.

This all-sufficient satisfaction of Christ takes hold upon the individual subjectively, in justification. This is a judicial, declarative act on the part of God, by which he first pronounces the sin-crushed, contrite sinner free from guilt as it regards the past, for the sake of his only-begotten Son, and then ("freely," Romans 3:24; "without the deeds of the law," 3:28; by grace, through faith, and not of himself, Ephesians 2:8) makes over to him, in boundless mercy, the full righteousness of the same, to be counted and to be in fact his own. It is in this way (1) negatively *remissio peccatorum* (Psalm 32:1-2; Romans 3:25; 4:7; Luke 11:4; 2 Corinthians 5:19) and (2) positively *imputatio justitiae* and *adoptio in filios Dei* (Romans 4:5; 5:9; 2 Corinthians 5:21; Galatians 3:6; Philippians 3:9). Man by justification steps into the place of Christ, as Christ had previously stepped into the place of man. What he did altogether, he did not for himself, but out of free, self-sacrificing love toward the human race, of which he is the head.*

---

* *Conf., Aug.,* Art. 4., p. 10; *Apol. Conf.,* Art. 2, pp. 71 ff.; *Form. Conc.,* Art. 3, pp. 683 ff.: Unanimi consensu credimus, docemus et confitemur, . . . quod homo peccator coram Deo justificetur, h.e., absolvatur ab omnibus suis peccatis et a judicio justissimae condemnationis, et adoptetur in numerum filiorum Dei, atque haeres aeternae vitae scribatur, sine ullis nostris meritis aut dignitate, et absque ullis praecedentibus, praesentibus aut sequentibus nostris

In this way, all Pelagian and Semi-Pelagian self-righteousness is torn up by the roots; humility is exhibited as the ground of piety; and all rightful honor is secured to Jesus Christ, as the only and all-sufficient Mediator between God and man.

While the merit of Christ is thus viewed as the only ground, the efficient cause *(causa efficiens* and *emeritoria)* of this righteousness, the only means of its appropriation *(causa instrumentalis, instrumentum, organon lepticon)* is presented to us in *faith.* This is not a natural product of man, although it finds a basis in the possibility and want of redemption belonging to his fallen nature; but the free gift of God, which is offered and imparted to him through the word and sacraments.* Nor is it moreover, as regarded in the Romish system (and this is a very essential point), a mere historical assent, and so a theoretic process simply; but along with this, and principally, a cordial unconditional *trust* in the atoning efficacy of Christ's merit, a *personal appropriation* of it to the entire spiritual life of the subject.† It holds, back of

---

operibus, ex mera gratia tantummodo, propter unicum meritum perfectissimamque obedientiam, passionem acerbissimam, morten et resurrectionem Dom. nostri J. Chr. cujus obedientia nobis ad justitiam imputatur. Reformed symbols—*Conf. Helv.,* c. 15, pp. 494 ff.: Justificare significat Apostolo in disputatione de justificatione, peccata remittere, a culpa et poena absolvere, in gratiam recipere et justum pronunciare, etc. *Cat. Heidelb.,* quaest. 60, p. 443: Ut . . . sine ullo meo merito (Rom. 3:24) ex mera Dei misericordia (Tit. 3:5; Eph. 2:8-9) mihi perfecta satisfactio (1 John 2:2), justitia et sanctitas Christi (1 John 2:1) imputetur ac donetur (Rom. 4:4-5; 2 Cor. 5:19), perinde ac si nec ullum ipse peccatum admisissem, nec ulla mihi labes inhaereret, imo vero quasi eam obedientiam, quam pro me Christus praestitit, ipse perfecte praestitissem (2 Cor. 5:21)—a most clear, complete, and valuable definition. *Art. Anglic.,* Art. 11-12, pp. 603 f.; *Conf. Gallic.,* Art. 18, p. 334; *Conf. Belg.,* Art. 22, p. 374; *Conf. Scot.,* Art. 12, p. 346; *Declar. Thorum.,* de gratia, p. 673; *Can. Syn. Dordr.,* III, c. 10, p. 710; *Conf. Westmonast.* cap. 11, de justif. § 1—6, and c. 12.

* *Conf. Aug.,* V, p. 11: Nam per verbum et sacramenta, tanquam per instrumenta, donatur Spiritus Sanctus, qui fidem efficit, ubi et quando visum est Deo, in iis, qui audiunt Evangelium, etc. *Conf. Helv.,* Art. 16, p. 496: Haec autem fides merum est Dei donum, quod solus Deus ex gratia sua electis suis, secundum mensuram, et quando, cui et quantum ipse vult, donat, et quidem per spiritum sanctum, mediante praedicatione evangelii et oratione fideli.

† Besides the passages already cited, comp. *Conf. Aug.,* Art. 20, p. 18. More fully in his *Loci theologici,* p. 226 (1562 ed.), Melanchthon[23] describes the nature of faith, first as an *assentiri universo verbo divino,* and further as a *fiducia misericordiae Dei,* and then proceeds: Fiducia est *motus in voluntate,*

the psychological distinction of understanding and will, in the inmost depth of man's personality, and so works with like influence upon both. The later Protestant theologians tried accordingly to exhaust the conception of faith, as much as might be, under three characters. The first is *notitia,* the knowledge of its object, Jesus Christ namely and his all-sufficient merit; the second, *assensus,* free inward consent to all the Scriptures teach of the mercy of God in Christ; the third, which is most essential and full of comfort, *fiducia,* or the act of the will moving toward Christ and resting in him for redemption, the confidence that this grace is not only of general objective force, but personally proper also to the believing subject himself.

In what relation now does this justification stand to *holiness;* faith as thus described, to *works?* Decided as Protestantism is in limiting all justifying efficacy to the apprehension of Christ's merit by means of faith, it is just as far from denying, however remotely, the necessary connection between this grace and a godly life. This even the most shrewd, clear-sighted, and profound of modern opposers of the system, has been constrained to admit when he says: "It would be *in the highest degree unfair,* however, not to add that according to the Lutheran theory, the apprehension of this free remission of sins must always draw after it the renewal of the sinner, and a transformation of his life to holiness."

Genuine Protestantism has ever in its eye the faith of Paul, that works of love—or to speak with the Helvetic Confession—the

---

necessario respondens assensioni, seu quo voluntas *in Christo acquiescit.* Comp. Calvin's *Instit. Chr. Rel.,* III, 2, 8; *Conf. Helv.* II, Art. 16, p. 496. Fides enim Christiana non est opinio et humana persuasio, sed *firmissima fiducia* et *evidens ac constans animi assensus,* denique *certissima comprehensio veritatis Dei,* propositae in scripturis et symbolo apostolico, atque adeo *Dei ipsius,* summi boni, et praecipue promissionis divinae et Christi, qui omnium promissionum est colophon. Most masterly also, and drawn from the deepest experience, is the definition of faith by the Heidelberg Catechism, in its answer to the 21st question. No such deep views of the constitution of faith had been taken since the time of the apostles. Sarpi[24] relates that the bishops of the Council of Trent were not able to conceive of it as anything more than assent simply to historical truth; and that they were brought into the greatest embarrassment with the subject, since they could find no satisfactory light, either from the fathers or the schoolmen, on what had not before come under thorough discussion.

*fides, nulla operum fiducia,* is at the same time *operum foecundis-sima.* Its very being consists in the appropriation of Christ, the holy and the just. How then should it *not* produce good works, as necessarily as a good tree must yield good fruit? It is the parent of all virtues. As soon as we have known and believed the love which God has toward us (1 John 4:16), we cannot but love him in return (4:19).* This relation between faith and love is of such inward force that this last also can have no place without the first, as little as one may gather grapes from thorns.

Faith is always necessarily presupposed in love; for what does not spring from faith is sin, and so not love—the essence of which is a forsaking of self, while self-seeking forms the inmost nature of evil. "Good religious works make never a good religious man, but a good religious man maketh good religious works. So that always the person must first be religious and good before all good works, and good religious works follow and go forth from the religious good person. As the tree must be before the fruit, so must the man be first good or bad in his person, before he doeth good or bad works. The like we see in all handiwork. A good or bad house maketh not a good or bad carpenter, but a good or bad carpenter maketh a good or bad house. No work maketh a master, such as is the work; but as the master is, his work also is such. . . . Works, as they make not believing, so they make not pious

---

* *Conf. Aug.,* Art. 6, p. 11; Art. 20, pp. 15-16; *Apol. Conf.,* Art. 3, pp. 83, 85. In the same, pp. 133 f., it is said: Ideo justificamur, ut justi bene operari et obedire Legi Dei incipiamus. Ideo regeneramur et Spiritum Sanctum accipimus, ut nova vita habeat nova opera, novos affectus, timorem, dilectionem Dei, odium concupiscentiae, etc. *Form. Conc.,* epit. Art. 3, p. 586; Art. 4, p. 589; sol. decl. Art. 3, p. 688. The noble passage of Luther in his preface to the Epistle to the Romans is known: "Oh, it is a living, busy, active, mighty thing with faith, that it cannot possibly cease from working good. It does not ask either if good works are to be done, but before the question is put it has done them already and is doing them still . . . ; so that it is impossible to sunder works from faith, as much so verily as that burning and shining should be sundered from fire." The Reformed symbols, without exception, press this point in terms equally strong, and in actual life indeed this church has shown herself more zealous for good works even than her sister. I refer only to *Conf. Helv.* II, Art. 16, pp. 496 f.; and *Cat. Heidelb.,* Q. 64, p. 444: neque enim fieri potest, quin ii, qui Christo per fidem insiti sunt, fructus proferant gratitudinis.

either. But faith, as it maketh pious, so doth it make good works also."*

Protestantism in this way only places faith and love in their natural relation to each other, without detracting in the least from the dignity of the last. Rather, with the apostle Paul, it puts this highest, for the very reason that it comes last; as the beginning is always the less perfect, that points to a more complete form of existence. The evangelical morality, as the product of free love and gratitude, is also much more sound, pure, deep, than the Roman Catholic, which even in its highest exhibitions must be allowed to include a sinful mixture of spiritual pride or mechanical formality.

Good works then, in the Protestant system, are held to be acceptable to God; and it is taught even that God rewards them graciously.† But no room is left for the imagination that we can earn salvation by their means, much less to think of any surplus

---

* Luther's sermon "Liberty of a Christian Man"; one of his most profound productions (edition by Gerlach, Vol. V, pp. 37 f.). The two theses of Luther, *"If faith be not without all work, it maketh not righteous,"* and *"It is impossible that justifying faith should be without constantly many good works,"* have been tiresomely paraded by the papists as an irreconcilable contradiction. To this however, Sartorius[25] (*Evangel. Kirchenzeitung,* 1835, p. 826) has rightly answered that both agree admirably, and the more the truth of the one is seen, the more true must the other show itself to be at the same time. In proportion as the man, renouncing himself, ascribes his salvation only and altogether to God's preventing love, the more deep and inward will be the devotion of his love in return, and his grateful zeal in all good works; which flow the more richly from faith, as its fruit, the less they are made to go before it, or take rank with it, in the way of principle or ground. As for the dictum finally of the same great Reformer, so ignorantly misconstrued: *Si in fide fieri posset adulterium, peccatum non esset;* we must bear in mind the bold, reckless, wholesale, sweeping style in which he was accustomed to speak; and then reflect further that with him no such sin *could* be committed in faith, so that he argues simply *ex impossibili.*

† *Apol. Conf.,* Art. 3, pp. 96, 135; *Form. Conc.,* Art. 4, pp. 700 f.; *Conf. Helv.* II, c. 16, p. 498: Placent vero approbanturque a Deo opera, quae a nobis fiunt per fidem. —Etenim docemus Deum bona operantibus amplam dare mercedem. —Referimus tamen mercedem hanc, quam dominus dat, non ad meritum hominis accipientis, sed ad bonitatem, vel liberalitatem et veritatem Dei promittentis atque dantis, qui cum nihil debeat cuiquam, promisit tamen, etc. *Conf. Belq.,* Art. 24, p. 376: Interea non negamus, Deum bona opera in suis remunerari; sed id mera sua gratia fieri dicimus, ut qui dona sua in nobis coronet.

merit. The entire Christian life is made to appear as a *debt of gratitude,* for the boundless, eternally to be praised love and mercy of God manifested toward us in Jesus Christ.* When we have done all accordingly, we have at best done only what was our duty (Luke 17:10).

Sanctification, however, is in its nature a continually progressive work that becomes complete only when the whole body of the church, of which the individual Christian is a member, has reached its state of perfection. Yea, strictly considered, even the best works of the believer, so long as he sojourns in the body, by reason of the continued presence of sin in his person, are not good absolutely, but only so much and so far as they are wrought in him and through him by the Spirit of God.† If he might say even with the apostle, "I know nothing by myself," that is, am conscious of no wrong, he must with him also still add, "yet am I not hereby *justified.*" His confidence of salvation consequently can never rest upon his works of love, but only upon the objective rock of Christ's merit, whose he feels himself to be in faith. Even Paul himself, the apostle, at the end of his career—a career such as no saint of the Romish Church certainly can exhibit—declares it to be the highest object of his desire that he might *not* have *his own* righteousness, which was of the law, but a foreign righteousness, which was of faith in Christ, the righteousness namely that is of God by faith (Philippians 3:9).

The last point of difference in the case before us regards the *assurance* of justification. Being justified by grace through faith, we have peace, the apostle tells us, with God (Romans 5:1–5). This peace is a state of mind, which necessarily attends the exercise of faith. For God is the fullness of all blessedness, and faith

---

* With admirable judgment accordingly, the Heidelberg Catechism has comprehended all Christian practice under the article of "Gratitude." The *Conf. Helv.* II, Art. 16, p. 497, agreeing with this says: (Bona opera) fieri debent, non ut his promereamur vitam aeternam, Donum Dei enim est, ut Apostolus ait, vita aeterna; neque ad ostentationem, quam rejecit Dominus Matth. 6; neque ad quaestum, quem et ipsum rejecit Matth. 23; sed ad gloriam Dei, ad, ornandam vocationem nostram gratitudinemque Deo praestandam, et ad utilitatem proximi. *Art. Anglic.,* Art. 14.

† *Conf. Helv.* II, c. 16, p. 499: Sunt multa praeterea indigna Deo, et imperfecta plurima inveniuntur in operibus etiam sanctorum. Luther's word is known: *Justus in omni bono opere peccat.*

is the possession of God; consequently in itself of beatifying nature, in itself the assurance of salvation. To be united to God in Christ is to be saved. But faith is the consciousness of this communion. As nothing makes a man living but life, nothing makes him joyful or loving but joy or love, so he can be made blessed only by faith, which is the same thing with blessedness itself.* At the same time to be sure, since faith is at one time large and strong, as Luther says, at another small and weak, this assurance of justification must naturally rise and fall in the same way.†

Before passing over to the formal principle, it may be well, in view of the immense importance of the Protestant doctrine of justification, to notice the most acute and weighty objections that have been urged against it on the part of Roman Catholic and pseudo-Protestant, or rationalistic opposers.

1.   One of the most common reproaches is that "the Protestant theory of justification encourages a thoughtless reliance on grace and neglect of good works." Here, however, the curse turns into a blessing. For the same reproach was brought against the doctrine of the apostle Paul‡; and it serves to show consequently that

---

* This assurance of salvation, as secured to us by faith, is proclaimed in the loftiest style by the old church psalmody, and by Luther himself in a thousand places, as for instance in his sermon on the gosp. D. 20. p. trin.[26] where among other things he says: "If death make onset, so have I Christ; he is my life. If sin make onset, so have I Christ; he is my righteousness. If hell and damnation make onset, so have I Christ; he is my salvation. Set in upon me thus what may, still I have Christ; him I can hold forward as my shield, so that nothing can do me harm." Calvin's *Instit.,* III, 2, 16—In summa: vere fidelis non est, nisi qui solida persuasione Deum sibi propitium benevolumque patrem esse persuasus, de ejus benignitate omnia sibi pollicetur; nisi qui divinae erga se benevolentiae promissionibus fretus, indubitatam salutis expectationem praesumit.

† Calvin's *Instit.,* III, 2, 17: Nos certe dum fidem docemus esse debere certam ac securam, non certitudinem aliquam imaginamur, quae nulla tangatur dubitatione, nec securitatem, quae nulla sollicitudine impetatur; quin potius dicimus, perpetuum esse fidelibus certamen cum sua ipsorum diffidentia. Tantum abest ut eorum conscientias in placida aliqua quiete collocemus, quae nullis omnino turbis interpelletur.

‡ Romans 3:8: "We be slanderously reported, and some affirm that we say, Let us do evil, that good may come." Romans 5:10 compared with 6:1; Galatians 5:13. When Peter says in his 2d Epistle, 3:16, that there are some things in the epistles of Paul hard to understand, which they that are unlearned and unstable wrest to their own destruction, he has the doctrine of justification mainly in his eye.

we agree with him. As he could triumphantly point such calumniators to the moral exhortations contained in all his epistles and also to his own life, so do we with like confidence hold up to our opponents our symbolical books and the lives of the Reformers themselves, whose moral earnestness and untiring practical activity were such as to cast all their contemporaries into the shade.

2. "It is not possible that God, who is truth itself, can declare a man to be righteous, and treat him as such, when he is not such in fact." The mere *treatment* involves no difficulty. Even in the sphere of the natural life, God treats us better than we deserve, causing the sun to shine, and giving rain, for the benefit of the ungodly as well as of the good and pious. The nature of grace, which falls, it is true, beyond the range of abstract justice, consists always in this, that the offender is released from merited punishment, and put into the positive enjoyment of freedom; that being thus subdued and humbled, he may be led to pursue a better life.

Love also in general, of which grace is only a particular modification, shows in its highest utterances the very same character, without which it could never be exercised toward an enemy. When some unfortunate has fallen into the water, the philanthropist stops not to inquire, even if it be his own enemy, whether he is worthy of being rescued, but plunges at once into the stream, and by his noble, self-forgetting conduct wins the heart of him whose life he saves.

The whole difficulty then in the case before us must turn, not upon God's treatment of the believer, but upon the idea of his *declaring* a man to be what he is not in fact. If, however, practice and judgment are to be saved from irreconcilable contradiction with each other, the first must involve here the supposition again of the second. When God is represented by the apostle as having loved men while they were yet sinners, it does not mean that he loved them *as* sinners, which would be to have loved sin itself in them, whereas this is always his abomination; but he loved them as creatures, who were capable of redemption, and in this view worthy of being loved. He loved the divine nature which was in them potentially, having reality indeed only in his own purpose, but destined, through the manifestation of his grace and love, to actualize itself and become real subjectively also in man himself.

Men are declared righteous then by God, not so far as they are sinners, but so far only as they are in Christ, and have thus in this objective way the principle of righteousness in fact; and this justifying act becomes itself the occasion, by which the principle is actualized in its subject, having creative force, quickening the dead, and calling into existence that which had no existence before. The justifying grace of God does not stand over against the convicted sinner in an abstract form, but passes over to him through the medium of faith, sets him in its own element, and thus lodges in his person a life germ altogether new, in which is comprehended from the start the entire growth of holiness. So Abraham was called a father of many nations, before he was so actually. Ideally, however, in the divine plan he was such in the fullest sense.

God, before whom the dimensions of time all give way in the same vast eternity, looks upon men in their inmost nature as rooted in Christ, with whom they are brought into living union by faith. For the relation of Christ to humanity is not outward, but inward and essential. He is the second Adam, the spiritual head of the race, the true center of all its individual personalities, in which only the idea of the whole is fully realized and made complete. This whole objection then proceeds upon a perfectly abstract conception of the doctrine of justification, which admits the thought of a judgment in the divine mind that is not at the same time creative; and only against such a conception of the case can it be allowed to have any force.

Many of the Lutheran theologians did indeed lean toward this extreme, in their anti-Pelagian zeal; but it was not so with the Reformed. They always acknowledged the true element here in the catholic doctrine, without sanctioning its Pelagianistic trait.*

---

* Comp. particularly the whole 11th chapter of the third book of Calvin's *Institutes;* for example, § 6, where this agreement and difference are both very clearly stated: Sicut non potest decerpi Christus in partes, ita inseparabilia esse haec duo, quae simul et conjunctim in ipso percipimus, justitiam et sanctificationem. Quoscunque ergo in gratiam recipit Deus, simul spiritu adoptionis donat, cujus virtute eos reformat ad suam imaginem. Verum, si solis claritas non potest a calore separari, an ideo dicemus luce calefieri terram,

For there still remains always this great distinction, that the principle of righteousness in man as answering to the justifying act of God never flows even in part of his own subjective constitution, but only and altogether from his believing union with the objective Christ, and that the actualization of this principle in his person, is itself conditioned by the declaratory act, creative at the same time, going before.

3. "It is unreasonable to ascribe all justifying and saving power to faith, and to deny such virtue to love, when the apostle Paul nevertheless, who is in such great authority with Protestants, places love above faith—1 Corinthians 13:13."* We, too, proclaim love to be the highest, the always-abiding; but precisely for this reason it is not to be found in guilty man, immersed in selfishness and sin, but only in God himself, the fountain of all love. So the only way of coming to God, and becoming assured of his love in Christ, through the knowledge and apprehension of which we are made first capable of love in return, is no other than faith itself; which is simply what our doctrine asserts. The fruit is better than the root; and yet this last carries the tree, and not the first. In this objection moreover, it is forgotten, that all justifying and saving power, causatively considered, is lodged according to our view, neither in human faith, to which we attribute only instrumental efficacy, nor in human love, but exclusively in God's grace, that the glory of this may remain complete.

4. Adroitly constructed is the objection: "Faith in the Protestant view is justifying, not as a dead historical assent, but in the character of inward humility and trust, as a longing after the Redeemer, as love consequently though in its infancy; and thus the theory, to preserve itself, falls back again unwittingly to the Roman Catholic dogma." Now we may well allow that there *is* an

---

calore vero illustrari? Hac similitudine nihil ad rem praesentem magis accomodum: sol calore suo terram vegetat ac fecundat, radiis suis illustrat et illuminat: hic mutua est ac individua connexio, transferre tamen quod unius peculiare est, ad alterum, ratio ipsa prohibet.

* In similar style the argument was pressed by an opponent upon Melanchthon: dilectio est maxima virtus; ergo dilectio justificat. Melanchthon, however, draws from the proposition just the opposite conclusion: dilectio est maxima virtus, atqui nos eam *minime* praestamus; ergo per dilectionem *minime* justi sumus.

ultimate point where faith may be regarded as a constituent in the development of love, taken in its broadest sense. But unless all ideas are to lose themselves in one another promiscuously, we must distinguish and separate on the one hand, as closely as we seek connecting relations on the other. Only in the use of such reflective separation is any scientific knowledge possible. We say then that fallen man—sold under the power of selfishness, which is the very opposite of love, in order that he may come to the exercise of this grace in its true Christian, self-renouncing, self-sacrificing form—must first become conscious of the divine love in its relation to himself personally, must *yield* himself to *Christ's love;* and this is itself the exercise of faith. The receptive element must go before the spontaneous; humble apprehension, before self-subsisting action. We are always brought back accordingly to the Protestant thesis that man is justified and saved, not by the love which he exercises himself, but by the love he receives from abroad, that is, by faith.

## THE FORMAL PRINCIPLE OF THE REFORMATION

So much for the *material* principle of Protestantism, by which direct and full access has been made good for man to the grace of God in Christ. This doctrine was brought to the consciousness of the Reformers in their inward spiritual conflicts, by means of the written word of God. While tradition as it then stood contradicted it entirely, directing men for salvation, not to faith, but to mechanical outward observances and forms; the almost forgotten Bible was felt to preach the glorious truth, distinctly and loudly, from beginning to end.* Thus as Christ became to them all in

---

* This experience is described in a lovely way by Luther himself: "Then (after coming to a clear sense of justification by faith), at once I felt that I was newborn, and had now found a wide open door to enter paradise itself; *saw now moreover the precious Scriptures in a very different light from all they seemed before; ran accordingly soon through the whole Bible, and gathered in other passages also according to this rule all its expositions of what is meant by God's work, God's righteousness, and God's faith.* And as before I hated this little word right heartily—God's righteousness—so I began now to hold the same high and dear as the sweetest and most comforting to me of all words, and this same passage in Saint Paul became to me of a truth the very gate of paradise."[27]

all, his word also was taken for the separate and sufficient fountain of their religious knowledge. To the material or life principle of the Reformation accordingly is joined as its necessary
complement the *formal* or *knowledge principle,* which consists in
this, that the *word of God,* as it has been handed down to us in
the canonical books of the Old and New Testaments, *is the pure
and proper source as well as the only certain measure of all saving truth.*

We find here now a similar relation to that which we have already met in the case of the material principle, and a correspondence between the terms on both sides. The word of God answers
to faith; and tradition, to love. As the doctrine of justification refers back to the doctrine of sin as its necessary presupposition, so
does the doctrine of the authority of the Scriptures also to a corresponding view of the relation of the natural reason to revelation. The more favorable the view that is taken of the will of
man in its natural state, the less will be the account made of the
blindness of the understanding as going hand in hand with sin,
and the higher the consequence attached to the word of man, as
well as to his works, in the business of salvation; and so the reverse will hold also in every point. Hence Romanism, as it makes
faith and works to be parallel sources of justification, and lays
the main stress in fact practically upon the last, is only consistent
with itself, when it invests, here also in the sphere of the formal
principle, the word of God and human tradition with equal authority as sources of religious knowledge, and gives the second in
reality the preference above the first. Protestantism, on the contrary, places both powers in each case in their natural relation
to each other, in the relation namely of ground and consequence,
cause and effect, origin and process. Faith alone justifies, but produces at the same time good works as its necessary fruit; the word
of God is the only fountain and norm of knowledge, but it flows
forward in the church, and comes there continually to clearer
and deeper consciousness. As moreover, according to this view,
the value of works is estimated by the measure of the faith which
forms their ground, so the worth of tradition also is determined by
its organic connection and agreement with the word of God.

Inasmuch however as history is ever developed by means of more or less one-sided antagonisms, it was natural that with the Reformation, in opposition to the reigning overvaluation of *man's works* and *man's word,* the principal emphasis should be placed upon *God's grace* and *God's word;* not with the repudiation indeed, but with some neglect at least of the other side. This was the case particularly with regard to tradition.* The neglect here is the more to be excused, since the Church of Rome under the credit of apostolical tradition had smuggled into her communion the most shocking errors, and brought the word of God almost entirely into oblivion, had repeatedly prohibited it to the laity indeed in express terms. Tradition was in fact, as Chemnitz says in his *Examen. Conc. Trid.*[28] the box of Pandora, *cujus operculo omne genus corruptelarum, abusuum et superstitionum in ecclesiam invectum fuit.*

As both principles are thus inwardly connected, being only two different sides indeed of one and the same principle, our exposition of the formal, which is now before us, will be materially assisted by the acquaintance we have formed with the other.

The Council of Trent accepts, according to the first decree of the fourth session, two sources for the knowledge of divine revelation, the word written or the sacred Scriptures, and the word unwritten or tradition; and these she makes coordinate, in the first instance, as the product of the same Holy Spirit (*pari pietatis affectu ac reverentia suscipit et veneratur*). Such a coordination

---

* We may notice here incidentally a very important fundamental peculiarity of the Lutheran Church as distinguished from the Reformed. This communion, in its genuine form and life, has more respect for tradition than the Reformed, and its development accordingly has been more historical and gradual, and more largely conservative of what was old; while the Reformed, in Puritanism particularly, proceeded more violently, and by its contempt for history furnished occasion, in part at least, for the multiplication of sects. However, the Reformed Church is more strenuous than the Lutheran in its view of the necessity of good works, and has always displayed accordingly uncommon practical activity in the Christian life; while the sister body, reveling in free justification, presses hard on the confines of antinomianism; having been carried in the person of one of her principal champions quite over to the maxim "Good works hinder salvation!" An exaggeration, which of course the church soon disowned.

serves itself to depreciate the written word.* But this is done still
more effectually through the further definitions and restrictions to
which it is subjected. In actual practice, the Scriptures fall behind tradition, as in the case of the material principle, faith falls
behind works. For under the written word of God, the Church
of Rome understands not merely, as we do, the canonical books
of the Old and New Testaments, but in open contradiction to
the oldest and purest tradition of an Origen, Athanasius, Eusebius, Hilary, and even her otherwise so much respected Jerome,
incorporates into it also the Apocrypha; mere human productions, whatever may be their worth.† The distinction between
the divine and human is thus unsettled. This pantheistic feature
runs through the whole system, culminating in the respect shown
toward the pope, as lawfully holding and exercising the threefold
office of Christ himself. Too much again is allowed to human
agency in the formation of the sacred Scriptures, by limiting the
inspiration of the Holy Spirit to mere assistance and guidance
*(assistentia et directio).*‡ Still further, the Latin translation of
Jerome, a work of course proceeding from a particular church position and reflecting its image, is not only placed on a par with
the original text, but in actual use preferred to it altogether.§
In the fourth place, the charge of darkness and ambiguity is

---

* For it involves the assumption that there is much wanting in the Scriptures that is necessary to salvation, and that they are consequently incomplete;
as Bellarmine, *de verbo Dei,* IV, 3, expressly asserts.

† *Conc. Trid., Sess. IV, decr. de can. script.,* where at the same time the
Protestants, for rejecting the Apocrypha, are laid under an anathema.

‡ Bellarmine, *de verbo div.,* I, 15. Aliter Deus adfuit prophetis, aliter his-
toricis. Illis revelavit futura et simul adstitit, ne aliquid falsi admiscerent in
scribendo; his non semper revelavit ea, quae scripturi erant, sed excitavit
duntaxat, ut scriberent ea, quae vel viderant, vel audierant, quorum recorda-
bantur, et simul adstitit, ne quid falsi scriberent; quae assistentia non exclude-
bat laborem. The Jesuits proceeded further and admitted without reserve the
possibility of error, and even of falsehood outright in the Gospels; as, for
example, Alb. Pighius,[29] *Hierarch. eccles.* 1, 2. Matthaeus et Ioannes evangelis-
tae potuerunt et *labi memoria* et *mentiri,* etc.

§ *Conc. Trid.,* S. IV, decr. de edit. et usa s. libr., where the Vulgate is pronounced *authentica* and the rejection of it, that is, all departure from it in
interpretation, is prohibited. Comp. Bellarmine *(de verbo Dei,* II, 10) who
with proper consequence maintains that the Vulgate is free from all material
error in translation.

brought against the Scriptures*; whence tradition is held to be necessary for their interpretation; and it is counseled that the laity should not read them, except in cases of special qualification, of which the bishop is to be the judge.† In short, the whole tendency of the Roman Catholic Church has for its object to subordinate the Bible to tradition, and then to make itself the infallible judge of both, with power to determine at pleasure what is God's word and the doctrine of the church, and to anathematize everything that may go beyond its past decisions, even though, as in the case of the Reformation and Jansenism, it should be an actual deepening of the Christian consciousness itself.

As already remarked, tradition in the Romish sense, is the unwritten portion of divine revelation; by which is meant simply that it was not committed to writing in the beginning by its author, however it may have been reduced to this form since, in the symbolical books and other productions of the church. Its contents are partly expository and partly supplementary to the Bible; it springs in part from Christ himself, and in part from the apostles under the guidance of the Holy Spirit; it is thus of like origin and like dignity with the written word; and has trans-

---

* Comp. Klee's *katholische Dogmatik,* Vol. I, p. 277, 2d ed. Lindanus (de opt. script. interpret.)[30] is not ashamed to say even that the Scriptures without the aid of tradition have no more value than Aesop's fables: Sacram scripturam, si auctoritas ecclesiae disideratur, non plus per se valere quam Aesopi fabulas. Comp. also the *Instruction pastorale* I, of Bossuet, cap. 43.

† The symbols, it is true, are silent on the point, and in all times there have been Catholics who have earnestly recommended the study of the Bible. (Comp. extracts on the necessity and use of Bible reading from the fathers and other Catholic writings by Leander van Ess,[31] 2d ed., Sulzbach, 1816). But in strict Roman Catholic lands, such as Italy and Spain, the people are fearfully ignorant of the Bible, and the priests oppose every effort of the Protestants to circulate it, frequently indeed have committed large numbers of Bibles to the flames. It is a fact further that the reading of the Scriptures has been prohibited to the laity by several popes, from Gregory VII down to our own time, and also by several provincial councils; as the *C. Tolosanum,* 1229[32] (*can.* 14. Prohibemus etiam, ne libros Vet. T. aut N., laici permittantur habere: nisi forte Psalterium, vel Breviarium pro divinis officiis, aut horas B. Mariae aliquis ex devotione habere velit. Sed ne praemissos libros habeant in vulgari translatos, arctissime inhibemus); so the *C. Tarraconense,* 1234.[33] In any case, according to the whole system of the church, the reading of the Scriptures is not regarded as necessary, and the people are referred to the priests as a nearer and surer fountain of instruction.

mitted itself through the church all along, pure and true, under the constant care of God's Spirit.* Articles of tradition are, for example, infant baptism, the worship of the saints, the doctrine of purgatory, the sacrifice of the Mass, the forty-day fast before Easter. Its compass is determined of course by the church, that is, by the Roman Catholic Church, which is taken to be the church universal, and so the rightful bearer of this trust. What she has declared to be apostolical tradition, through her organs, the popes and councils, must be received in this character. She decides in the case however according to a fixed rule, the criterion of catholicity namely presented by Vincentius Lirinensis[35]: *quod ubique, quod semper, quod ab omnibus creditum est.* All valid traditions consequently must have been universally acknowledged by the Christian Church from the beginning.

But just here comes the knot which the Church of Rome is not able to unloose, but only to cut in a violent way. The universality in time and space, which is called for by the criterion now mentioned, cannot be shown in favor of a single one of all her tradi-

---

* The Council of Trent speaks on this difficult subject in its 4th Session, but for reasons easily understood does not go into it minutely. Even to have raised a question here, must have been to put at stake a number of her most important doctrines and usages. Bellarmine, *de verbo Dei,* IV, 2, divides traditions into 1st *traditiones divinae,* communicated by Christ to the apostles; 2d *traditiones apostolicae,* proceeding from the apostles, though not in their writings; and 3d *traditiones ecclesiasticae,* ancient church usages and customs. The first stand parallel in value with the Gospels; the second, with the writings of the apostles; and the third, with the written decrees and constitutions of the church. Moehler's[34] view of tradition, on the contrary, is by no means strictly orthodox, but ideal, showing a Protestant tinge. Here, as in his celebrated book also on the unity of the church, the theology of Schleiermacher was evidently felt. Thus he distinguishes in his *Symbolik,* pp. 362 ff. of the 5th ed., 1838, between a tradition in the subjective and a tradition in the objective sense. The first is nothing more than "the Christian sense belonging to the church, and handing itself down by means of church training, the word continuously living in the hearts of the faithful"; the same thing thus with what Schleiermacher styles the Christian consciousness. Tradition in the objective sense is made to be "the aggregate faith of the church through all ages as exhibited in external historical testimonies." But this is to say nothing characteristic of it as distinguished from the sacred Scriptures, which also belong to the aggregate faith of the church in this form. It is easy enough, in such fashion, to escape the difficulties of the case; which begin precisely where it comes to the question of the concrete contents of tradition as differing from the Bible.

tions as different from the Bible. This point has been largely handled by Chemnitz, with great learning. Very many dogmas and usages rose clearly in the Middle Ages, or at least after the time of Augustine; and in the best cases, the alleged universality reduces itself to a relative majority of voices merely, which was often very small, and not unfrequently besides the result of outward influences entirely. In the discussion on tradition itself, in the fourth session of the Council of Trent, nothing like absolute unanimity was to be found.[36] The bishop of Chiozza maintained that the Gospels contain all that man needs for salvation; and another prelate declared decidedly that God's word consisted not of two parts, that it was a reproach to divine providence to assume that a portion of its revelation had not been committed to writing, and that we must rather follow therefore the example of those fathers, who confined themselves always to the Bible alone. In the discussion on the doctrine of justification a still more considerable want of unity appeared. The archbishop of Sienna, the bishop della Cava, Giulio Contarini, bishop of Belluno, and with them five theologians, joined in declaring faith to be the only ground of justification; love and hope, its attendants; and works, its evidence or proof; while the general of the Augustinians, Seripando, brought forward the view of Gaspar Contarini, which took a middle course between the two systems.

But the voice of history, with its thousand tongues, is overwhelmed, not answered, by the Church of Rome, with the declaration that she is absolutely infallible, the unerring organ of the Holy Spirit, to which all private judgment, all historical inquiry, must yield implicit submission.* To this point in the end the

---

* The Council of Trent of course takes this position everywhere for granted, and utters all its decisions accordingly. In the nature of the case, at the same time, it could not be subjected to particular investigation and proof. This would have been nothing less than a *petitio principii;* since to be able to show its divine authority, the Synod must have assumed the fact as already given. The *Cat. Rom.,* I, 10, 18, ascribes to the Roman Church, and to this exclusively, freedom from all error in *fidei ac morum disciplina tradenda;* and so likewise Bellarmine, *eccl. milit.,* c. 14. Nostra igitur sententia est *ecclesiam absolute non posse errare,* nec in rebus absolute necessariis, nec in aliis, quae credenda vel facienda nobis proponit, sive habeantur expresse in scripturis, sive non: et quum dicimus, ecclesiam non posse errare, id intelligimus tam de universitate fidelium quam de universitate episcoporum.

whole controversy of right comes; with it the entire Roman Catholic system stands or falls. But this highest principle precisely of the infallibility of the papal hierarchy, like the highest principle of most philosophical systems, is merely asserted, *never proved.* It forms the *proton pseudos,* the grand falsehood, on which the whole system rests; and at the same time its central sin, creature deification, making itself identical with the universal church, yea, with the absolute kingdom of God, out of which all are heretics only and children of perdition.

Protestantism has shaken this foundation from its place. It plants itself on the principle that infallibility belongs to Christ and his word alone, and to all else so far only as it may be joined to him in living union. This union however, in the present world, is progressive, and so always incomplete. In the case of the single Christian, this is as clear as day. As in the best works of the regenerate, sin still continues to work with more or less power so that they can never become the ground of justification; so also error still cleaves to his knowledge, as long as he tabernacles in the body, and on this account the truth which is unto salvation can never be built on human tradition. For error and sin are ever inseparably related, like the understanding and the will. Sin is practical error, and error is theoretic sin. If this holds in the case of the individual, it is hard to see why the same should not be true of the church also, since this is nothing else than the organic complex of individual Christians. A bishop does not become another man, in appearing as the member of a synod, made free as by a magic wand from error and sin. As little is this the case with the whole body. Many sinners make no saint, many blind make no seer, as little as a quantity of wood can yield iron, or a quantity of stones, bread. Error and truth differ not gradually, but specifically.

If the church militant then be not free from sin, which no one in the face of history will maintain, so neither is she free from error. True, she has the unerring word of God, and is styled by Paul "the pillar and ground of the truth." The truth accordingly can never disappear from her communion; and this is the right and sound side of the Roman Catholic dogma. But this by no means involves the idea of a positive infallibility. Rather, the

church has error along with the truth, by which this may be corrupted and obscured, though never absolutely lost. She bears the
golden treasure in earthern vessels; along with her ideal, divine
nature, she possesses also a real, human existence, which is subject to the conditions of the finite, and thus also to the laws of
process and growth. In the church herself, as well as in her members singly taken, we must distinguish different periods of life.
She is not made perfect at once, but is engaged in a gradual process
of development, which holds just in this, that she is ever extricating herself more and more from the Judaism and paganism,
sin and error, that still cleave to her by nature; by entering always
more deeply into the word of God, in her hands but not for this
reason fully understood from the beginning; and by incorporating
it more fully always with her thinking, feeling, and acting; till in
the end she shall appear the full-grown body of Christ, without
spot or wrinkle, infirmity or disease, thus ceasing at the same
time to be a militant church, and passing over into the kingdom
of God triumphant.

For every unprejudiced person, history confirms this by incontrovertible facts. Even the most celebrated councils have been sufficiently characterized by contention and strife, contradictory feelings and views; and human passions and errors have come into
play in their proceedings, as fully as in other places. Add to this,
that popes and councils have not unfrequently appeared in direct
contradiction; a circumstance fatal at once to the claim of infallibility. Thus, in the Arian controversy, several synods, just as large
and constitutional as those afterward acknowledged to be orthodox, declared in favor of this heresy; and while the Council of
Constantinople (754), by imperial will the Seventh Ecumenical,[37]
composed of 338 bishops, fanatically damned all religious images,
the next universal synod, held at Nicaea in 787, proclaimed the
whole proceeding to be wind. More frequent still have been the
cases of contradiction, [partly by the popes among themselves,
partly between the popes and] the great reformatory synods of
Constance and Basel; so that with regard to this point, the Roman
theologians themselves have not been able to agree.

The Protestant Church however can appeal, in favor of her
view, not simply to the history of councils and popes, but also

to the express testimony of the most ancient church fathers; as Athanasius and Augustine, for example, without qualification *allow the possibility of error even in the highest administration of the church.** The idea of a positive infallibility, excluding all and every error, and clothing the decisions of councils with the character of divine oracles, was first uttered by the Council of Chalcedon, A.D. 451, with reference to that of Nicaea; whose decrees it was directly affirmed, were given not by the fathers of the synod themselves, but by the Holy Spirit speaking through their persons.

If there be then any unerring fountain of truth needed to satisfy religious want, it can be found only in the *word of God,* who is himself the truth; and this becomes thus consequently the *highest norm* and *rule* by which to measure all human truth, all ecclesiastical tradition, and all synodical decrees.† Having in this way no rival at their side, the sacred Scriptures must take a far higher place in the Protestant system than they are allowed to hold in that of Rome, similarly to the view taken of faith also in the two

---

* Thus [Augustine says in] *de baptismo contra Donatist,* II, 3: Quis autem nesciat S. Scripturam . . . omnibus episcoporum litteris ita praeponi, ut de illa omnino dubitari et disceptari non possit, . . . episcoporum autem litteras, . . . per sermonem forte sapientiorem cujuslibet in ea re peritioris, et per aliorum episcoporum graviorem auctoritatem doctioremque prudentiam et per concilia licere reprehendi, si quid in eis forte a veritate deviatum est: et ipsa concilia, quae per singulas . . . provincias fiunt, *plenariorum conciliorum* auctoritati, quae fiunt ex *universo orbe christiano,* sine ullis ambagibus cedere, *ipsaque plenaria saepe priora a posterioribus emendari,* cum aliquo experimento rerum aperitur quod clausum erat et cognoscitur quod latebat. If the general councils themselves admit and require thus improvement and correction from those that follow, they cannot be infallible.

† *Artic. Smalc.,* I, 2, 15, p. 308: Ex Patrum enim verbis et factis non sunt exstruendi articuli fidei. . . . Regulam autem aliam habemus, ut videlicet verbum Dei condat articulos fidei, et praeterea nemo, ne Angelus quidem. Luther, as early as the conference at Augsburg would be "confuted only from the Scriptures"; and at Worms, as is known, he put forward the *testimonia scripturarum,* and declared his conscience bound by God's word. *Form. Conf. praef.,* p. 570, where the Bible is styled *unica regula et norma* of all doctrines; also *sol. decl.,* p. 632.[38] The Reformed Church proclaims this formal principle throughout with still more distinctness and decision, so that it is almost superfluous to refer to proof passages. *Conf. Helv.,* II, Art. 1-2, pp. 467 ff.; *Artic. Anglic.,* Art. 6; *Conf. Belg.,* Art. 3-5, pp. 361 f.; *Conf. Gallic.,* Art. 2-5, pp. 329 f.; *Conf. Westmonast.,* c. 1, § 1—10.

churches. Our older theologians cannot be charged certainly with
any want of respect for the Bible; rather fault is to be found with
the inspiration theory of the seventeenth century, that it did not
sufficiently recognize the individuality of the sacred writers, which
without the least prejudice to the divinity of the matter, mirrors
it nevertheless in every case under a peculiar form. These Bible
fathers, as I may style them with Daub,[39] have resolved the excellence predicated on the Scriptures into the following properties:

1. The character of *fontal* and *normal authority* immediately
in view.

2. *Perfection* as to compass and contents *(perfectio s. suffi-
cientia)*; not of course in the absolute sense, as containing all that
can possibly be known of God and divine things; but relatively,
reaching to all that is necessary to salvation, as distinctly expressed
in the symbolic books *(continet omnia, quae ad salutem consequendam sunt necessaria)*. All traditions accordingly, unless they
be mere consequences drawn from the Bible, are either positively
false, or contain only subordinate and unessential truth.* It might
be presumed indeed beforehand that the divine wisdom and goodness, in the case of the new covenant as well as in that of the old,
would provide for a true and full record of the truth, as needed
for salvation, in a written form; since a merely oral tradition, in

---

* Schleiermacher *(Der christl. Glaube*, Vol. II, § 103, p. 120 f., 3d ed.) says
with much truth: "This original revelation of God in Christ is moreover so
sufficient, and at the same time so inexhaustible, that so far as this first point
is concerned Christ stands forth at once as the crown and consummation of all
prophecy. For it is not possible, either for any representation of our relation
to God to take place, out of the sphere in which Christ is already known, that
shall not fall behind this revelation; or for any such advance ever to be made
within the Christian Church, as may show anything imperfect in the doctrine
of Christ itself, for which something better might be substituted, or to conceive
for the understanding of man, as it regards his relation to God, anything
more spiritual, deep and complete, than has been done by Christ. With the
idea of such a perfectibility of the Christian doctrine, as might allow us to go
beyond Christ himself, the idea of his peculiar excellence must fall to the
ground. On the contrary, all later excellence here can never be anything else
than the right development of what is either comprehended in his declarations
as handed down to us, or in such relation to them as to have been necessarily
present to his mind." That Schleiermacher has in his mind the contents of
the Bible here, as the measure which none can transcend, must be clear to all
who are acquainted with his system.

the nature of the case, must be subject to change and distortion, making it impossible at last to distinguish truth from falsehood. In such passages as Acts 20:27; 26:22; 2 Timothy 3:14-17; Galatians 1:8; Revelation 22:18, the Scriptures ascribe this character to themselves quite directly; and the claim is made good continually in practical life. The more anyone enters into the contents of the Bible, the more he learns to say with Luther that it resembles an herb, that by every rubbing becomes only the more odoriferous, a tree, that by every shaking throws down only a richer supply of golden apples. Every valuable exegetical work discloses to us new treasures; and our church, after having lived upon it already three hundred years, must still with Paul exclaim in amazement, "O the depth of the riches both of the wisdom and knowledge of God!"

3. As regards form, the Bible has the quality of *perspicuity (perspicuitas);* not absolutely again, as excluding every mystery; but so, as that all things indispensably necessary to salvation may be known by every member of the church from the Scriptures, without the aid of tradition or councils, if only the proper conditions are at hand for the purpose. These include not simply the general command of intellect and knowledge that are requisite for the understanding of every human book, by which the loose spiritualism of the Quakers is disowned, but a living sense also of spiritual need, and a proper affinity with the Spirit from which the Scriptures proceed. And here the Protestant Church appears in full opposition to rationalism, in the case of which the natural understanding, that cannot discern the things of the Spirit according to Paul (1 Corinthians 2:14; 12:3; 2 Corinthians 3:5), is made the principle of interpretation. That it is properly the Holy Spirit only which can interpret the Scriptures, is admitted by the Romish Church also; and so all controversy here turns upon the question: Where is this Holy Spirit?* The Church of Rome of course arrogates its presence, and with this the right interpretation of the Bible, entirely to herself, her bishops and her popes; and thus

---

* Bellarmine, *de verbo Dei,* III, 3. Convenit etiam inter nos et adversarios, scripturas intelligi debere eo spiritu, quo factae sunt, i.e., spiritu sancto. . . . Tota igitur quaestio in eo posita est, ubi sit iste spiritus.

in fact exalts herself above the Bible, as its infallible judge.* The
Protestant, however, binds the Spirit that "bloweth where it list-
eth," not to a particular form and section of the church, but to the
word alone (comp. John 8:31-32). Where the word is read and
preached, there the Spirit lives and moves and creates light; in
other words, the Scriptures interpret themselves.† When, notwithstanding, controversies arise, as they unavoidably must, and opposite parties contend for different senses of the word in their
own favor, the Protestant requires, it is true, a subjection of the
individual to some general authority; whether it be a small body
of theologians, as that which framed the Formula of Concord, or
a regular synod, as of Dort, Westminster, and others, which estab-
lishes a standard of faith for all within its jurisdiction. On this
ground, it is known, the Reformers were earnestly urgent for a
general council in which the controversies of the time might be
decided. But here still this important difference prevails between
the Protestant and Romish systems, that in the view of the first
no such ecclesiastical authority is permitted to draw its decision
from tradition, but always again from the Bible itself only; and
thus the principle of its self-interpretation in the Holy Spirit remains unimpaired.‡

---

* Bellarmine, I, c. 3, 9, has poorly sustained his usual logical acumen at
this point. He maintains that as the Bible is the subject of controversy, we
must not appeal to it as judge in the case, but only something external to it,
that is the church. But the church is also a party; and so not qualified to act
as judge, unless in the most partial, and in the worst sense, extra-biblical
style.

† *Scriptura sacra est sui ipsius legitimus interpres.* Comp. especially the Reformed symbols; for example, *Conf. Helv.* II, c. 2, p. 469: illam duntaxat
scripturarum interpretationem pro orthodoxa et genuina agnoscimus, quae
ex ipsis est petita scripturis . . . cum regula fidei et caritatis congruit et ad
gloriam Dei hominumque salutem eximie facit.

‡ The Lutheran divines distinguish accordingly thus: (1) Index *principalis*
est spiritus s.; (2) judex *instrumentalis* est s. scriptura; (3) jud. *ministerialis*
(also *inferior*) est ministerium ecclesiasticum. This last however may not "pro
suo arbitrio sententiam pronunciare, sed juxta normam a supremo judice prae-
scriptam, videl. juxta scripturam s., quam propterea vocem judicis supremi
et normam judicis inferioris et judicem directivum appellamus." Calvin treats
of the point in *Instit.*, IV, c. 9, § 13, where the remarkable passage occurs:
"Nos certe libenter concedimus, si quo de dogmate incidat disceptatio, nullum
esse nec melius nec certius remedium, quam si verorum episcoporum Synodus
conveniat, ubi controversum dogma excutiatur. Multo enim plus ponderis

The last character of the Scriptures is the power *(efficacia)* with which they operate through the Holy Spirit on the soul of man, in the way of illumination and renewal. This however is of no essential consequence to our present investigation.

When all this is taken together, we may say, leaving out of view a number of fathers and medieval divines, very prominent men it is true, that the holy Scriptures were first instated in their proper rights, in a general way, by the Reformers. It is felt accordingly to be a sacred duty with Protestantism, which in this view also forms a decided advance in the history of the church, to circulate them as widely as possible in the languages accessible to the people; while it lies in the interest of popery universally, to restrain their circulation, and to anathematize all Bible societies; under the convenient plea of course, that the editions are heretical, and the translation, corrupt.

We are now to investigate the relation of the Protestant Bible principle to *tradition*; or the place assigned to tradition in the Protestant system. To do justice however to this difficult point, we must first reduce the idea to its constituent parts; since the word is used in very different senses, and by the Council of Trent in particular is made so general as to embrace the whole mass of what has been handed down in the church. We may take up the whole compass of its meaning under the distinction of *ritual, historical,* and *dogmatic* tradition. To all these forms, the general relation of Protestantism is such that it *affirms their historical necessity, while at the same time it places them neither parallel with the Scriptures, nor over them, but under them only, and measures their value by the extent of their agreement with this standard.*

1. The first class corresponds in the main with what Bellarmine styles ecclesiastical traditions. It comprises the ancient customs

---

habebit ejusmodi definitio, in quam communiter ecclesiarum pastores, invocato Christi spiritu, consenserint, quam si quisque seorsum domi conceptam populo traderet, vel pauci homines privati eam conficerent." He then goes on to establish this view, in part exegetically (from 1 Corinthians 14:29), in part historically; adding in the end however that the Holy Spirit may forsake an entire synod, so that the decisions of such a body are not necesarily free from error, as history shows. Hoc autem perpetuum esse nego, ut vera sit et certa scripturae interpretatio, quae concilii suffragiis fuerit recepta.

and usages pertaining to order and worship, which have gradually
acquired the character of catholicity; for example, the distinctions
of the clergy, the church festivals, the arrangement of divine service, the specifications of church discipline, and the whole range
of church symbolism, as the custom of praying with the face
toward the East, the consecration of the baptismal water, making
the sign of the cross, and so on. That these points in general were
established *after* the age of the apostles, needs in the present posture of historical inquiry no further argument. It entered not
into the design of Christ and the apostles to lay down more than
the most essential ground regulations for the order and worship of
the church. They wished not to burden the new organization
with forms and ceremonies. This would have been wholly contrary also to the free genius of the gospel, which was expected
rather to create its own body according to time and circumstances,
as its wants might require (comp. Romans 14; Galatians 4:9-10;
5:4; Colossians 2:16-18). To insist on *one* constitution and *one*
worship as alone true and valid, in the case at least of the militant
church, is to fall back again into fleshly Judaism. So in the Church
of Rome itself, many primitive customs have gone into disuse,
and others again have been introduced much later, which now
form an essential part of the system; as the papacy in its present
form, the pomp connected with the Mass, the splendid clerical
attire, the festivals of Mary and the saints, the details with regard to fasts and penances, praying by the rosary, and the like.

Now in all these secondary things, Protestantism recognizes
throughout no normative force, as is done by the Church of
Rome, but claims the right to exercise a free evangelical criticism in the case; rejecting absolutely all that conflicts with the
true life of the church, and serves merely to promote a dead mechanical religion; while it retains only what is found to embody
with suitable form and expression the Christian spirit.* As how-

---

* *Conf. Aug.,* Art. 15, pp. 13 f.: De ritibus Ecclesiasticis docent, quod ritus
illi servandi sint, qui sine peccato servari possunt et prosunt ad tranquillitatem
et bonum ordinem in Ecclesia, sicut certae feriae, festa et similia. De talibus
rebus tamen admonentur homines, ne conscientiae onerentur, tamquam talis
cultus ad salutem necessarius sit. Admonentur etiam, quod traditiones humanae institutae ad placandum Deum, et promerendam gratiam et satisfaci-
endum pro peccatis, adversentur Evangelio et doctrinae fidei. Quare vota et

ever at the time of the Reformation, the church had well-nigh
petrified in these outward forms, with the loss in a great measure
of all inward life, as it was with Judaism at the time of Christ;
while the apostolic age, as far as we can gather from the New
Testament, was characterized by the greatest simplicity and spirituality; it was quite natural that the Reformers should have
been carried too far at times in opposition to the existing system. At the same time, this was not the case so much with the
Lutheran and *German* Reformed Churches, as it was with the Reformed Church in Scotland and France. For the Romanic nations,
and the English also, are much more disposed to attach an undue
value to form, than the inward-minded, idealistic Germans; and
for this very reason it was natural for them, when the spirit was
roused to the consciousness and assertion of its superior rights,
to fall over unduly to the opposite side, on the principle that one
extreme begets another. Puritanism in particular, I am constrained here openly to acknowledge, through a false spiritualistic tendency and an utter misapprehension of the significance of
the corporeal and outward, showed itself in this case rash in its
zeal, and has sacrificed many beautiful customs, by which religious
ideas were sweetly interwoven with common life, and outward
opportunities continually supplied for the favorable application
of truth to the heart. All this, it is much more difficult to recover,
than to cast away. It is always more easy to destroy than it is to
build. The culminating point of this abstract spiritualism has
been reached in the system of the Quaker, which rejects even the
ministry and the sacraments as mere forms; but strangely enough,
against its own will, swings clear over at the same time to the
very opposite extreme. For of all others, the Quakers are the
greatest slaves of form, and the most barren and unmeaning besides in their profession; a palpable satire upon all such naked

traditiones de cibis et diebus, etc., institutae ad promerendam gratiam et satis-
faciendum pro peccatis inutiles sint et contra Evangelium. Comp. Art. 22,
p. 20 (falsa enim calumnia, etc.), and the whole admirable 8th section in the
*Apol. Conf.* de traditionibus humanis in eccles., pp. 205-223. Chemnitz,[40] in
his *Exam.* lays down in relation to ritual traditions the following very sound
rule: Ceremoniae [in ecclesia] sint genere indifferentes, numero paucae, sint
piae et utiles ad aedificationem, ordinem et decorum . . . extra casum scandali,
liberas habeat observationes.[41] Cf. *Conf. Helv.* II, Art. 27, pp 530 f.

inwardism, an involuntary argument for the necessity of exter-
nalization.

2. To the *historical* tradition must be referred, as of first account, the testimonies of Christian antiquity on the genuineness
and integrity of the sacred books, the time and place of their
composition, and the settlement of the canon. This tradition the
Lutheran and Reformed Churches hold to be of great account,
and they have retained, as is known, the canon of the Catholic
Church. But still faith in the Scriptures is made to rest, in the
end, not on these testimonies of the fathers, but on the inward
testimony of the Holy Spirit, and is not allowed to have any
true worth, while it continues a simple blind trust in authority.
Then again, these traditions are for Protestantism by no means
infallible and binding, but simple historical testimonies only,
whose worth is to be estimated, partly according to the general
credibility of the writer concerned, and partly also, and mainly,
according to the measure of their connection with the apostolic
age. It is sufficient to show them not infallible, that before the
Council of Hippo in the year 393, they are known not to agree
with one another in relation to several books of the New Testament, the so-called *antilegomena* of Eusebius. The Church of
Rome has so much the less room for casting reproach upon us
here, since in open contradiction to the oldest and best accredited
tradition, which we have once more restored to its rights, she
has rejected the distinction of canonical and apocryphal books,
and so invested with traditional authority this false coordination
itself.

Under the same head, in a wider sense, may be reckoned *exegetical* tradition. The Council of Trent understands by this the pretended consent of the fathers; and it was ordained, in the fourth
session, that this should govern the interpretation of the Scriptures.* This tradition also Protestantism prizes, without overvaluation. It is well pleased to find a church father in harmony
with the true explanation of a passage; as may be sufficiently seen
for instance, from Chemnitz' *Examinis Concilii Tridentini,* and

---

* Ut nemo . . . contra unanimem consensum Patrum ipsam scripturam
sacram interpretari audeat.[42]

Gerhard's[43] celebrated system of theology. The religious life rests on the deepest feeling of communion. It may be safely affirmed, moreover, that for every peculiar exposition of the Reformers, at least an analogy may be found in the ancient church, particularly with Augustine. But still the Reformers by no means allow a normative authority to the fathers. Respect for them is not suffered to shackle the further progress of exegesis, as in the Church of Rome.* The fathers, in their interpretation, proceeded in part on wholly unsound principles, as those of Alexandria for instance with their extravagant allegory; and of a full agreement, except only in the most essential particulars, it is idle to speak.† The scripture expositions of the Reformers show not only far more agreement, but also sounder sense and tact, and saving the single case of Augustine, who however like all philosophical thinkers is a better theologian than interpreter, are characterized by much greater acuteness and depth.

3. The *dogmatico-moral* traditions finally, on which most hangs, may be taken first in the *material* view; comprehending thus, in the Romish system, all doctrines that are referred to Christ or the apostles, without being found in the Scriptures. These we might look for most naturally, in the apostolical fathers and the ecclesiastical writers of the second and third centuries. But we find here no utterances of Christ and the apostles, that

---

* *Conf. Helv.* II, Art. 2, p. 469: Proinde non aspernamur sanctorum patrum Graecorum Latinorumque interpretationes neque reprobamus eorundem disputationes ac tractationes rerum sacrarum cum scripturis consentientes; a quibus tamen recedimus modeste, quando aliena a scripturis aut his contraria adferre deprehenduntur. Nec putamus illis ullam a nobis hac re injuriam irrogari, cum omnes uno ore nolint sua scripta aequari Canonicis. . . . Eodem in ordine collocantur etiam Conciliorum definitiones vel Canones. With this agrees the whole practice of the orthodox Protestant interpreters and theologians.

† This Moehler[44] himself is constrained to allow, *Symbolik,* p. 390 (5th ed.): "With the exception of the interpretation of a very few classic passages, a general agreement here is to be found only in this, that all educe from the holy Scriptures the same doctrinal and moral views" (even this however holds only in the case of the veriest essentials); "everyone, at the same time, in his own peculiar way; so that some as expositors are distinguished models for all times, others rise not above mediocrity, and others still are entitled to respect only for their good intention and their love to the Savior."

are not more clearly and fully presented to us in the New Testament. At times besides, something wholly unsuitable and absurd is attributed to them; as *Papias* for instance, in Irenaeus,[45] puts an allegorical saying into the mouth of Christ, which he could never have uttered. It becomes necessary accordingly to proceed here with the utmost critical caution, and there remains no rule by which to discriminate the true from the false but the Scriptures. Our Romish opponents however set more store by the dogmatic traditions of the *Middle Ages;* which are referred at once to a divine origin, on the grievously arbitrary principle of Peter à Soto[46]: *quarum observationum initium, auctor et origo ignoratur vel inveniri no potest, illas extra omnem dubitationem ab apostolis traditas esse.* All these doctrines, however, which not only have no foundation in the Bible, but for the most part contradict it outright, such as the worship of the virgin Mary and the saints, the scholastic theory of justification, purgatory, satisfactions, and indulgences, are with full right rejected by Protestantism; under the authority of the apostle's word: "Though an angel from heaven should preach unto you any other gospel than that which we have preached unto you, let him be accursed." For how can the Spirit of Christ contradict itself? And where do we find it written that the church has the power at pleasure to create or sanction new doctrines? These then are no apostolical but, in their later Romish form at least, altogether human, arbitrary traditions; like the self-made Jewish ordinances of the Pharisees and Sadducees, and the false doctrines against which we are expressly warned by Christ and his apostles (Matthew 15:2; Mark 7:3, 5, 13; Galatians 1:14; Colossians 2:8).

Quite different, however, in the second place, is the case of the *formal* dogmatic tradition. This is such as has not for its contents something different from what is contained in the Bible, but forms the channel by which these contents are conducted forward in history; the onward development thus of church doctrine and church life, as comprehended first dogmatically in the so-called rules of faith, above all in the Apostles' Creed, and then in the ecumenical creeds—the Nicene and Athanasian—and still further as orally carried forward, apart from all written statement, through the entire course of church history, so that every-

one, before he wakes even to self-consciousness, is made involuntarily to feel its power. Tradition in this sense is absolutely indispensable. By its means we come first to the contents of the
Bible; and from it these draw their life for us, perpetually fresh
and new; in such way that Christ and his apostles are made present, and speak to us directly, in the Spirit which breathes in the
Bible, and flows through the church as her life's blood. *This tradition therefore is not a part of the divine word separately from
that which is written, but the contents of scripture itself as apprehended and settled by the church against heresies past and
always new appearing; not an independent source of revelation,
but the one fountain of the written word, only rolling itself forward in the stream of church consciousness.* Much to the same
purpose, Martin Chemnitz says: "Haec est vera et vetus apostolorum traditio, quae nihil tradit extra et praeter scripturam, sed
complectitur summam totius scripturae."*

This tradition Protestantism can and must allow without a
surrender of its principle. For the Reformers in their great controversy had always in their eye, not this conception, but the
material tradition only, as a fountain of knowledge independent
of the Scriptures, and having different contents. Many Protestants
are to be found, to be sure, in our own time particularly, who entirely overlook the importance of this point; which makes it so
much the more necessary to give it emphasis. But we can appeal
boldly to history for its support.

In the first place, an argument for holding fast to tradition in
this form is found in the whole historical connection of the Reformation itself with the period going before, as this has been already brought into view. Then we have it expressly declared by
the leaders of this vast movement that men can be saved only in
connection with the true Christian Church, as it has stood from
the beginning, against which the gates of hell cannot prevail;
and that all reformation therefore, and further development of
doctrine and life, must maintain essential unity with the collective consciousness of the Christian Church.† Lastly, our affirma-

---

* *Examen Conc. Trident.*, Part I, p. 120, ed. Francof.

† Particularly worthy of note in this view is a passage found in a letter of
Luther to Duke Albert of Prussia, in the year 1532.[47] He is speaking of the

tion is confirmed by the practice of the Reformed and Lutheran Churches. For these have appropriated to themselves unhesitatingly the ecumenical symbols, as true expressions of this church consciousness, that is as agreeing with the Scriptures; to which they refer still as the unerring fountain and norm of religious

---

real presence of the Lord in the Eucharist—a doctrine denied it is true by Zwingli, but firmly held by Calvin, as he expressly declares particularly in his *defensio ad Westphalum,* and also in his *Instit.* "This article moreover," the letter proceeds, "has been clearly believed and held from the beginning of the Christian Church to this hour—*a testimony of the entire holy Christian Church,* which, if we had nothing besides, *should be sufficient for us. For it is dangerous and terrible to hear or believe anything against the united testimony, faith and doctrine, of the entire holy Christian Church,* as this hath been held now 1,500 years, from the beginning, unanimously in all the world. Whoso now doubted thereon, it is even the same as though he believed in no Christian Church, and he condemneth thus not only the entire holy Christian Church as a damnable heresy, but also Christ himself and all the apostles and prophets, who have established and powerfully attested this article, where we say, '*I believe in a holy Christian Church*'; Christ namely, Matthew 28:20: 'Lo I am with you always, even unto the end of the world'; and Paul, 1 Timothy 3:15: 'The Church of God, which is the pillar and ground of the truth.'" *Conf. Helv.* II, c. 17, p. 503: *Communionem vero cum ecclesia Christi vera tanti facimus, ut negemus eos coram Deo vivere posse, qui cum vera Dei ecclesia non communicant, sed ab ea se separant.* Nam ut extra arcam Noë non erat ulla salus, pereunte mundo in diluvio, ita credimus extra Christum, qui se electis in ecclesia fruendum praebet, nullam esse salutem certam: et proinde docemus, vivere volentes non oportere separari a vera Christi ecclesia. The idea of the church is developed in a masterly style by Calvin, *Instit. Chr. Rel.,* IV, c. 1, § 1 ff. He who has God for his Father, he tells us, has the church also for his mother; and this not simply under the law, but after the coming of Christ likewise, who will have us to be children of the new and heavenly Jerusalem (Galatians 4:26). He then goes on to say, § 4: Verum quia nunc de visibili ecclesia disserere propositum est, discamus vel uno *Matris* elogio, quam utilis sit nobis ejus cognitio, imo necessaria: quando non alius est in vitam ingressus, nisi nos ipsa concipiat in utero, nisi pariat, nisi nos alat suis uberibus, denique sub custodia et gubernatione sua nos tueatur, donec exuti carne mortali similes erimus angelis. Neque enim patitur nostra infirmitas a schola nos dimitti, donec toto vitae cursu discipuli fuerimus. Adde quod extra ejus gremium nulla est speranda peccatorum remissio, nec ulla salus, teste Iesaja (37:32) et Joele (2:32). With the greatest severity he then reproves all those who without imperious necessity of conscience separate themselves from the reigning church. This whole section in fact sounds so strongly Catholic that Moehler (*Symbolik,* pp. 443 f.) accuses Calvin of being in perfect contradiction here with himself, in leaving the Catholic Church. But this reproach is fully answered by the second chapter of the same book, where Calvin, with that overwhelming moral earnestness

knowledge.* Then again, they formed in their own bosom a peculiar Reformed and Lutheran tradition, carrying forward thus
the stream of church consciousness in themselves, and giving it
representation in their symbolical books. This too is in no respect
contrary to their Bible principle. For the Protestant symbols are
likewise *formal* dogmatic traditions, which contain nothing different from the Scriptures, but simply express the faith of Protestantism in the Scriptures themselves, and its apprehension of
their contents. They are *the evangelical answer to the interroga-
tion of the divine Word*†; which founded the church at first, and
by which it must be continually set free from remaining alloy,
and carried forward from one degree of light and power to another, till at last the word itself shall be fully corporealized in its
life, and the written letter thus will be no more needed in the
plenitude of the spirit.

With this view firmly secured in our minds, we escape the in-
superable difficulties, which do in fact encumber the Protestant
position as held by many—particularly in our own time—who invest the Bible with the most abstract, isolated character, inter-
posing a lifeless void of eighteen centuries between its completion and the present time, while yet, in spite of their own theory,

---

which is peculiar to him, exhibits the papacy as a false church, because by its
ordinances it directly contradicted the word of God. He estimates thus the
worth of a church by its agreement with this unerring standard, the charter
of the covenant, and the depository of all truth. Till the papists can show
what has not yet been done, that their church agrees with the word of God,
Calvin stands fully justified. For the sake of his connection with the true
Catholic Church, he was compelled to separate from a communion, which in
its spiritual insolence claims to be the only true church, without being able
to bring anything more than its own assertion in proof of the pretension. The
true church, before the Reformation, existed no doubt in the dominion of
the pope; but the papacy must by no means be identified, for this reason, with
the true church; as little as Christianity in the beginning was to be considered
one with Judaism, because Christ and his apostles stood in this system, visited
the temple, and took part in its service.

*Conf. Gallic.*, Art. 5, p. 330: Quamobrem etiam tria illa Symbola, nempe
Apostolicum, Nicaenum et Athanasianum, idcirco approbamus, quod sint illi
verbo Dei scripto consentanea.

† Hence the known expression, *symbola non imprimunt credenda, sed ex-
primunt credita.* They are not *norma fidei,* but *norma doctrinae,* according to
which the Scriptures are to be taught.

they do themselves in fact hold it only through the medium of tradition, and see and understand it too only as mirrored in the present consciousness of the particular church to which they belong. A gross inconsequence truly, and glaring contradiction, of which the Romish theologians are well pleased to take advantage.

Before closing this part of our discussion, and passing over to the consideration of the *present* posture of Protestantism, we have still to notice the principal Roman Catholic objections to the scripture principle, and then to make clear, in a comprehensive view, its relation to the *material* principle.

Some of the most frequent objections are:

1. "The church is older than the holy Scriptures; these proceed from her; this relation between them ought not then to be reversed, as it is with Protestantism." True, the church was in being before any book of the New Testament existed; but not before the unwritten word of Christ and the apostles, which rather was the foundation of the church, and in substance is the same with the written.* Now however this originally oral communication is fixed and secured against corruption by the Scriptures. Why then should we have recourse besides to unwritten tradition, as though these were not sufficient? As long as the apostles lived, the inspired bearers of the divine word, such tradition was sufficiently safe. In case of corruption or perversion, the apostles might apply the necessary correction. But the case must be wholly different, after the death of these unerring witnesses. If the gospel was to be perpetuated in its purity, it became indispensable that it should be committed to writing; since all merely oral tradition, in proportion as it becomes removed from its source, is found to grow more and more turbid through the accession of foreign matter, till in the end it is no longer possible, without the intervention of a new revelation, to make any sure distinction between the truth and the error. Against such disaster God has provided under the new dispensation, as before

---

* Quenstedt[48] replies to the objection in hand: Quando Pontificii argumentantur in hunc modum: Ecclesia est antiquior scriptura, ergo majorem habet auctoritatem, etc., respondeo: Distinguendum inter verbum Dei in scripturis propositum et ipsum scribendi actum, sive inter scripturae *substantiam,* quae est verbum Dei, et hujus accidens, quod est scriptio. *Syst. Theolog.,* 1702, p. 93.

under the old, by causing his word to be committed to writing, and wonderfully preserving it in this form from age to age. Allowing then, as all reasonable Protestants will be ready to do, that the written word was not necessary for the *rise* of the church, it must still be considered indispensable for its *continuance* as the perpetual, pure fountain, and only certain measure of saving truth.*

2. "It is through tradition only we have the Scriptures themselves, and are assured of their authenticity, integrity, and divine character. So likewise we are referred to the church for the de-

---

* We can appeal here even to the testimony of the most important Roman Catholic theologian of the present age. Moehler, in his spirited work *Ueber die Einheit der Kirche* (Tübingen, 1825), p. 60, says: *"Without the holy Scriptures,* in which the gospel was first embodied, *the Christian doctrine would not have been preserved in its purity and simplicity; and it is certainly a great want of right feeling toward God, to speak of them as accidental"* (which however is just what many Romish theologians, in opposing Protestants, have done, and are doing still) *"because they may seem to have sprung from merely accidental occasions. What a conception of the regency of the Holy Spirit in the church!* Without the Scriptures, moreover, the first link of the church would be wanting, leaving it thus without any proper beginning, and for this reason unmeaning, confused, and chaotic. But without a continuous tradition, all higher sense for the Scriptures would fail us too, since without intermediate links we could be conscious of no connection. Without the Scriptures we could form no complete image of the Redeemer, as *trustworthy* material would be wanting, and all must be *made uncertain through fables;* without a continuous tradition the spirit and interest would be wanting to form for ourselves any such image, and the material again likewise, for without tradition we should have no scripture. Without the Scriptures the peculiar form of the discourses of Jesus would be withheld from us; we should not know how the God-man spoke, etc." What is here said, with as much beauty as truth, of tradition, impairs not at all the force of the passage in favor of Protestantism. For tradition is not taken here in the true Roman Catholic sense, as we have before noticed in the case of Moehler, but as the regenerated reason, the Christian consciousness of the church; which stands not beside the Scriptures as an independent fountain, but is simply the stream of their contents reaching to us through the life of the church, embracing always only what is contained in the Scriptures themselves; the same view accordingly that we freely and cheerfully admit on Protestant ground itself. The distinguished champion of popery says indeed explicitly that without the Scriptures we should be left without trustworthy matter, *all being involved in fables;* and this, of course applies with fair consequence also to tradition in the Romish sense, so far as it is made to hold contents of its own, not derived from the Scriptures. Comp. also Baur, *Der Gegensatz des Katholicismus und Protestantismus,* 1834, pp. 348 f.

termination of the sacred canon, which fixes the limits of the written word. Now it is inconsistent when Protestants accept the canon thus handed down to them by the church, and yet in theory reject tradition." With regard to this, it has already been observed that these testimonies of the church on the genuineness, integrity, and number of the sacred writings, have no claim to infallible authority; but are primarily of mere historical character, subject fairly to critical trial, external and internal, and become fully valid to the individual Christian at last, only through the self-evidencing power of the Scriptures themselves to his spirit by the Holy Spirit. Properly too they utter nothing new, give no contents, are no voice beyond the Scriptures, but only *upon* the Scriptures. "The church," as Nitzsch[49] says, "has not made the Scriptures genuine by acknowledging them, but the Scriptures have demonstrated themselves to her, and now make the church genuine."* And in the same way, apart also from these patristic testimonies, they still demonstrate themselves as genuine and divine, to every earnest reader, by the Spirit of God speaking through them to his heart.

3. "By rejecting tradition, which imposes definite rules and limits on the interpretation of scripture, we throw open the door to lawless objectivity. This is shown by the actual state of the Protestant world, as rent into various conflicting parties, which without exception appeal to the Scriptures in support of the most opposite doctrines and principles." Here indeed a disadvantageous side of Protestantism is brought to view, which we are constrained to acknowledge with deep sorrow, as will appear hereafter. Still, however, while we readily allow that the curse of sects is to be ascribed, in large part, to the contempt of church authority and the abuses of Protestant liberty, we must decidedly reject the allegation that tradition alone, and that in the Romish sense as an infallible judge of scripture, forms a sufficient remedy for the cure of this disease. The prescription at best leaves us where we were before, if it bring us not into a plight still worse. For tradition itself is capable also of various interpretations, and to a greater extent indeed than the Bible, in proportion as the writ-

---

* *System der christlichen Lehre,* 4th ed., p. 93.

ings in which it is to be found are of greater compass. It is pro-
digious injustice to ascribe all clearness to man's word, and all
darkness to the word of God. The history of the church besides
informs us plainly that different sects have stayed themselves on
tradition as well as upon the holy Scriptures. This was done, for
instance, by the Gnostics, and again by the Arians at the Council
of Antioch*; also by the Artemonites,[50] who according to Eusebi-
us† affirmed that their error with regard to the person of Christ
had been held by the apostles and the whole church down to the
time of the Roman bishop Victor, and was first exchanged for a
different view under his successor Zephyrinus. It is known too that
different views still prevail in the Church of Rome, without loss
of orthodoxy, on several by no means unimportant articles of the
Tridentine system; and it is owing only to the outward force
she employs to restrain all tendencies of the more free sort, as
in the case of Jansenism and Hermesianism,[51] that these differences come not to more open contradiction and collision. In this
way, however, the disease is not cured, but only covered over; to
break forth the more dangerously again, in its own time. Such
tyranny over the conscience and against free inquiry, is contrary
in the view of our church to the free nature and spiritual constitution of the gospel. As little as the present so sadly divided condition of the Evangelical Church may be considered her proper,
normal, and perfect state, it still forms an advance as compared
with the posture of the Church of Rome, to which the crisis is still
future. What vital energy must not Protestantism possess to endure so long and renew its youth continually, in spite of such
distraction!

In directing our view now to the relation of the two principles
to each other mutually, it may be observed that they are inseparably joined as contents and form, will and knowledge, and
strictly taken constitute but two sides of one and the same principle, which resolves itself into the maxim: *Christ all in all.* All
sects accordingly, which either deny justification by faith alone, as
the Socinians, Unitarians, and Swedenborgians, or reject the
written word, as the Schwenkfeldians and Quakers, are to be ex-

---

* Socrates, *Hist. Eccles.,* II, 10.
† *Hist. Eccles.,* V, 28.

cluded from the territory of orthodox Protestantism, however they
may claim to belong to it and seem to stand in its connection.
Wherever either element comes to be held in a one-sided way, a
deviation has already taken place from the original character of
the Reformation. Christ, or in an immediate view of his Spirit, is
ever in the word and with the word; never without or beyond
the word, written or preached; yea, he is himself the living, personal word. The word again can be understood only by faith, in
union with the Spirit of Christ speaking to us through the letter.
By the word the objective Spirit bears witness to the subjective
spirit that it is born of God.* The material element without the
objective basis of the formal becomes swarming inwardism, and
in the end sheer subjectivity. The formal element without the
material, however, conducts to stiff, lifeless, and soulless external-
ism, the idolatry of the letter; and comes besides to no right understanding of the Scriptures, to which the key is found only in
justifying faith as produced by the Spirit of God. We have a like
result in philosophy, where idealism and realism come not to a
living interpenetration. The first sundered from the second becomes a barren, merely formal thought-thinking; the second without the first sinks into rough empiricism and materialism.

In thus breaking through the interposed obstruction of hierarchical authority, vindicating to Christ his exclusive and all-sufficient mediatorial rights, bringing man back from the dead works
to God's grace, from vain traditions to God's word, and thus by
means of both obtaining for him direct access to his Savior, and
through him to his heavenly Father, Protestantism at the same
time gave no countenance to loose and unrestrained willfulness
in thought or practice. On the contrary, the freedom it has introduced is such as has solid contents, not excluding but including allegiance to law and order. *It has bound the religious spirit*

---

* The relation is happily exhibited by Calvin, *Instit.*, III, c. 2, § 6: Prin-
cipio admonendi sumus, perpetuam esse fidei relationem cum verbo, nec
magis ab eo posse divelli, quam radios a sole, unde oriuntur.—Quare si ab hoc
scopo, in quem collimare debet, vel minimum deflectit fides, naturam suam
non retinet, sed incerta est credulitas et vagus mentis error. Idem verbum
basis est, qua fulcitur et sustinetur, unde si declinat, corruit. Tolle igitur verbum, et nulla jam restabit fides.—Unde et fidem definit Paulus obedientiam,
quae praestatur, evangelio (Romans 1:5).

*indissolubly to God's grace and God's word, and by so doing set it free from all human ordinances running counter to the same.* The positive element is accordingly the first. Our church is primarily evangelical. Protestation is its second character, and has respect only to that which invades destructively the objective ground of the gospel. Positively evangelical, it becomes at the same time negatively protestant toward all opposing error. In short, its freedom is the blessed liberty of the children of God, which stands in unconditional obedience to the Lord and to his word, and is identical thus with moral necessity.*

---

* Excellent instruction on this point is to be found in the truly masterly sermon of Luther, the *Liberty of a Christian Man;* where he handles the seemingly contradictory propositions: "A Christian man is a free lord over all things," and "A Christian man is a bound servant of all things, and subject to every man in Christ."

## PART TWO

## The Principle of Protestantism
## in Its Relation to the Later Development and
## Present State of the Protestant Church

THE NEW RELIGIOUS VIEWS comprehended in Protestantism accomplished a remodification of the entire world, in government, science, art, and social life. Modern history is an inexplicable riddle without the Reformation. We are not called however to quit the strictly theological sphere. Rather, having now completed the historico-doctrinal part of our subject, we must pass on to consider the relation of the Protestant principle to the posture and wants of the church in our own age.

It must be acknowledged something remarkable always, that the last days of Luther and Melanchthon, who had attained to such a full measure of evangelical liberty and joy, should have been characterized nevertheless by a deep melancholy. Only ill will can attribute this to their personal character, and only the most superficial reflection reckon it the discredit of their work.*

---

\* The distinguished critic and historian Thomas Carlyle, who has well apprehended and described the character of Luther, at least in its human greatness and historical significance, observes of his melancholy very beautifully (*Heroes and Hero Worship*, p. 164): "The basis of his life was sadness, earnestness. In his latter days, after all triumphs and victories, he expresses him-

125

They were sad, not on their own account, but on account of the church, which lay immeasurably nearer to their hearts than all personal prosperity. And the men were not imposed upon by their own imagination; their sad forebodings, in view of the perils outward and inward to which Protestantism stood exposed, after its glorious pentecostal period, had in fact a prophetical character. The great rent, from which Christendom still continues to bleed, had now taken place; the church hitherto one was divided; individuals and whole nations were set loose from the bonds of hierarchical discipline. The Reformers had not sought the separation; it was however unavoidable. They must themselves set their seal to it, after the pope had uttered his damnatory sentence, if they would obey God and their own conscience rather than men, and honor Christ's crown of thorns above the triple crown of gold with its arbitrary decrees.

It was simply the objective course of history itself, and with this, one would think, they might have set their hearts at rest. But history, since the presence of sin, unfolds itself only through extremes in the way of action and reaction. A religious principle, once uttered, becomes the property of the whole world, communicates itself like fire to all other departments of life, rushes onward restless and one-sided to its extreme consequences; and then, by inherent dialectic process, strikes over into its opposite. Dislodge a heavy rock from its place on the summit of a mountain, and it rests not till it finds the bottom of the valley below, and there breaks into a thousand pieces. All flesh is as grass; only the word of God abideth forever. This was well understood by

---

self heartily weary of living; he considers that God alone can and will regulate the course things are taking, and that perhaps the day of judgment is not far. As for him, he longs for one thing: that God would release him from his labor, and let him depart and be at rest. They understand little of the man, who cite this in discredit of him! I will call this Luther a truly great man; great in intellect, in courage, affection and integrity; one of our most lovable and precious men. Great, not as a hewn obelisk, but as an alpine mountain—so simple, honest, spontaneous, not setting up to be great at all; there for quite another purpose than being great! Ah, yes, unsubduable granite, piercing far and wide into the heavens; yet in the clefts of it, fountains, green beautiful valleys with flowers! A right spiritual hero and prophet; once more a true son of nature and fact, for whom these centuries, and many that are yet to come, will be thankful to heaven."

the great men of whom we speak. Already indeed they had been compelled to witness with their own eyes much fleshly misunderstanding of their pure work, false consequences drawn from it, confusion and division by its means, though not by its fault. In all this, they saw now the slender beginnings of greater distraction to come and were made sorrowful by the prospect. Time has since verified their fears. What they thus despondingly anticipated, lies painfully disclosed before our eyes.

Protestantism has now a history of three hundred years behind it—a short, but most stirring and active life. True, it has built no Gothic domes, painted no Raphaelian madonnas, founded no monastic orders; in such spheres its laurels are not found. But it possesses a scholasticism, less philosophically deep perhaps, but quite as acute, as that of the Middle Ages, and at the same time much more biblically sound and solid. It carries in its bosom a mysticism, not less inward and full of feeling, speculative and practical, than that which preceded it in the Roman Church. Its hymns and chorales, in Germany at least, may stand comparison with the richest creations of church art in earlier times. From the snows of Greenland to the islands of the South Sea, from the sundered walls of the mammoth Asiatic State to the western shores of America, its missionaries are scattered among the heathen, vying in devoted and untiring zeal with those of the ancient church. It calls a literature its own, which is truly a literature for the *world,* and the power of which continues to be felt with boundless influence upon the civilization of the human race. To it belongs, at all events again in Germany, a theology, to which, in point of mobility, learning, spirit, penetration, freedom from prejudice, and skillful delineation, nothing equal is to be found in the earlier history of the church. From it also has sprung the modern philosophy with its succession of systems, which in their kind are something no less bold and grand than the papacy itself and its dogmatic image, the metaphysics of the schools. It has organized states and given them immunities, which our age for no price could commute again with the servitude of the ancient hierarchy. Compare Prussia with Italy, England with Spain, the Free States of North America with Brazil, and the truth of this declaration will be at once felt.

To Romanism itself, though serving on the one hand to fix it in its own principle, it imparted on the other a new impulse—calling into life the Jesuits, for its defense, purifying like a storm its moral atmosphere so that it could venture no more to nominate such a pope as Sixtus IV, Alexander VI, or Julius II. It stands indeed continually over against its powerful adversary still as a corrector and waker from sleep, and who will not admit that the greatest modern defenders of popery, a Moehler,[1] a Goerres,[2] for instance, are so formidable as they are simply because they have sharpened their weapons on the whetstone of Protestant science. In short, without this influence the vast communion of Rome, like the Greek Church (at least in great part), must have passed over into a state of putrefaction, so as to present at best only the spectacle of a praying corpse.

Traverse the lands in which Protestantism has established its seat, from the northern boundary of Sweden to the Sandwich Islands, from the southern declivities of the Himalayas to the banks of the Mississippi; almost everywhere you may find theologians victoriously contending against infidelity and superstition; preachers, who like Paul are not ashamed of the gospel of Christ crucified, but hold all the glory of the world in contempt for its sake; a strict moral order; a blooming domestic life; an acquaintance with the Bible; a freedom and joy of faith in the inward man; such as you may seek in vain in the central seat itself of the Church of Rome. There is still sufficient salt in the system with all its diseases to save it from corruption; full as much certainly as belonged to the Catholic Church toward the close of the Middle Ages; material enough therefore for a new Reformation. High and low, learned and unlearned, die happily within its bosom every day with nothing but the Bible in their hands and faith in the free unmerited grace of God in their hearts. Only blindness itself can deny that Protestantism still continues the great moving force of the time, holding the helm of the world's political and spiritual history; while every other form of action comes to have deep significance, only as standing with it in hostile or friendly relation.

# . 3 .

## The Diseases of Protestantism

---

WE MAY NOT HOWEVER, and will not, for this reason, close our eyes to the shadow that falls from this gigantic system, on the other side. In its inmost center there is lodged, as in the heart of the Catholic Church at the time of the Reformation, a dangerous disease; and woe to us, if we look not round betimes for a remedy. This must be sought, not beyond the system itself, but only again within its own bosom, in that same apostolic circle into which the Judas has crept, as was the case also, according to our previous showing, with the Reformation itself. Along with the bright aspects just noticed, Protestantism has also its *revolutions,* its *rationalism,* its *sects,* which are all the more dangerous as foes inasmuch as they all claim to be its truest and most legitimate offspring.

With the first, the spirit of political revolution, we have here no concern. It falls not within the theological territory. To the other two however our attention must now be directed, then to the reaction of Puseyism, and finally to the true remedy for these diseases in its most essential points.

RATIONALISM: OR ONE-SIDED THEORETIC SUBJECTIVISM

*Rationalism* has developed itself mainly in the Lutheran Church upon what may be styled its classic soil. Germany is the proper home, not only of the Reformation, but of all the deeper spiritual movements which have been called forth by this during the last three hundred years. Thither then we must first direct our view. To the creative period of the Lutheran Church, which came to a close with the Formula of Concord, succeeded immediately that of logical comprehension; as in the Catholic Church the patristic, dogma-producing time was followed by the scholastic. This Protestant school learning was accompanied indeed, like that which preceded it in the Church of Rome, with mystical tendencies of various sorts[3]; but still it gave tone to the age. Its great effort accordingly was to reduce to system the theological acquisitions of the period of the Reformation, with a demonstration, in part dialectic and in part biblical, extending to the smallest separate particulars. Our business here, is not to bring into view the many merits of this period, in which such men as Johann Gerhard, Hutter, Quenstedt, Calovius,[4] rise before our vision, but only to show in what respect it tended necessarily to call forth opposition. Shutting itself up from the start within the narrow circle of the Formula of Concord, it stood in a perfectly exclusive relation, not only toward the Reformed system of doctrine, but also toward the diverging peculiarities of the Melanchthonian school[5]; and thus gradually degenerated, like the scholastic theology of the Middle Ages, into dry dogmatism and stiffened orthodoxy, in which religion was made to consist in sound knowledge, and its practical nature thrust wholly out of sight. Justification was separated abstractly from holiness; while as it regarded the formal principle, the theory of inspiration, contrary to the freer view of the Reformers, became so overstrained that the Scriptures were made to assume a magical character in which their human, natural side was not allowed at all to appear. All this opened the way for an opposite movement.

The reaction showed itself first in the sphere of the material principle, under the form of Spenerian Pietism[6]; which in opposition to such forms of outward intellect successfully asserted the

vast importance of holiness and the verification of faith in practice. This mission it fulfilled with great earnestness; but not
without a certain one-sidedness, particularly in its later character, which gave its orthodox adversaries, with their superior
science, the advantage of right in many points. Pietism contributed much—along with its kindred spirit among the United
Brethren,[7] by whom all confessional distinctions were undervalued—to disseminate a religion of sickly sentiment and sighs,
aversion to clear definite conceptions, and to a regularly digested
system of theology, and since the confession of the truth is the
ground of the church, along with all this a want of true church
feeling.

This was the first step, we may say, toward rationalism; the nature of which holds in this, that it allows the idea of religion to
resolve itself into simple morality, or in the end into mere good
citizenship—a result fully as one-sided as the error of identifying
it with theoretic orthodoxy. Men who could acknowledge the
truth belonging to Pietism, while they still continued to stand
firm on the solid ground of the old church faith, such as the great
J. A. Bengel,[8] who stands out to view as the religious ornament
of the eighteenth century and of his native Württemberg in particular, were not common; and their number grew always smaller
as the century advanced toward its close. The chord once struck
found every day a clearer response. The undervaluation of the
church and her symbols led gradually to the undervaluation of
the apostles and their writings, and terminated finally in a denial
of the divinity of Christ himself. The transition of the pietistic
tendency over into the rationalistic, is strikingly exhibited in
the case of the celebrated professor of Halle, Semler[9]; who was
brought up in the pietistic school, and continued to adhere to it
all his life also, in the way of what he called "private piety," but
became nevertheless, through his special dislike to doctrine, and
his bold critical and historical investigations, the proper father
of the German neology, and contributed beyond all others to unsettle the received views, with regard to the canon and the subject
of inspiration. Other elements, in part foreign—the English deism, the French infidelity—whose leaders found unfortunately
so powerful a protector in Frederick the Great, and lastly the

immeasurably flat philosophy of Wolff,[10] making all in heaven
and on earth clear by making all shallow, came in to support this
fatal tendency; so that toward the close of the revolutionary century it had almost universal possession of the pulpit and the professor's chair, and was fairly and fully at home with the visible
rulers of the church, the general superintendents and counselors
of consistory.

Rationalism again, however, has its own historical development. In its first stage it appeared as a shallow, popular *aufklaer-
ung*, by which religion and the church were both cleared of all
deeper meaning. Afterward, by means of the philosophy of Kant,
which had in the meantime taken hold on the consciousness of
the age, it assumed a more scientific form. The familiar, every-
day style of thinking was made to give place to intellectual, philosophically cultivated reflection. Finally, it culminated in the destructive speculative theology, or *untheology* rather, which within
a short period past has burst, like a wild monster, with terrific
desolation, from the camp of the negative criticism and Hegelian
logic. Compared with this, the old common rationalism is only
a harmless child. The critical and doctrinal writings of Strauss,
Feuerbach, Bruno Bauer,[11] and their associates, may be regarded
as a complete concentration, full of spirit and keen penetration,
of all assaults heretofore made upon Christianity; so that if they
should be fully overcome, apologetic divinity might hold a true
triumph and allow her armor to hang long without use. Rationalism, it is true, even in its first stage, had exchanged the Protestant doctrine of justification for Pelagianism, and put the holy
Scriptures into the same class with mere human books. It still
left standing however some fundamental religious truth, as the
being of God, his providence, the freedom and immortality of
man, and paid great respect particularly to the morality of Christianity. It is not to be denied that Kant's *Critique of the Practical
Reason* is animated with great moral earnestness, and may have
served as a schoolmaster to bring some to Christ. Being separated
however in itself from the personal ideal of morality, Jesus Christ,
the absolute God-man, it was pervaded with the poison of stoic
self-righteousness, and could make no stand therefore against the
evergrowing stream of the negative movement.

The speculative rationalism has now fully demolished the brittle structure, and thus realized in the world of thought, what the French Revolution under Robespierre accomplished in actual life. The entire sacred history of our Savior is resolved into a collection of myths, unconsciously produced by the imagination of the infant church, and forming a tissue of inward and outward contradictions. One church dogma after another is given to the winds as an imperfect conception, self-annihilated gradually by the onward course of scientific criticism. Yea, the whole supernatural world is drawn over into the present life as a mere product of the religious fancy without all objective reality, and the infinite Godhead itself must shrink into the finite spirit of man. This is pantheism in the most scientifically complete and perilous form the world has ever yet seen, exalting the general idea of humanity to the throne of the universe, and proclaiming it the creator, preserver, and redeemer of all things. No further progress seems possible in this direction, unless it be to reduce the theory to practice by building temples for the worship of genius, as has been already proposed, and in some parts of the New World actually carried into effect; and by composing liturgical forms, in which the human spirit may offer prayers and sing speculative hallelujahs, in measured logico-dialectic process, to the honor and glory of itself.

It would be an error, however, to suppose that the representatives of this tendency are agreed among themselves. They stand to one another, in part at least, in the most contradictory relation; so that the negative theological literature of Germany, at the present time, appears a tumultuating chaos of systems and theories, whose affinity often is such as holds between fire and water. In the nature of the case, when the human understanding is raised to the highest tribunal, full scope is given to the willfulness of private judgment at the same time.

This extreme climax of unbelief proclaims itself to be the ultimate necessary result of Protestantism. To this we answer however, in the words of the apostle John, concerning the anti-Christian errorists of his own day: *They went out from us* (in the way of outward, historical derivation), *but they were not of us;* for if they had been of us, they would no doubt have continued with

us (1 John 2:19). It belongs to the very nature of the Reformation, as we have seen, that it makes the clearest distinction between sinful man and a holy God, prostrates utterly the imagination that the human will may redeem itself, or the natural understanding know the truth by its own power, and requires an unconditional submission on the part of the sinner to God's grace
and God's word. Here, on the contrary, the divine grace is taken
to be a mere objective reflex of the power belonging to man himself, and the subjective reason, or understanding rather,* is made
the fountain and norm of knowledge. If there was ever a radical
confusion of things totally heterogeneous, we have it in the pretension just mentioned. The tendency in question deserves to be
regarded only as a Christianly refined paganism, whose very character stands in a deification of the universe, and the worship of
the forces, either physical or spiritual, in which it has its constitution. It might be shown that all the heathen mythologies find
their image in this modern infidel cultivation.

From this it may now be seen clearly that the standpoint of our
time is wholly different from that of the Reformers. The most
dangerous enemy with which we are threatened on theoretic
ground is not the Catholicism of Rome, but the foe within our
own borders; not the hierarchic papacy of the Vatican, but the
worldly papacy of the subjective understanding, and Protestant
infidelity; not the *Council of Trent,* but the theology of unbelief,
as proclaimed by a Roehr,[12] a Wegscheider,[13] a Strauss, a Feuerbach, and others of the same stamp. Must not all serious believing
Protestants feel themselves more closely related in spirit to a Bellarmine or a Moehler,[14] who agree with them in acknowledging
the Trinity, the deity of Christ, atonement by his blood, and the

---

* Rationalism arrogates to itself the title of rationality or reason as specially its own. In truth, however, it moves not at all in the sphere of reason,
but only in that of the abstract understanding, the region of mere finite
thinking, entangled in contradictions and external appearances, the standpoint of reflection. Reason, on the contrary, is the power of perceiving the
supernatural, the infinite, the harmonious unity, the essence of things, the
primal idea of the absolute. It is the longing of the spirit after its true country, its home-drawing toward God and the revelation he has made of himself
in Christ; just as conscience is the point of contact between the human will
and the ground of all will in God. Reason, then, in its inmost nature, is a
receptive faculty that must go beyond itself for its contents.

divine inspiration and infallibility of the Scriptures, than they
are to Strauss and Bruno Bauer, by whom all these articles are
rejected? I will by no means deny indeed that a certain affinity
also may be traced, in another view, between Protestant rationalism and the Catholicism of Rome; in the fact that the tradition principle of the one corresponds with the reason principle
of the other, while both rest upon a Pelagian basis in which all
right apprehension of the deep corruption of sin is wanting.\*
Even the pantheistic character of the latest rationalism is not
without its analogies in the absolute infallibility and supremacy
in church and state claimed by the papacy, and in the doctrine of
transubstantiation, according to which the priest by his consecrating act produces the body of the Lord—the creature, the Creator—and sensible elements are taken to be the immediate contents of the Savior's flesh and blood. But a great difference holds

---

\* This is allowed by the more discerning and honorable Roman theologians.
Thus the powerful Moehler, in the preface to the first edition of his *Symbolik,*
from which all the recent apologists of popery, who are of any account, draw
their material (p. xi): *"The Catholic has this advantage moreover, that his
system includes, as well what the rationalists honor one-sidedly or exclusively
in Christianity,* as what is made prominent in the same Christianity just as
one-sidedly or exclusively by the orthodox Protestantism. *These two extremes
are in fact, in his faith, balanced and fully reconciled. It holds as much affinity with the one as with the other;* and the Catholic accordingly can comprehend both *since his system is the unity of both.* The naturalistic Protestants are indebted to Luther directly only for this, that he has procured for
them the freedom of daring to profess what is directly opposite to him and
to the religious communion which he established; and the orthodox Protestants are bound with them by nothing but the oppressive feeling that Luther
has founded a church, whose conception constrains them to tolerate patiently
such opposers in their midst, as a case admitting no help. The Catholic on
the contrary has an inward affinity on the ground of his faith with both, and
thus stands higher than both and overlooks both. He has what belongs to
both, only without their one-sided defects." Compare the description which
Melanchthon gives of the rationalistic and Pelagianistic theology of his time
in the *Apol. Conf.* and his *Loc. Theol.* We may refer also to the fact that the
more free investigations which gradually led to rationalism had their origin
in part in the Catholic Church, as we may see in the case of Petavius[15] in
dogmatic history, and Rich. Simon[16] in the criticism and history of the Bible.
The Jesuits first proclaimed the principle of the sovereignty of the people,
which produced the French Revolution, and by their casuistry opened the
way for the formal overthrow of all morality, with which all religious faith
also must necessarily fall at the same time.

notwithstanding between the two systems, of which we must not lose sight, if we would be equal to the questions of the time.

For Romanism, in the first place, is in this respect at most only *half* Pelagian and *half* rationalistic, that it makes the grace of God and the sacred Scriptures coordinate with works and tradition, and equally necessary as the ground and fountain of salvation; while rationalism, in true stoic style, dreams of being able to do *all* by its own strength, and to know *all* by reason simply, separated from its proper divine contents and contradicting thus its own design; on which account the idea of a supernatural revelation is rejected, and Christ himself is degraded to a natural hero of virtue, a second Socrates, a mere man accordingly, however ideally apprehended. A further difference consists in this, that Romanism in making works necessary to justification and salvation looks to the deeds of the *whole church,* and by tradition, as a fountain of knowledge and rule of faith supplementary to the Bible, intends properly the reason of *all Christian history,* showing itself thus in the character of *objective, churchly semi-Pelagianism and semi-rationalism;* while Protestant rationalism holds the *isolated* will and reason of the *individual* sufficient for the purposes of salvation, and in this way is altogether *subjective and unchurchly* in its nature.

This then, as already said, stands in vastly more direct opposition to the essence of Christianity and orthodox Protestantism than the enemy which the Reformers were called to combat. Luther and Calvin, if they should make their appearance now, would act very differently, in the altered state of things, from what they did three hundred years ago. Their main zeal would be directed no doubt against such purely negative pseudo-Protestantism, as something altogether worse than popery itself.

We need to bear this in mind, in our activity for religion and the church at the present time, that we may not lose sight of our true character and calling as Protestants, in view of the false pretensions with which we are surrounded on the part of the unbelieving and ungodly, who profess to stand upon the same ground and to glory in the same name, and who show themselves loudest possibly in their cry against popery and Jesuitism, only to cover their hostility to all faith and righteousness. Such have a nominal title only, but none that is historical, to appear in the Protestant character. That caution is needed here in a high degree, in our present circumstances, is not to be doubted. By making common cause with such destructive Protestants in their opposition to Catholicism, whether the immediate object be political or religious, we must render the most efficient support and aid to this interest itself; which has already indeed, with serpent wisdom, contrived to draw immense advantage from such anti-Protestant connections between Christ and Belial. The attack intended to overwhelm the enemy, recoils in this case necessarily, in the way of self-annihilation, upon its source. Rather let us never forget the much that we hold in common with the Roman Church, the bond of union by which she is joined with us in opposition to absolute unbelief, whose wild ravages are displayed also in her own bosom, particularly in France. Let us first with united strength expel the devil from our own temple, into which he has stolen under the passport of our excessive toleration, before we proceed to exorcise and cleanse the dome of St. Peter. At least, let this be our main business.

It may be said however perhaps that rationalism, at least in the philosophical form now described, has for our own country no danger. But it should be remembered that the evil does not hold simply in the form. The main thing is the principle from which it grows; the general standpoint of a cold, abstract intellection, to which all that is mystical or supernatural in Christianity is found displeasing. In this view, we may discover affinities with the German rationalism, not only in the Unitarian and Universalist heresies of this country, but in much also that passes for orthodoxy. That unbelief has not yet acquired here the same giant force, is not owing so much to the greater prevalence of personal piety, or to the moral earnestness of the English character, as to the one-sided practical tendency and want of scientific spirit generally predominant. Where a man does not think, it requires no great skill to be orthodox. But the orthodoxy that includes no thought, is not worth a farthing. In countries where scientific feeling has prevailed, though with less force, as Holland and France, results have appeared quite analogous with the course of things in Germany. In Holland particularly the old established orthodoxy, having degenerated in great part into dry and lifeless forms, found itself assailed by Arminianism, which itself again ran out finally into formal Pelagianism and rationalism.

In the case before us, it may be expected that the disposition to explore a given principle, and carry it out to its proper consequences, will continually gain ground; and with this change, if no scientific counterpoise be provided in season, rationalism must assume among us a more dangerous form. Why should it not find its way into England and America, even as the deism of the first country, from which it is descended, wandered formerly over into Germany, to complete there its university training? Time and space are continually becoming more compressed; the intercourse of the nations more active and free. Emigration from the Old World is on the increase. Acquaintance with German literature is extending daily; and it would not be difficult to show that many respectable divines of this country, who employ themselves with it only under its abstract intellectual form, have without their own knowledge or will admitted the rationalistic principle, which needs only to be cultivated as a germ in the earth, by those who may come after them without their piety, to grow upward in a short time into a mighty tree. Shall I say that even in the liturgies and hymnbooks of the German American Churches rationalistic elements are by no means rare, without being perceived by those who use them? In many cases, clergymen who were educated at the German universities in the palmy day of rationalism have been here improved indeed in their hearts under the salutary influence of practical piety, but have at the same time retained the poison, for which no scientific antidote was at hand, in their heads, and communicated it also involuntarily to others.

I will simply notice the fact besides, as of a kind to justify anxiety, that so many of the German periodicals of the country, particularly in the West, are lending themselves, as organs more or less expert, to the service of infidelity, with the worst influence on the more common class especially of our immigrant population. True, these sheets, so far as they are known to me, are mostly both in matter and style beyond description miserable; such as dare not show themselves in Germany at all, unless in the lowest alehouses. The great body of their readers however, of

course, are not aware that all this style of pretended light and
liberality has been fairly exterminated by German science in its
most recent form, or we may say even by the romantic school itself; and then, practically, it comes to much the same, whether
infidelity goes about in the antiquated coat and cue style of a
Bahrdt[17] and Edelmann,[18] or in the modern philosophical cloak
of a Strauss or Feuerbach. We have good reason therefore to stand
on our guard in this quarter also, and to prepare ourselves beforehand for the crisis that may come.*

---

* As many of my readers probably never see the publications referred to,
while at the same time it is important that they should know something of
the infernal spirit, which is at work to undermine the faith of the German
population in America, I will submit here to the by no means pleasant task
of furnishing a sample of its character; selecting for the purpose a few striking passages only from the collection of various papers I have received, on
account of attacks they have contained against me for my ordination sermon,
as mentioned in my introduction. I might bring forward quite a body of political sheets, published only by immigrant Germans; but it may be better to
limit myself to two of religious, or much better antireligious, pretension
which appear in wholly opposite sections of the union.

The *Licht-Freund,*[19] published by Muehl and Strehly in Hermann, Missouri, contains in No. 6. of its 5th year, along with other products of the most
superficial, spiritless, and jejune form of rationalism, an essay on *baptism;*
in which it is represented as an old usage of pagan and Jewish origin, which
"Rabbi Jesus" was pleased to retain in his system, but that has now become
wholly unmeaning, or rather "irrational" and "grossly superstitious."—"Of a
trine immersion or sprinkling with water," we are told, "nothing was known
in the beginning; but this was introduced only after the introduction, at a
later period, of the nonsensical doctrine *of one God consisting of three persons;* of which, as we have shown on a different occasion, no trace is to be
found in connection with early Christianity."—"Have children sins then,"
sneeringly inquires this apostle of infidelity, this jack-o'-lantern philosopher,
"that call for forgiveness? On the topic of original sin, as discussed by us in
our preceding year, we have handled this point at large and exposed the
*ridiculousness of the church doctrine.*"—"It is said of baptism further (the
reference is to Luther's Catechism) that it redeems us from death and the
devil. But this is still more false, since baptized and unbaptized alike die;
and as for the devil, it is well understood that *this is an invention simply of
diseased imagination, that carries us back to the times of the most gross superstition and rudeness.* The devil, who plays specter in the doctrine of the
church, is long since killed dead and no longer creates fear; though it cannot
be denied that there is still devil enough in the world, and particularly in
America." This last remark has certainly much truth, of which the writer
himself may be taken as good practical proof.—In the same number we read:
"This bugbear (of the *orthodox* Lutheran and Reformed Churches) is the

## SECTARISM: OR ONE-SIDED PRACTICAL SUBJECTIVISM

We turn now to the other grand disease which has fastened itself upon the heart of Protestantism, and which must be considered only the more dangerous, because it appears ordinarily in the
imposing garb of piety, Satan transformed into an angel of light.
This is the *sect system*, which reigns especially in our own land,
favored by its free institutions and the separation of the church

old theology which has long since outlived itself. For who in our time can
still believe in three Gods, a propitiation of God by blood, a descent into
hell, and other devil's play, as expounded here to a hair in the largest style.—
Let no one say however that people do not play with puppets when they
grow large and old. This history of religion, ancient and modern, teaches us
that men continue to be children, however old they may be." The religious
history of Hermann in Missouri appears however to form a special exception;
and the most learned Messrs. Muehl, Strehly, and company, are to be regarded, we presume, as the only truly rational men the world has yet seen.
What a pity no one should think of making them professors of theology and
philosophy! It is enough to drive one mad, such a perverse world, with its
childish religious history.—In No. 10 of the same year a characteristic article
is found abusing the Pennsylvania synods, which however is too long to be
presented here; also a report on the rationalist associations in Hermann and
Augusta, exhibiting in the case of the first, among others, the following spirited resolution: "That we hold all and every title, assumed by the clerical
tribe, such as Reverend, Ehrwuerdig, Hochwuerdig, etc., for a ridiculous,
aristocratic pretension, repugnant to free, republican feeling, which every
free man should reject with scorn." That these honest heroes of liberty should
abolish such titles among themselves, must be approved as altogether rational
and natural; though we should think it hardly necessary; for none surely who
care for decency or truth are likely to burden them with any titles of the sort.
    The *Licht-Freund* however sheds but the pale glimmer of a glowworm, as
compared with the full blazing brightness of another periodical, which makes
its appearance at New York, edited by Samuel Ludvigh, under the blinding
title *Die Fackel*[20]; with the motto: "Out of the ruins of Judaism and Christianity, rationalism will raise its head; out of the rubbish of temples and
churches will rise halls of science." Here we read, in No. 4 of the 2nd year
(14, Dec., 1844) among other things, such blasphemies as we find it almost
too much to copy: "Dass nach der Lehre des Herrn V. die Asteroiden Bruech-
stuecke eines grossen Planeten seien, ist in meinen Augen ebenso richtig, als
der heilige Geist einen Gottessohn machen koenne. Wenn Planeten Junge
machen koennen, so bleibe man doch ja fein im Glauben des alten Gottes,
und lasse ihn durch seinen heiligen Geist hier auf Erden noch andere goett-
liche Jungfern-Kinder erzeugen. Wie aber seine keuschen Marien in jenen
Planeten aussehen muessen, das begreift mein Hirnkasten nicht!" The same
writer presents his confession of faith, or no faith rather, which is pronounced
by Herr Ludvigh, "the quintessence of the highest human spirit." [He has it
on display, engraved on glass, at his home], and all "whose means allow them

from the state, and is entitled accordingly to our particular attention. While rationalism has been nurtured mainly in the bosom of the Lutheran Church, the poisonous plant of sectarianism has flourished most on Reformed ground, and with the practical nations, England, and her now full-grown, emancipated daughter America.

---

to honor such a pearl" can be furnished with it there for five dollars. It is of such sort, as to throw Feuerbach himself into the shade, whose *Wesen des Christenthums* is diligently turned to account by the *Fackel.* "I believe (thus speaks this 'very distinguished scholar' of Boston) in an inexplicable, exalted eternal existence, whose name no tongue has ever yet uttered, which was, is, and shall be, past, present, and future, in all three externally without change; which was, is, and shall be, one and the same in endless union with itself and the majestical whole; whose power comprehends itself and all, from eternity—that I also have sprung from its bosom, and as a shoot of its eternal endure forever—that my eternal deposited in my mother as seed, impregnated into a germ and brought into the world, formed my present—that I have here heaven and hell, joy and sorrow alike—that when my present shall here dissolve, its elements will be reduced again to the mass out of which I was taken by my birth—that no miracle can occur in the course of the whole —that man and spirit are but spokes in the eternal wheel, no one of more account than another to its movement—that no dead shall or can come ever again—that the judgment of the living must have place here as the consequence of their actions, and that for the dead none is needed—that the most glorious temple is nature under the vault of heaven, and that a God among the stars, crowned with suns, must blind us to the pomp and splendor of churches, and is too high for human worship—that what the priests teach is only falsehood and delusion, and the hope of a life to come a mere contrivance for gain—that the consciousness of praiseworthy actions is a true paradise and a state of divine peace—that an affectionate, faithful wife, and loving children, are the true heavenly angels, and in the opposite case also they are the hateful devils—that man needs a wise teacher, for his own welfare and that of others—that I must respect myself, before I can deserve to be respected by others—that I must do right, before I exact right—that the noble man is a god of the earth; but a rough, unprincipled one, the most hateful of all venomous monsters—that when I have lived as a man, and loved my fellowmen, I can peacefully resign my ashes to corruption in the urn of oblivion, and finally that something from my eternal thus laid down shall be my resurrection." What this residuum shall consist in, we are informed by the great dogmatist himself. Moscow leather for boot soles! And this nauseous filth of a demented brain is offered for five dollars! Utilitarianism, in such a case, may well be indulged with its *Cui bono.* The Bostonian philosopher seems himself to have but small hope of replenishing his hungry purse from the profits of his system. He confesses to his friend Ludvigh: "A real dog's life among men, who are like asses and tigers! I have had much, and still have much to bear; my old skin is tanned to moscowy leather. Whoever shall work it into boot soles hereafter, he will have soles that may be expected to last."

This difference has its ground in the national character of the Germans and the English, who stand in a relation to each other similar to that of the ancient Greeks and Romans. For the better understanding then of this part of our subject, a short ethnographic digression may not be out of place.

The German, when true to his better nature, is distinguished by inwardness, heartiness, and a tendency to contemplation and deep thought. His favorite home is the ideal region of truth and beauty. He possesses at the same time inexhaustible energy and endurance. He can devote his whole life to the development of a philosophical thought or some learned investigation, and feel himself happy while so doing under the most unfavorable circumstances, even sitting on a shoemaker's bench, like Jakob Boehme,[21] or suffering hunger with Kepler.[22] He reckons among his countrymen the greatest philosophers and artists. An idealist by profession, he has but little tact for practical life. Readily and easily he adapts himself to all outward relations, foreign countries, and new tongues, not setting himself to remold them to his own taste, if only he may be left free to follow his inward theoretic bent. He seeks his highest crown in the *Gemuetlichkeit* that forms especially the ornament of the German woman, and in science, the pride and joy of the man. Hence accordingly almost all movements in the German Church have turned upon doctrine. She produced all the leading ideas of the Reformation, but left to other nations the business of outward organization. She presents at this time in particular a mixed mass of systems and schools, a pattern chart of all possible views and tendencies. But they all continue notwithstanding in one church connection, only in rare instances run into separation, schism, sectdom. In Germany one may often meet with disputations among the younger class, where different persons contend, amid clouds of tobacco smoke, with the greatest keenness and most thorough learning, bringing out the inmost principles of their subject, making them stand forth like day and night, and not resting till they are pushed to their most extreme consequences. But at last, their strength exhausted, they join in a friendly glass and song, and exchange a general kiss, as though nothing had occurred. When however it does come to separation, a case exemplified too often among Germans in this country, we find this usually in an eccentric style. For the German cannot well observe moderation. He has a decided tendency to extremes, both in politics and religion. As he can rise very high, so he can fall very low.

Quite different is the Englishman, and the American resting on the same basis. True, he shares with his kindred Germanic race the same ethical force, which no storms can overcome. But since the time of William the Conqueror, a strong Romanic element has been found associated with his nature. The energy of his will accordingly takes a different direction, one which is outward namely, into practical life. A born realist, he possesses the greatest talent for organization; shrinks from no difficulty, where the call is for order and form; his character is marked and strong. For philosophy and art in their higher forms he cares but little; single praiseworthy examples excepted, as among later writers, particularly Coleridge and Carlyle. Such studies are for him not sufficiently practical, useful, tangible. He laughs at the speculations of the modern German philosophers, as unfruitful, baseless, fantastic visions, and still continues to cherish a truly superstitious veneration for the empiricism of Locke. The German *Gemuetlichkeit*, with its expression of full, warm, heartfelt tenderness, he regards with distrust as effeminate weakness, or sickly sentimentality. So far is he from making himself at home, with passive self-renunciation, in foreign relations; he seeks rather everywhere to bend and cut them to his own nature. Go where he may, he remains always an Englishman. Even when he travels into other lands, he expects more accommodation to his national peculiarities on the part of the people, than he is prepared to yield to theirs. So in this country, his will, language, manners, and customs are made the measure to which Spaniards, Swedes, Hollanders, and French must adjust themselves as they best can; and it is quite possible that the German nationality also, as it now holds among us under a distinct form, both in language and life, may gradually be swallowed up at last in the same Anglican ocean. A result however that must be considered calamitous, and which all Germans should endeavor with all their might to avert. In conformity with this character, the controversies belonging to the history of the English and North American churches turn not so much on doc-

trine, as on the constitution and forms of the church. In place
of schools and systems we have parties and sects, which in many
cases appear in full inexorable opposition, even while occupying
the platform of the very same confession. The mere question of
patronage has produced in Scotland, during the last century and
in our own time, very important secessions; though the freedom
of the Established Church in that country is of a high order, as
compared with the condition of the German Church; which nevertheless has no thought of a separation from the state on this
account; content if she may be internally free, in the midst of
the deductions of philosophy and the creations of art.

Sects, it is true, do not owe their origin to the Reformation.
They have root in the general nature of man, its sinful ambition
and pride. The apostles were called to oppose the evil in the very
infancy of the church, as we may learn from 1 Corinthians 1:10 ff.,
as well as from other passages. The first centuries exhibit a vast
number of sects, and they extend through all of the Middle Ages.
The Catholic Church however has gradually overwhelmed them,
partly by spiritual superiority and partly by outward force.
Through the emancipation of a large portion of Christendom
from the Roman yoke, in the sixteenth century, much more
ample scope was secured for the action of subjective freedom, so
that it became possible for such separations to acquire independent strength and clothe themselves with a regular constitution.
Still they were held back, at the beginning, by the thunder of
Luther's voice, and the colossal weight of his person. Calvin too
had such a religious horror of heresies and sects that he hewed to
pieces without mercy the unprincipled Libertines of Geneva with
the sword of his spirit, and even suffered the distinguished Spanish physician, Michael Servetus, to be burned for denying the
doctrine of the Trinity.

In England the energetic government of Elizabeth was enabled to unite the conflicting tendencies of Protestantism, though
not indeed without violence toward the most stubborn opposers, under a common head, in the form of a complete state-church
organization. But under her successors this degenerated continually more and more into mere external formalism. The consequence was the *Puritan* revolution, by means of which under

Cromwell the more free Protestant element gained the ascendancy, though only for a short time. [With his own life], Laud atoned for the hierarchical Charles I and for the political sins of the new Protestant popedom. The deep moral earnestness, the stern self-discipline, the unbending force of character, exhibited in Puritanism, must fill the unprejudiced historian with high admiration. There was reason in its war against the tyranny of false forms. When it is beheld, with inexorable zeal for the first and second commandments, storming the altars and turning St. Paul's Cathedral into a stall for horses, it strikes us as a divine judgment, the scorn of the Most High himself, directed against the proud creations of men, and one is reminded of the conduct of Moses, when with indignation at the calf-worship of the Israelites, he dashed the Tables of the Law to pieces.

But here precisely lies the weakness also of this tendency. Puritanism has a zeal for God, but not according to knowledge. Inflamed against the deposition of bad forms and the abuse of such as are good, it makes war upon form in every shape and insists on stripping the spirit of all covering whatever, as though the body were a work of the devil. If the choice were simply between a bodiless spirit and a spiritless body, the first of course must be at once preferred. But there is still a third condition, that of a sound spirit in a sound body; and this is the best of all, alone answering to the will and order of God. For the body is the divinely formed, natural habitation of the spirit, without which it wanders about ghostlike, exposed to all inclement powers, and must in the end perish with cold. It is worthy of notice that a large part of the Puritan or Presbyterian congregations in England, and also a considerable section of the Congregational interest in North America, in the beginning of the last century, fell over to Unitarianism. The failure of life was a failure of orthodoxy at the same time. Whereas in the case of organizations better secured by forms, the orthodoxy in the same circumstances has still maintained itself at least with statute force, so that when life has returned again, after a period of collapse (against which no constitution as such can make the church secure), it has found at once its established church channels, by which to flow forth among the people.

With this rugged, abstract spiritualism stands closely connected the unhistorical, revolutionary tendency of Puritanism. It has no respect whatever for history. It would restore pure, primitive Christianity, with entire disregard to the many centuries of development that lie between, as though all had been labor in vain, and the Lord had not kept his own promise to be with the church always to the end of the world. It is not surprising, on this account, that Cromwell, who overturned in such stormful style the ecclesiastical creations of an older time and even stained himself with the blood of a king and an archbishop, should hardly be named without horror in the bosom of the Episcopal Church, and that the great and lofty qualities which undoubtedly belonged to his character should be so generally overlooked, or regarded without respect.* He that tramples father and mother underfoot has no reason to find fault with his children, when they treat him in the same way, and prove the instruments of a divine Nemesis to bring him to a sense of his own wrong committed against history.

With vastly more wisdom, prudence, and moderation, did the founders of Methodism commence and carry forward their work of reformation. Whitefield and the two Wesleys never laid aside their respect for the mother church, but notwithstanding its degeneracy labored in its communion and died within its bosom. The Wesleyan movement, it is true, included a secessional element from the beginning, which the force of circumstances soon rendered too strong to be restrained; and the result was the establishment of a separate church. The divorce however was unnatural and wrong; and the form into which Methodism has since run, in this country particularly (the fair evolution of its original one-sided subjectivity), is not suited certainly to unsettle this judgment. In the nature of the case, the contemporaneous secession from the Church of Scotland, notwithstanding the eminent piety of the principal actors in it, must fall under the same con-

---

* An attempt indeed to do him justice has been made recently by Thomas Carlyle, in his book *Heroes and Hero Worship,* Sect. VI: "The Hero as a King." Carlyle however is constitutionally no Episcopalian, but a Scottish Presbtyerian.

demnation. The results of it as transplanted again to American soil furnish a painfully ridiculous commentary on the false tendency involved in it from the start.

Puritan Protestantism forms properly the main basis of our North American church. Viewed as a whole, she owes her general characteristic features, her distinctive image, neither to the German or Continental Reformed, nor to the German Lutheran, nor to the English Episcopal communion, but to that band of Independents, who for the sake of their faith and a good conscience forsook their native land before the time of Cromwell, sought refuge first in Holland, and finally landed with prayers and tears on the shores of Massachusetts Bay. To this New England influence must be added indeed the no less important weight of Presbyterianism, as derived subsequently from Scotland and Ireland. But this may be regarded as in all essential respects the same life. The reigning theology of this country is neither that of the Heidelberg Catechism, nor that of the Augsburg Confession, nor that of the Thirty-nine Articles. It is the theology of the Westminster Confession.

We may never ungratefully forget that it was this generation of godly Pilgrims which once for all stamped upon our country that character of deep moral earnestness, that spirit of strong intrepid determination, that peculiar zeal for the sabbath and the Bible, which have raised it to so high a place in the history of the Christian Church, and enable it now to compare so favorably with the countries of the Old World. For our German emigration in particular it must be counted a high privilege that it is here brought into contact with the practical piety of the English community, and by degrees also imbued more or less with its power; though with the loss, to be regretted on the other side, of many German peculiarities. Thousands of souls, that might have died in vanity and unbelief in their native land, have been thus rescued, we may trust, from eternal perdition.

But while we thankfully and joyfully acknowledge this, we have no right still to overlook the fact that along with the same tendency an unhistorical and unchurchly character has inserted itself also into the inmost joints of our religious life. The Scriptures are the only source and norm of saving truth, but tradition is the channel by which it is carried forward in history.* The letter of revelation transforms itself continuously into life and action, and this not simply in the individual believer as such, but in the Christian Church as a whole, to which, as his mother, the individual must hold himself subordinate as indeed it is only through her he receives the Scriptures themselves. The plan of redemption, moreover, calls for more than the rescue simply of individual souls. God's will is that the body of the redeemed should exhibit an organic communion, that may be the image of the union that holds between himself and the only-begotten Son. This conception of the communion of the church, however, as the Body of Christ, few here seem to have reached, in its depth and glory.

The principle of Congregationalism, which has exercised such vast influence upon the entire conformation of our religious views and relations, leads legitimately to full atomism. The Bible principle, in its abstract separation from tradition or church development, furnishes no security against sects. They make their appeal collectively to the sacred volume; the devil himself does so, when it suits his purpose. Strongly also as Puritanism and Congregationalism, in their theocratic, state-church period, endeavored to secure a religious and civil union of their members, a subordination of the individual to the general, the system is clearly impotent in this direction. It includes no limitation for the principle of sects. In its own nature it is unhistorical and one-sidedly spiritualistic, and has no reason on this account to require or expect that its children should be bound by its authority, more than it has itself been bound by the authority of its own spiritual ancestry. The theocratic period accordingly soon ran its course.

With the Revolution, the separation of church and state became general and fixed. As there was now no hierarchic bond on the

---

* When we speak here, and afterward occasionally, in favor of tradition, the reader is requested to bear always in mind what we have already said of the different kinds of tradition. We plead for it, not of course in the Romish sense, which makes it a source of knowledge independent of the Bible, and coordinate with it in rank, but as exhibiting the consciousness the church has of the contents of the Bible, the Christian reason in the form of history, the *living* word of God in the church as it flows forth from the written word.

one hand, as in the Church of Rome, so neither was there any civil supremacy on the other, as in Germany, the Episcopal Church of England, and the Greek Church of Russia, by which the single elements might be held together. The emigration from the Old World increased meanwhile with every year, transporting with it the germs of sectarian distinction and material for new religious formations. Tendencies, which had found no political room to unfold themselves in other lands, wrought here without restraint. All the circumstances of the country, in one word, have contributed to precipitate the church into those evils precisely with which she was least qualified in her original character successfully to contend.

Thus we have come gradually to have a host of sects, which it is no longer easy to number, and that still continues to swell from year to year.* Where the process of separation is destined to end, no human calculation can foretell. Anyone who has, or fancies that he has, some inward experience and a ready tongue, may persuade himself that he is called to be a reformer; and so proceed at once, in his spiritual vanity and pride, to a revolutionary rupture with the historical life of the church, to which he holds himself immeasurably superior. He builds himself of a night accordingly a new chapel, in which now for the first time since the age of the apostles a pure congregation is to be formed; baptizes his followers with his own name, to which he thus secures an immortality, unenviable it is true, but such as is always flattering to the natural heart; rails and screams with full throat against all that refuses to do homage to his standard; and with all this though utterly unprepared to understand a single book, is not ashamed to appeal continually to the Scriptures, as having been sealed entirely, or in large part, to the understanding of eighteen centuries, and even to the view of our Reformers themselves, till now at last God has been pleased to kindle the true light in an obscure corner of the New World! Thus the deceived multitude, having no power to discern spirits, is converted not

---

* The latest work on the American church, *An Original History of the Religious Denominations at Present Existing in the United States, Etc.* by I. D. Rupp (Philadelphia, 1844), gives an account of not less than forty-one Protestant sects, but is notwithstanding by no means complete.

to Christ and his truth, but to the arbitrary fancies and baseless opinions of an individual, who is only of yesterday. Such *con*version is of a truth only *per*version; such *theo*logy, *neo*logy; such *ex*position of the Bible, wretched *im*position. What is built is no church, but a chapel, to whose erection Satan himself has made the most liberal contribution.

Such is the aspect of our land. A variegated sampler of all conceivable religious chimeras and dreams, in connection with more sober systems of sectarian faith! Every theological vagabond and peddler may drive here his bungling trade, without passport or license, and sell his false ware at pleasure. What is to come of such confusion is not now to be seen.

Nor is it enough that all these poisonous weeds shoot up thus wild and luxuriant in our Protestant garden. Even those divisions of the church that are essentially rooted in the same evangelical soil, and that cannot well be included in the category of sects, stand for the most part in such hostile relation to one another, and show so little inclination or impulse toward an inward and outward union in the Lord, that one might weep to think of it. There are indeed single cases of honorable exception, which I know how to value. Without them we might wellnigh despair. In a broad general view of the case, however, particularly as it is exhibited in the periodical organs of the different denominations, the evidences of a wrong spirit are sufficiently clear. Jealousy and contention, and malicious disposition in various forms, are painfully common. We see but little of that charity, which suffereth long and is kind, envieth not, vaunteth not itself, is not puffed up, doth not behave itself unseemly, seeketh not her own, is not easily provoked, and thinketh no evil: that rejoiceth not in iniquity, but rejoiceth in the truth, wherever it may be found; that beareth all things, believeth all things, hopeth all things, endureth all things. No, alas; with shame and humiliation be it confessed, the different sections of our orthodox Protestantism also are severally bent on securing absolute dominion, take satisfaction too often in each other's damage, undervalue and disparage each other's merits, regard more their separate private interest than the general interest of the kingdom of God, and show themselves stiff-willed and obstinately selfish wherever it

comes to the relinquishment, or postponement even, of subordinate differences for the sake of a great common object.

To the man who has any right idea of the church, as the communion of saints, this state of things must be a source of deep
distress. The loss of all his earthly possessions, the death of his
dearest friend, however severely felt, would be as nothing to
him, compared with the grief he feels for such division and distraction of the Church of God, the Body of Jesus Christ. Not for
the price of the whole world, with all its treasures, could he be
induced to appear as the founder of a new sect. A sorrowful distinction that, in any view; and one besides that calls for small
spiritual capital indeed in these United States.

I am well aware that many respectable Christians satisfy their
minds on the subject of sectism, by looking at it as the natural
fruit of evangelical liberty. In the main matter, the leading orthodox Protestant parties, they tell us—Episcopalian, Presbyterian,
Methodist, Lutheran, and Reformed—are all one; their differences have respect almost altogether to government and worship
only, that is, to the outward conformation of the church, in the
case of which the Lord has allowed large freedom; and so far as
they may have a doctrinal character, they may be said to regard
not so much the substance of the truth itself, as the theological
form simply under which it is apprehended. The separation of
these churches, in the meantime, is attended, we are told, with
this great advantage, that it serves to stimulate their zeal and activity, and to extend in this way the interest of religion. This last
point we shall not pretend here to dispute; but the advantage,
so far as it may exist, is to be ascribed, not to the divisions in
question as such, but only to God, who in his wisdom can bring
good out of all evil. In the balance of the Last Judgment, moreover, good works that proceed from ambition and emulation only
will be found to carry but little if any weight.

From those however who undertake to justify the sect system
as a whole, the apologists of religious fanaticism and faction, I
would fain require some biblical ground in favor of what is thus
upheld. Not a solitary passage of the Bible is on their side. Its
whole spirit is against them. The Lord is come to make of twain
one; to gather the dispersed children of God, throughout the

whole world, into one fold, under one Shepherd. His last command to his disciples was that they should love one another, and
serve one another, as he had loved and served them. His last
prayer, before his bitter passion, was that all his followers might
be made perfect in one, as he was in the Father and the Father in
him. Of the first Christians we read, in the Acts of the Apostles,
that they were of one heart and one mind, and continued stead-
fast in the apostles' doctrine and fellowship, and in the breaking
of bread and prayer. Paul exhorts the Corinthians in the name
of Jesus Christ that they should all speak the same thing and
that there should be no divisions among them, but that they
should be perfectly joined together in the same mind and in the
same judgment. They must not call themselves after Paul, or
Apollos, or Cephas, or Christ in the way of party or sect. For
Christ was not divided; and Paul had not been crucified for
them; and no one had been baptized into the name of Paul, but
all into the name of Christ. The entire view taken by this apostle
of the nature of the church, as the one Body of Christ, whose
members all partake of the same lifeblood and are set for mutual assistance; having one hope of their calling, one Lord, one
faith, one baptism, one God and Father of all; endeavoring to
keep the unity of the one body and one spirit in the bond of
peace; this view, I say, inflicts a death blow, with one stroke, on
the whole sectarian and denominational system. Peter describes
the church as a single spiritual temple, built up with living stones
on the same living foundation, Jesus Christ. John places one
great mark of Christianity in love to the brethren; and when in
his old age he was carried to the church, having no strength more
for any long address, he would still repeat that one exhortation,
as comprehending all besides: *Children, love one another.*

Perhaps however the sect system must still be regarded as at
all events the last necessary consequence and unavoidable fruit
of Protestantism. So many Protestants even, and of course all
papists, affirm. If such were the fact, the Reformation must stand
in direct contradiction to the holy Scriptures, and be adjudged
by its own umpire to condemnation, as a sinful work of man. But,
God be praised, the case is not thus bad. The reproach is of the
same order with that other, which as we have already seen would

shove us into the arms of rationalism and pantheism, as our only legitimate resting-place.

As in that case, so in this we repel the alliance as unnatural and false. The sect system, like rationalism, is a prostitution and caricature of true Protestantism, and nothing else. We have shown, in the first part of this tract, that the Reformation was no arbitrary novelty, but the fruit of all the better tendencies of the Catholic Church itself; that the Reformers aimed at no separation from the reigning church, but that this was wholly the work of the pope. Had they been permitted to preach the pure word of God with freedom, and to administer the sacraments according to Christ's appointment, they would have remained in their original communion. But in what orthodox Protestant party of our day is this forbidden? No man is in danger with us of being burned or deposed for preaching the gospel. Both in the Reformed Church and in the Lutheran, thank God, the word may be proclaimed in its purity; in both the conversion of souls may go forward without hindrance. In this view therefore our position is wholly different, so that modern sectaries have no good reason whatever for breaking communion with the church. True, there are defects and faults enough in each of these churches. But these may and should be reproved *within* the communion itself, that so if possible the whole body may be healed. When, moreover, the Reformers, for conscience' sake, and because they would obey God and his word rather than men and their ordinances, proceeded to form a communion of their own, nothing could be further from their intention in doing so than to throw open the door for the system of sects. Their object was not to upset the church, and break the regular course of its historical life; but only to restore to it once more the clear light and sure rule of God's word; not to emancipate the individual to uncontrolled freedom, but to bind him to the definite objective authority of God's truth and grace. Luther exhibited the doctrine of justification as precisely the true ground of Christian union, and fought with all the strength of his gigantic spirit against the fanatical and factious tendencies of his time. His last wish, as that of Melanchthon also, [was concerned] for the unity of the church. His most depressing fear was still: "After our death, there will rise many harsh and terrible sects. God help us!" Calvin utters himself against sectaries, with his own peculiar cutting severity,* and repulses the reproach that Protestantism itself was a sect, in the strongest terms.†

From all this it appears that in this practical respect also, as well as in its theoretic relations as before considered, the posture of the Protestant principle is different now from what it was at the time of the Reformation. The most dangerous foe with which we are called to contend, is again not the Church of Rome but the sect plague in our own midst; not the single pope of the city of seven hills, but the numberless popes—German, English, and American —who would fain enslave Protestants once more to human authority, not as embodied in the church indeed, but as holding in the form of mere private judgment and private will. What we need to oppose to these, is not our formal principle; for they all appeal themselves to the Bible, though without right; but the power of history, and the idea of the church, as the pillar and ground of the truth, the mother of all believers, with due subordination always to the written word. In this controversy we may be said rather to have the Roman Church, in a certain sense, on our side; though we may never employ against sects the same carnal weapons, and propose not for ourselves *such* unity as is offered to us from her hand. For this in the end is an outward sameness only, in which the divinely ordained prerogatives of

---

* *Instit.,* IV, c. 1.

† *Ibid.,* IV, c. 2, § 5. Jam vero quod reos schismatis et haereseos nos agunt (Romanenses), quia et dissimilem praedicemus doctrinam, et suis legibus non pareamus, et seorsum conventus ad preces, ad baptismum, ad coenae administrationem aliasque sacras actiones habeamus: *gravissima* quidem est *accusatio,* sed quae nequaquam longa aut laboriosa defensione opus habet. Haeretici et schismatici vocantur, qui dissidio facto ecclesiae communionem dirimunt. This communion however with the true church and her only head Christ, he goes on to say, the Protestants have maintained, and for this reason have been thrust out from the false church, as the apostles formerly, who had the true spirit of the Old Testament, were expelled from the Jewish synagogues. Eant nunc (§ 6) et clamitent haereticos nos esse, qui ab ipsorum ecclesia recesserimus, *quum nulla alienationis causa fuerit, nisi haec una, quod puram veritatis professionem nullo modo ferre possunt.* Taceo autem, quod anathematibus et diris nos expulerunt. Quod tamen ipsum satis superque nos absolvit, nisi apostolos quoque schismatis damnare velint, *quibuscum similem habemus causam.*

the individual subject are disregarded and trampled underfoot, and all opposition as it rises from time to time, is either covered with a hypocritical mask, or kept down by the strong hand of power. Hence accordingly when it comes to full strength, and can no longer be repressed, its violence proves vastly more destructive than it would be in connection with Protestantism; as we see strikingly illustrated in the case of the French Revolution. We ought never to forget, however, that Romanism has already drawn, and continues to draw still, its principal advantage from the pseudo-Protestant sect system, as well as from rationalism. Its recent show of new life and power finds here precisely its proper explanation. Continually its laugh of malicious triumph is going up, in view of our cancerous affection. If then we would contend successfully with Romanism, we must first labor to put away from ourselves the occasions that now lay us open so broadly to its attacks. Away with human denominations, down with religious sects! Let our watchword be: One spirit and one body! One Shepherd and one flock! All conventicles and chapels must perish, that from their ashes may rise the One Church of God, phoenixlike and resplendent with glory, as a bride adorned for her bridegroom.

*Rationalism and sectarism then are the most dangerous enemies of our church at the present time. They are both but different sides of one and the same principle—a one-sided false subjectivity, sundered from the authority of the objective. Rationalism is theoretic sectarism; sectarism is practical rationalism.*

# . 4 .

## Puseyism, the Reaction to These Diseases,
## but Not Their Remedy

WHO NOW WILL GUIDE the vessel of orthodox Protestantism safely between these rocks? In such peril, the helmsman looks anxiously around for help, come whence it may. Possibly the reefs draw still closer together, so that the ship proceeding in the same course must at last inevitably founder. Were it not best then that it should tack about, and seek again the old haven from which it started?

So think the Puseyites, so named from their leader, or the Tractarians, as they are styled from their principal organ, the "Tracts for the Times," or the Anglo-Catholics,[23] as they choose to be called themselves. Let us see whether they have found the true remedy for the complaints of the Protestant Church.

It is scarcely more than ten years since the tendency in question appeared in the ancient metropolis of English theology, in the midst of the venerable remains of church antiquity, and upon the same seats of instruction, where once along with schoolmen and papists the voice of Wickliffe sounded, and where the *Institutes* of Calvin were afterward for a long time honored as the highest dogmatic authority. Within this short period it has spread throughout the Old and New Worlds. Sympathies long prepared for its reception have been met by it in every direction; partic-

157

ularly in the old antiunion Lutheranism of Germany, which has
been transplanted also to this side of the Atlantic. It has brought
into clear consciousness, on all sides, spiritual tendencies and
wants which were not previously understood. Already thus it appears clothed with a world-historical importance. I have myself
hardly ever before had such an impression of the objective power
of the "idea," as during the course of my late travel through
Germany, Switzerland, Belgium, England, and North America;
encountering as I did everywhere, in the persons of distinguished
ministers and laymen, if not precisely Puseyism itself, at least as-
pirations and endeavors of a more or less kindred spirit. [Against
such a life question, such a question of the age, what sense is there
to the foolish cry of "Popery," "Romanism" by our intellectual
and anti-intellectual press?] Grapple with the subject in earnest.
Bring the fire engines. Extinguish the flame. If you do but idly
stare at it, or stand before it lamenting and railing with folded
hands, assuredly it will soon burst triumphantly through the
roof, and leave you at last houseless and bare. Nothing can well be
more shallow and miserable, and full of senseless pretension
withal, than the style in which the controversy with popery and
Puseyism is to a great extent conducted in our religious periodicals. It may be said to be for the most part ammunition expended
in vain, time and labor lost for writer and reader alike. If the
tendencies in question encounter nothing more solid than such
ephemeral opposition, their victory may be counted sure.

I look upon Puseyism as *an entirely legitimate and necessary
reaction against rationalistic and sectaristic pseudo-Protestantism,
as well as the religious subjectivism of the so-called Low Church
Party;* with which the significance of the church has been forgotten, or at least practically undervalued, in favor of personal
individual piety; the sacraments, in favor of faith; sanctification,
in favor of justification; and tradition in its right sense, in favor
of the holy Scriptures. I make indeed no question, but that
with many who belong to this neo-Catholic school a feeling of
poetical romance is more prevalent than true religious conviction; that others again, among the clergy especially, are swayed
more or less by hierarchic interest; and that still a third class,
largest of all perhaps, are carried along with the alluring move-

ment by the current of mere fashion. But with all these allow-
ances, when we take the movement in its whole compass as exhibited in its authors and leaders in England, we must admit that
it rests upon decidedly religious and true church ground, and
springs from grief on the one hand over the disjointed, discinc-
tured character of the age, and an endeavor after Christian catholicity and unity on the other. Hence we find it characterized by
deep moral earnestness, reverential solemnity, and a certain spiritual dignity of tone and manner even in controversy itself.

It has a proper feeling of respect for history, looks reverently
after the remains of the religious life of other days, cherishes a
filial homage toward the Christian past. It exalts the authority
of the general over all that is simply single, and makes the reason
of the church to be more than that of the individual, counter-
acting thus the rage for independence that rules the time. It
holds fast to the importance of the sacraments as objective institutions of the Lord, that hang not on the precarious state of the
subject, but include an actual living presence of Christ for the
purposes they are intended to secure, as real as that by which
he stood among his disciples in the days of his flesh. It restores the
week services, the church festivals, and frequent communions after
the example of the first ages; lays stress on religious discipline for
the whole man, outward as well as inward; seeks to revive the sense
of sacrificial consecration to God; has an open eye for church art,
and takes pleasure in beautifying sanctuaries and altars; on the
principle that what is best should belong to the Lord, and that
such decoration is only the natural expression of childlike love,
as it might be expected to show itself even toward a human friend,
being well suited at the same time to assist devotion in the way
of support and elevation through the senses. With all this it de-
signs not at all to fall back to Romanism, but only to revive once
more the fair usages, lost and forgotten, of the undivided, universal primitive church, as nearest to the age of the apostles and so
to the fountain of Christianity; and thus also to hold within the
Protestant communion such as feel themselves urged to forsake
it, through dissatisfaction with the usual nakedness and barren-
ness of its worship.

In all this, considered by itself, I find nothing that is absolutely wrong. Rather it is my firm conviction that we must ourselves appropriate fully some of the more general views lying at the ground of Puseyism, to be secure against its advances, and to prevent its errors from spreading continually more and more along with its truth. We too must take a wider range, and our faith in the one universal Christian Church must show itself to be, not merely a confession of the mouth, but power and truth, life and act. We too may not seek the perfection of our own communion, apart from the perfection of the entire Christian Church. We too must be like the good householder who gathers up even the fragments, appropriating to ourselves from the stores of early Christian history in particular, what has sprung from God and proved a blessing to thousands and millions. We too must bear in mind that the single can hold with advantage only in due subordination to the general, and that there can be no true freedom save in the form of subjection to the authority of God.

So far we go hand in hand with young Oxford, even at the hazard of being called reformed Catholic, or catholic Protestant. So soon however as it comes to the choice of the means, by which the object in view is to be reached, we are constrained to part with it as unsound and unsafe. Its "tracts for the times" are not just "tracts for eternity." Its grand defect, forming an impassable gulf between it and our position, is *its utter misapprehension of the divine significance of the Reformation, with its consequent development, that is, of the entire Protestant period of the church.* As to Romanism, so to Puseyism also, there is wanting the true idea of *development* altogether. It regards the church as a system handed down under a given and complete form, that must remain perpetually the same. It confounds with Christianity itself, which we may never and can never transcend, and which is always equally perfect, the measure of its *apprehension* on the part of mankind, or its *appropriation* into the consciousness of the church, which like the life of the spirit universally, from first to last, has the character of a genesis or process, and passes through different stages of growth. With all their historical feeling, the Puseyites show themselves absolutely unhistorical with regard to the Reformation. They wish to shut out of view the progress of the last three centuries entirely; to treat the whole as a negation, if possible; and by one vast leap to carry the church back to the point where it stood before the separation of the Oriental and Western communions, when however the tendencies were already at work which led with historical necessity afterward to the popish system in its worst form. Turn and twist as they may, with their external, mechanical conception of the church and episcopacy, the Reformation can be to them properly an *apostasy only* from the true church, and they must unchurch entirely all those Protestant bodies that have parted with the episcopal constitution.

Their doctrine of episcopal succession, with its denial of the universal priesthood of all believers, the episcopal and apostolical character of every inwardly and outwardly called minister of Christ, involving the papistical idea of a clerical mediatorship between God and man—this is the old leaven of the Pharisees, which has never been thoroughly purged out of the Anglican Church, and that may be said now to offend Protestant feeling in the writings of the Oxford school in particular, from beginning to end. If this succession were taken as one simply of doctrine and ministry, *successio Spiritus Dei, doctrinae evangelii* and *ministerii divini,* it would carry a perfectly rational meaning, necessarily included in the conception of the church, as the abiding and indissoluble communion of believers in Christ; and in this view it might be confidently claimed by the whole orthodox Protestant interest, with which both word and sacrament, ministry and ordination, are continued, and the founders of which derived their own ordination regularly from the Catholic Church. But instead of this, the idea is limited to the order of the bishops, unscripturally sundered from the laity and lower clergy, as though they were specifically different in their nature, and were alone competent to transmit ministerial power. All ends in a personal, outward, mechanical succession. The Spirit of God, whose very nature it is to be free, is thus bound to a particular ecclesiastical structure, for which no sure authority can be found in the New Testament; and the apostolical legitimacy of a church is made to turn upon a question of history, in the case of which besides by reason of the darkness that hangs over certain periods, during the earlier part especially of the Middle Ages *no satisfactory result* is possible. Altogether a most crazy foundation, on which to build so momentous an interest. According to this theory, Paul was illegitimate fully, because he had his ordination neither from the Lord nor from an apostle, but from a simple presbyter in Damascus. His judaizing adversaries, who had already in substance the Puseyite view, were right then in divesting him at once of all apostolical credit. How monstrous again is the position, necessarily involved in the same theory, that the dead Armenian and Greek denominations, because they have bishops, belong regularly to the Holy Church Catholic, while the German Reformed, Lutheran, and Presbyterian bodies, with all their religious life, are flatly denied any such character, and even their most godly and successful ministers are branded as ecclesiastical bastards, or mere hirelings privily smuggled into the sanctuary. God be praised for that word of the Lord, "By their *fruits* ye shall know them," and that *love* is made, in another place, the criterion of discipleship.

Let it be allowed that the Tractarians are right, and all unbishoped churches are left without hope, till their clergy submit to have their character made valid by the hands of his Grace of Canterbury, or some diocesan Onderdonk[24] on this side of the Atlantic; unless indeed they should prefer to have recourse at once to the holy father at Rome, or the patriarch no less holy of Constantinople. Preposterous imagination! Can the church be renovated by putting on a new coat? I have all respect for the episcopal system. It possesses in fact many undeniable advantages and by its antiquity besides must command the veneration of all who have any right historical feeling. But the thought must be utterly rejected, that it carries in its constitution as such the proper and only remedy for the existing wounds of Protestantism. Does it offer any sure guaranty for union? The contests with which the English Episcopal Church has been torn, especially for the last ten years (to say nothing of the posture of our American Episcopacy at this moment), sufficiently show the contrary. Or does it furnish more efficient means for the promotion of true inward piety? Let the state of the Greek Church, always true to the episcopal succession, be taken in reply; or the Roman Church as it stood toward the close of the Middle Ages, and as it stands still in entire countries; or the Church of England itself, as it appeared under the last Stuarts and during the eighteenth century. No, we need something higher and better than anointed lords and consecrated gentlemen. Such aristocratic hierarchs and proud bearers of the apostolic succession precisely, like the Pharisees and high priests of Judaism, have themselves again and again secularized the church, rocking it into the sleep of lifeless formalism or religious indifference. *Timeo Danaos et dona ferentes.* Little children, keep yourselves from idols, be afraid of false *gods* even under episcopal attire! It is the spirit that maketh alive; the letter killeth.

As the Puseyites, in this question of government and order, which they invest with undue religious importance both doctrinal and practical, stand upon essentially Roman Catholic ground,* it is quite natural that they should surrender in its behalf also what has been gained in point of doctrine by the Reformation. The points in which they still declare their system to be different from popery, are comparatively subordinate and unimportant. Of the true Protestant principle they have no conception, or else seek to cover it over, as Newman in tract No. 90 on the Thirty-nine Articles, with Jesuitical interpretation. The *sola fide* on which the Reformers lived and died, they have never had experience of probably in themselves, and accordingly they let it go for a small price. The sanctity on which they insist appears thus on

---

* The papists, at the time of the Reformation, appealed in just the same style to the *perpetua episcoporum successio.* Calvin (*Instit.,* IV, c. 2, § 2) answers well: Primum ab illis quaero, cur non Africam citent et Aegyptum et totam Asiam. Nempe quia in omnibus illis regionibus desiit sacra haec episcoporum successio, cujus beneficio se ecclesias retinuisse gloriantur. Eo igitur recidunt, se ideo veram habere ecclesiam, quia ex quo esse coepit, non fuerit episcopis destituta, perpetua enim serie alios aliis successisse. Sed quid si Graeciam illis regeram? Quaero igitur iterum ab ipsis, cur apud Graecos periisse ecclesiam dicant, apud quos numquam interrupta fuit illa episcoporum successio, unica, eorum opinione, ecclesiae custos et conservatrix. Graecos faciunt schismaticos. Quo jure? quia a sede apostolica desciscendo privilegium perdiderunt. *Quid? annon multo magis perdere merentur qui a Christo ipso deficiunt?* Sequitur ergo evanidum esse praetextum successionis, nisi Christi veritatem quam a patribus per manum acceperint, salvam et incorruptam posteri retineant ac in ea permaneant. Comp. § 3 where he refers to the relation of the prophets to the bearers of the Jewish hierarchy, who in the same way laid claim to temple, ceremonies, and succession, as all their own, and bitterly persecuted these divine messengers, the bearers of the Holy Spirit, and so the true succession.

closer examination to carry rather the character of an outward legalism, an unfree, anxious piety, reminding us of monkhood, with undue stress laid upon the observance of particular church forms, fasts, and self-imposed discipline. In the *Lives of the Saints*, as brought forward under the direction of Mr. Newman, the old Jewish work-righteousness presents itself again in its full arrogant parade.

With the scripture principle it fares no better in the hands of these gentlemen. It has been abandoned, almost from the start, for the Roman dogma of tradition. They wish to bind upon our necks all that has come down to us from the fathers, without any critical sifting by means of science or God's word, even the extravagant and utterly unsound, though often ingenious allegorical interpretations of the Alexandrian school. Quite a compliment to us certainly, not simply as Protestants in general, but as the friends also of a sound grammatico-historical scripture exegesis! So, very recently the organ of Puseyism in this country, the *New York Churchman*, has gone so far as to defend in many respects the last bull of his Holiness of Rome against Bible Societies. The case of Mr. Carey,[25] too, is well known, who was ordained by Bishop Onderdonk, though he had distinctly declared that he could subscribe to the decrees of the Council of Trent.*

Altogether Puseyism shows itself, in this way, to be no safe guide in the present great need of the church. Its mission must be regarded as preparatory only to that more full and perfect dispensation, by which in the end the captivity of Jacob is to be restored. It has done much, and may do still more, to bring the great problem of the age home to the consciousness of the Protestant world. But for the solution of the problem itself, it is found to be utterly incompetent. It were to be wished now indeed that the whole question might be wrested out of such unskillful hands, since the truth which lies at the ground of the movement is in danger of being brought into general discredit, at least for a time, by the false style in which it is here presented.

---

* According to the representation of Smith and Anthon, in their *Statement of Facts in Relation to the Recent Ordination in St. Stephen's Church*, New York, 1843.[26]

# · 5 ·

## The True Standpoint:
## Protestant Catholicism or Historical Progress

---

PUSEYISM then looks backward; we look forward. It tends toward Rome, and is there in spirit already, even though it should never outwardly complete the transition. We move toward Jerusalem, the new, the heavenly, the eternal. Its way is turned toward the fleshpots of Egypt, the old ignominious servitude of the house of bondage. Ours is onward to the land of promise that flows with milk and honey. Possibly when it shall have reached the last consequences of its principle, and stands confronted with the tyrannic scepter beyond the Red Sea, the better part of it at least may penitently smite upon its breast, and turn back again upon its own way; even at the hazard of being doomed to wander yet forty years in the Protestant wilderness. There are still to be found in this refreshing encampment, shady groves of palm and fruitful oases, heavenly manna and quails in abundance. Before us still moves the fiery, cloudy pillar of Israel; at our side, fresh water flows from the rock at the bidding of God; and full in view is the lifted brazen serpent, the symbol of the promised Messiah, to which every sin-wounded soul may look and be healed. Patience only, under the weight of our weary way! Canaan must be reached

165

at last. No premature catholicity and unity factitiously produced, that must prove after all only a transient mask! The Lord himself will help his people, and complete the work of the Reformation, in due time, by a new and more glorious creation; or conduct it rather to its own true and triumphant result. The less we presume to take the matter willfully into our own hands, the more we wait humbly on the leadings of the divine will, following step by step along the quiet, true historical way, the nearer and more sure is the hour, when he shall appear to gather the *disjecta membra ecclesiae* once more together, and form them into a more glorious body than the world has ever yet beheld.

Let us never forget that fidelity to her inherited patrimony, on the part of the church, is indispensable to her further prosperity. We must declare against Puseyism on the historical or catholic principle itself. For genuine catholicism holds in organic union with the pure history of the church, and through this with the apostles, through them with Christ, and through him finally with the eternal Father himself, whose thoughts of love and peace are unfolded in larger and more glorious measure always with the flow of time. We are faithless apostates, if we allow ourselves with overweening presumption to trample underfoot the work of the Reformers. Puseyism occupies extreme ground here, on two sides. Toward the church fathers it is *slavishly* true, taking upon itself the yoke of human bondage; toward the Reformers it is to the point of perfidy ungrateful. Luther and Melanchthon, Calvin and Beza, were indeed sinful and fallible men like ourselves. Of this they had the fullest consciousness themselves, and have declared us free accordingly from all bondage to men. We will not then fall into the error, which they have themselves most sharply reproved. We readily allow that in their zeal for the purification of the church, they threw away more than was necessary or wholesome. But we cannot consent to give up anything material of their *positive* conquest particularly in the form of doctrine. Assuredly they need not shun a comparison here with the deepest, most intellectual, and most pious, among the church fathers and schoolmen. They sought not their own, but the honor of God. No human doctrine, but God's word only, would they exalt to absolute supremacy. This they preached with unshaken boldness and the noblest disinterestedness; and so when their hard day's work was done died happily in the faith of Jesus Christ Crucified, as their righteousness and salvation. The Lord has spoken his *yea* and *amen* upon their work; and the church which sprang from it still stands fast in its strength, in spite of the numberless storms that have passed over it from without, in spite of the deadly foes to which it is still exposed within its own bosom.

But we must go still further. As the Puseyites in *contradiction to the Reformation* affect to be catholic (in the Roman sense; catholic in show, particularistic in fact), so as a matter of course they are unprepared altogether to understand or appreciate the subsequent development of the Protestant principle. In the history of the Protestant Church they can see *only* progressive *falling away;* in rationalism and sectarism, a work *purely of the devil.* This is a second point on which we differ from them; and where we come into collision also with the stiff confessionists, the hyper-orthodox Lutherans of the old stamp, the sons of Abraham Calovius[27] and Valentin Ernst Loescher.[28] These indeed acknowledge the divine character of the Reformation, at least in its Lutheran form, and in this respect we stand on common ground with them, against English and American Puseyism. But they will not allow the development of the church to extend beyond this point. Whatever progress may have had place before, all must be considered complete with the orthodoxy of the sixteenth century; circumscribed and made fast in the narrow bounds of the Formula of Concord. With blind misestimation of the rights and prerogatives of the Reformed Church, and of the special wants precisely of our time, they make Lutheranism to be the same thing with the ideal or absolute church itself, and fall thus into an error as bad as that of Rome, to whose view all that lies beyond its own borders is but damnable heresy and schism. This form of thinking bears, it is true, the name of Luther; but with his boundlessly free spirit it stands in no affinity whatever; just as little, we may say, as another section of the same *nominal* interest in this country, which has long since sacrificed the original spirit of the Lutheran Church, along with the German language itself, to the totally different genius of Methodism.

It is the presentiment and earnest hope of the greatest German

theologians that we stand at this time on the eve of a more comprehensive reformation than that which is past, which is to crown
and complete the work of our fathers, bind together again what
has been separated, and actualize the last absorbing wish of
Luther and Melanchthon, of which notice has already been taken.
Of course the Formula of Concord, worthy as it is in itself of all
respect, can never bring us to any such result as this. As little at
the same time however can we be helped toward it, by methodis-
tical "New Measures," the anxious bench and other such like
quack appliances and medicaments that work upon the nerves far
more than the soul. The old measures employed by Christ and the
apostles, which have stood the test of historical experiment from
the beginning, are vastly more to be relied upon. Eighteen centuries of use have not worn away their edge or force; rather it is
their invaluable quality that they become always more keen and
effective the more frequently they are applied. With such methods
moreover we reach results that are solid and radical, instead of
deceptive appearances only that soon pass away and leave the case
worse too often than it was before.

We condemn, without qualification, both rationalism and sectarism. Still our historical sense itself will not allow us to look
upon them as the work of Satan *only*. God, who brings good out
of evil, has been wisely active also in the immense system of destruction that has been going forward in the Christian world in
these forms since the beginning of the last century. "God writes
on a crooked line," says an old Portuguese proverb. Through the
heathenish larva of rationalist, pantheist, sectarian, and factious
irreligion, with which the age is marred, we discern the regenerated psyche; in the process of corruption, the still-living germ
that may be expected to burst its decaying shell, and leave the
earth behind, and grow upward into a tree beneath whose shadow
the world may rest. Like the development of the papacy during
the Middle Ages, the rationalism and sectarism of the modern
Protestant Church also has its conditional historical necessity, and
along with this a certain justification, an element of truth, that
needs to be incorporated into the process with which theology
and the church are to be still further developed. Let us illustrate
this, in the way of hint at least, by two or three general observa-

tions; though of a kind, it is true, to be fully intelligible only to
such as are thoroughly acquainted with church history. The details of the subject and its application to particulars may then be
carried out by the intelligent for themselves.

As Catholicism toward the close of the Middle Ages settled into
a character of hard, *stiff objectivity,* incompatible with the proper
freedom of the individual subject, now ripening into spiritual
manhood; so Protestantism has been carried aside, in later times,
into the opposite error of a *loose subjectivity,* which threatens to
subvert all regard for church authority. These extremes as such
are both equally false. Both however involve a principle that is
true and divine; the falsehood results from the one-sided way in
which this is held in each case. Necessity and freedom, dependence
and independence, generality and singularity, are the two poles,
around which human existence and all history revolve. The perfection of both is the union of both. The highest freedom stands
in the service of God. The divine law is at the same time the true
expression of particular will, the only form of free inward power.
Genuine obedience toward the church coincides with the highest
degree of personal piety. The life of the single member in the
body and for the body as a whole, constitutes also its own most
healthy and vigorous state. Separated from the body, it is given
over at once to a process of dissolution.

Rationalism and sectarism then are false and hateful, not simply
as they are subjective and appertain to the sphere of the individual, but as they are *one-sidedly* subjective, *in opposition* to the
general, and *with contempt* of the principle of authority, as embodied in the church. So far accordingly as the just claims of the
subjective reach, both may be said to have their vindication as
necessary and important in church history. In what this right, this
element of truth consists, is now to be shown.

Rationalism shows its bright and dark sides in this, that it fixes
its view one-sidedly on the human in Christ, in Christianity and
in the church, the earthly body only of their incarnate divinity,
and is so carried away toward what is natural and visible merely,
as to have no sense or perception of the supernatural, eternal, and
divine. Its principle is the abstract understanding, which walks the
treadmill of mere finite categories and contradictions, without

coming ever to the last ground and inmost unity of its subject. So far however as Christianity and the church fall within the finite, earthly sphere of man's existence, rationalism also must be considered in place, and not without its merits. It has served to overthrow many false prejudices and has made many contributions of permanent worth to history and criticism. But besides this, its influence has been salutary, in a certain sense, on the whole tone and spirit of the later evangelical German theology. Only ignorance or prejudice can deny that the older orthodoxy, including its first Protestant form also, made too little account of the conditions under which only the revelation of our religion in the way of history could take place. Hence, for instance, its resort to unsound and extravagant allegory, and its fairly magical conception of inspiration, overlooking entirely the human individuality of the sacred writers, which notwithstanding stares us in the face in every single book.

In this respect, the scientific rationalism of Germany, by bringing in a severe criticism and grammatico-historical exegesis, which form the natural ground and necessary condition of all theological knowledge of the Bible, has wrought clearly with purifying power in the church, the traces of which are not to be mistaken in the most orthodox works of the modern evangelical school. The old faith has sustained in this way no loss. It remains essentially the same. It has come forth from this critical fire, improved only in its form and argument, and cleared of all sorts of dross. It has lost nothing in living power, inwardness, and depth, while it has gained in freedom and solid scientific strength. We must not refer rationalism to sheer ungodliness as its source, but are bound to acknowledge in it also a scientific conscience which the old orthodoxy, though with the best intention, too often wounded in the most sensible manner. The latest speculative rationalism has this merit besides, that it has helped to destroy the common rationalism with which it was preceded; as Strauss, for instance, in his *Life of Jesus,* has exposed with great acuteness the unnaturalness of the so-called natural explanation of miracles, as conducted by Paulus[29] of Heidelberg; and the former style of attack also against the doctrine of the Trinity and the divine incarnation, has long since been shorn of its force by the Hegelian speculation. It must be admitted, however, that the most recent productions of this speculative rationalism fall back again rather to the old trivial and popular, scientifically surmounted standpoint, so that the system is involved thus in self-condemnation.

But readily as we allow that we are indebted to this transition phase of theology generally considered, for an understanding in part of history and the natural side of Christianity, we must still maintain that this understanding can become true and complete only where with the good side of the tendency in question, there is found united the determined faith of the old orthodoxy. For the body is the product of the soul, which it forms as an organ for its own use. It is the eternal Word, which has become flesh in the person of Jesus of Nazareth, in the sacred Scriptures, and in the church. He then who has the flesh only without the word, the body without the spirit, has in the end no more than a corpse.

As regards sectarism, in the second place, it must also be allowed that it almost always has its ground in certain practical defects of the church, as that of rationalism holds in the flaws and infirmities of the orthodox theology, and in this direction is not without right. Thus Quakerism appeared in opposition to the outward mechanism and dead formality that had taken possession of the Church of England in the beginning of the seventeenth century. Anabaptism finds its apology in the melancholy fact that many baptized persons in the church live like heathen, the consequence in a great measure of the want of proper Christian education. Modern Methodism in its various forms has its well-grounded complaints to present against a dead church orthodoxy, which is found too often along with unsound life, rejecting all life; along with protracted prayer meetings, all serious prayer; and along with wild fanatical awakenings, conversion in every form—making thus no distinction in its zeal. In almost every sect we may find some particular side of the Christian life clearly and strongly marked; where as in a mirror the church should see her own defects, the wrinkles or spots that mar her visage, so as to do penance for her unfaithfulness, by which so many of her best members have been led to forsake her communion. The divine significance of sects then, their value in the history of the church, consists in this, that they are a disciplinary scourge, a voice of awakening and admonition by which the church is urged to new life and a more conscientious discharge of her duties. The system has a favorable operation further, as it tends to spread religious interest and stimulate Christian zeal. In this country perhaps, if there were no sects, we should not have half as many congregations and houses of worship as we have now, and many sections in the West particularly would be destitute of the blessings of the gospel altogether.

But while this is thankfully admitted, two things still need to be kept in view. A sect, in the first place, loses its right to exist, in the same degree in which the body from which it is a secession, has corrected the faults that led to it. If it persists in its separation notwithstanding, it is either carried into full unbelief, or sinks into a slavish observance of particular lifeless forms, preparing in this way its own grave, as is strikingly illustrated by many cases in church history. Then again, a sect as such, can never, in its subjective isolation, provide successfully even for the particular interest to which it is pedantically devoted; since every single religious truth belongs to a great organically constituted whole, and can become complete accordingly only in connection with this as the source of all its life. Christianity is an indivisible unity; its truths are links only of an indissoluble chain returning into itself. Here exactly we may see the spiritual pride and narrow-mindedness of sectarism, that it fancies it can prosper and reach perfection, standing on its own frail feet, in abstract separation from the general life of the church. Break a branch from the vine, and it must soon wither. Separate a ray from the sun, and it is extinguished. Remove a child from the care of parents and guardians, and it will grow wild. Cut a hand from the body, and it will fall into decay. *If sects then would be true to themselves, they must as soon as they have fulfilled their commission unite themselves again with the general life of the church, that they may thus as organic members of the body acquire new vital energy; and the church, on her side, should make special efforts to gather once more under her motherly protection and care, the children that have forsaken her and are now estranged from her bosom. To this duty the Reformed Church is specially called, as the largest part of these modern separatistic movements have sprung from her communion.*

We must now quit for a moment the field of theology and the church, in the narrower sense, and cast a glance on the development of Protestantism, in its relation as a vast whole to the general course of the world's history; that we may discover how far there is included in it in this view also, the promise of a new, glorious future. We shall then be prepared to bring all together in a general image.

To the Lord and his kingdom belongs the whole world, with all that lives and moves in it. *All* is yours, says the apostle. Religion is not a single, separate sphere of human life, but the divine principle by which the entire man is to be pervaded, refined, and made complete. It takes hold of him in his undivided totality, in the center of his personal being; to carry light into his understanding, holiness into his will, and heaven into his heart; and to shed thus the sacred consecration of the new birth, and of the glorious liberty of the children of God, over his whole inward and outward life. No form of existence can withstand the renovating power of God's Spirit. There is no rational element that may not be sanctified; no sphere of natural life that may not be glorified. The creature, in the widest extent of the word, is earnestly waiting for the manifestation of the sons of God, and sighing after the same glorious deliverance. The whole creation aims toward redemption; and Christ is the second Adam, the new universal man, not simply in a religious but also in an absolute sense. The view entertained by Romish monasticism and Protestant pietism, by which Christianity is made to consist in an abstract opposition to the natural life, or in *flight from the world,* is quite contrary to the spirit and power of the gospel, as well as false to its design. Christianity is the redemption and renovation of the *world.* It must make *all things* new.

Such morbid views are powerfully counteracted in this country by the sound practical feeling which so generally prevails. A different mistake however, nearly as false, is widely established according to which science, art, and politics are placed in a relation, not of absolute hostility indeed, but of entire *indifference* to religion, that is, properly in no relation to it at all. The idea seems to be that a man's piety is deposited in one corner of his spirit; his politics, in another; and his learning in a third. All good and

necessary in their place, but having nothing whatever to do with
one another! According to this view, it might seem to be expected
further that religion should never come into any closer union with
the common secular departments of life. It must be counted pernicious if the church should be drawn into nearer contact with
the state, or art be made more extensively subservient to divine
worship, if Christian morality should seek to occupy all social relations, or Christian theology presume to incorporate with itself
the results of worldly science, philosophy in particular.

It were a vast object gained for the interests of American Protestantism, if this radically false and miserably narrow prejudice,
opposed as it is to all true and proper progress on the part of the
church, could be effectually subverted. The theme is indeed one
of the very highest consequence. It enters into the inmost life
of the time, and includes in itself the most momentous questions
with which the time is concerned. The following historical hints,
which we are not permitted here further to pursue, may serve
possibly, in some measure at least, to direct attention to the subject.

We set out then with the assumption that Christianity stands
in an absolutely negative, hostile relation only to sin and death,
while all that is properly human, the world with its several spheres
—government, science, art, and social life—is regarded by it as of
divine institution and force; which religion is required accordingly neither to annihilate nor yet to overlook as foreign to its nature, but on the contrary to occupy and fill with its own heavenly
spirit. This itself serves to show the universal character of the
gospel, and the catholicity of the church. It follows, of course,
that no one of these spheres of natural life can reach its highest
stage, its true perfection, until it has come to be thoroughly transfused with the leaven of Christianity. In the absolute view of the
case, therefore, there can be no perfect scholar or philosopher; no
perfect ideal artist, whether architect, or sculptor, or painter, or
musician, or poet; no perfect statesman; and finally no truly moral
man, who is not at the same time animated throughout with the
living power of faith. It follows again with equal necessity from
the same view, that the church cannot be said to have completed
its career, till the whole world shall appear transfigured with its

divine spirit, and states, and sciences, and arts, with all their glory, shall fall down before the altar of the Most High in full, free worship.

Let us now apply this standard to history for the purpose of determining according to it the relation between Catholicism and Protestantism, in the direction here noticed, and also the proper wants of our own time so far as the same view is concerned.

Catholicism, particularly in its medieval Romano-Germanic period, carried with it, if we put out of view its monastic institutions, a very distinct sense of the *nihil humani a me alienum puto* as just described. It is this precisely which renders the Middle Ages so grand and venerable, that religion in this period appears the all-moving, all-ruling force—the center around which all moral struggles and triumphs, all thought, poetry, and action are found to revolve. All sciences, and philosophy itself—the science of the sciences—were handmaids to theology, which based itself on the principle of Augustine: *Fides praecedit intellectum.* Before the pope, as the head and representative of Christendom, all states bowed themselves with reverent homage; and even the German emperor himself could not feel secure in his place, save as formally acknowledged by the chief bishop of the church. Princes and people arose at his bidding, forsook country and friends, submitted to the most severe privations, to kneel at the Savior's tomb and water it with thankful tears. According to the reigning idea, the state stood related to the church like the moon to the sun, from which it borrows all its light. All forms of life, all national manners, were suffused with magic interest from the unseen world. The holy sacraments ran like threads of gold through the whole texture of life, in all its relations, from infancy to old age. The different arts vied with each other in the service of the church. The most magnificent and beautiful buildings of the period are the cathedrals—those giant stone flowers with their countless turrets, storming the heavens and bearing the soul on high, and their mysterious devotional gloom, visited never by the light of the natural day, but only by mystic irradiations poured through stained glass; domes, the authors of which stood so completely in the general life of the church, and were so occupied only with the honor of God in their work, that with a divine carelessness they

have left even their own names to perish in oblivion. The maxim
was: Let the best house belong to the Lord. The richest paintings
were madonnas and images of the saints, as produced by a Fra
Beato Angelico da Fiesole,[30] a Fra Bartolomeo,[31] a Leonardo da
Vinci, a Perugino,[32] a Raphael, and a Michelangelo. It was felt
that the fairest among the sons of men, and the connections in
which he stood, must furnish the most worthy material for the
pencil. The most lofty and impressive music, according to Old
Testament example, resounded in the public worship of God.
Poetry sang her deepest and tenderest strains to the Lord and
his bride; and the greatest poet of the Middle Ages, Dante, has
left behind him in his *Divine Comedy* an image simply of the religious spirit and theological wisdom of the age, as occupied with
eternity itself and all its dread realities. Truly a great time, and
for one who is prepared to understand it, fraught with the richest
spiritual interest. He that has no heart for the excellencies of
this period, the beauty that belongs to the Middle Ages, must be
wanting in genuine culture, or at least in all right historical feeling.

The true church historian leaves to every age its own peculiar
advantages, without concern. He presumes not with narrow prejudice to reduce all to one measure, but recognizes with joyful
satisfaction, under the most different forms wherever found, the
footsteps of the Lord, the presence of his Spirit, as secured to the
church by his own promise through all ages. He does not *construct*
history, after the measure of some poor conceptions of his own;
he does not *correct* it by the standard of the time in which he
himself lives; but he takes it up and *reproduces* it, as God has
allowed it to occur in the progressive explication of his plan of
redemption, which apparent obstructions even, yea the rage of
diabolic passion itself, must only help forward in the end. However firmly settled he may be for himself in a particular standpoint, he thinks not of circumscribing the boundless fullness of
the divine life by the narrow horizon of his own view. With all
his respect for the Reformation as a true work of God, he is not
rendered insensible by it to what was excellent and beautiful in
earlier times, in which also men of immortal name lived and
worked and suffered, and when also God made his presence glori-

ously felt, and kept watch over the church continually with the eye of his love.

That must be regarded certainly as a most unwise policy, by which Protestants for a long time allowed themselves to renounce all interest in this period, and resign its treasures wholly to the Church of Rome, as though nothing but darkness and barbarism belonged to its history. The error indeed is still widely prevalent in this country—for the most part, however, a sin of profound ignorance—so that the stereotype title for that period is simply *the Dark Ages!* O thou light of the nineteenth century! How hast thou tarried with thy rising, hiding thyself for a thousand years behind the clouds, in cowardly fear of those dying men, the popes! Come now, ye poor unfortunate children of darkness—ye Leos and Gregorys, ye Emperors of the house of Saxony and the Hohenstaufen, Anselm, and Thomas Aquinas, Bonaventura, and Bernard of Clairvaux, Dante Alighieri and Petrarch, Erwin of Steinbach[33] and Bramante,[34] Leonardo da Vinci and Raphael, Francis of Assisi and Thomas à Kempis—come forth from your graves and be illuminated by the light that *now* reigns; learn how to govern church and state from our synods, consistories, and advocates; study philosophy and theology at Andover and New Haven; practice poetry, church building, and painting, amid the encouragement that is given to the arts in practical, money-loving America; and take lessons of piety from the "camp meetings" of the Albright Brethren and sects of the same spirit. But they have no desire to come back, the mighty dead! With a compassionate smile, they point our dwarfish race to their own imperishable giant works and exclaim, "Be humble, and learn that nothing becomes you so well."

In Germany this foolish prejudice, God be praised, has been happily surmounted, since through Herder and Wieland, and still more by the romantic school, particularly Tieck, Novalis, and the two Schlegels,[35] the poetic wealth of the Middle Ages has been brought to view; their significance in the general history of the world, by Moeser, Johann von Mueller, and Leo[36]; their universal human interest, by Goethe in his *Faust* and *Goetz von Berlichingen;* and finally their ecclesiastical magnificence and theological depth, scholastic as well as mystical, by the later works on church history and the development of doctrines,

and in particular also by various monographs on Innocent III,
Hugo of St. Victor, Anselm of Canterbury, Bernard of Clairvaux,
Henry Suso, Tauler, Savonarola, John Wessel, and others. It
should be borne in mind that the Middle Ages after all are the
cradle of the Reformation. They exhibit to us, not simply the
Roman, but the Romano-Germanic Catholicism, in whose arms
the Reformation is borne like the infant Christ by the madonnas
of Raphael. True, the madonna appears in the foreground, after
the Romish style. But still the highest beauty of the virgin mother,
surrounding her with the loveliness of heaven itself, flows mainly
from the adoring, blissful gaze with which she is absorbed in the
divine child, that smiles and plays upon her bosom, and yet bears
the world upon his hand. So too the Middle Ages have their richest
charm, in the longing and earnest expectation with which they
look forward to the Reformation as the ripe fruit of the previous
struggles of the church, the strong and joyous child of her deep
birth pangs endured for long centuries before.

Even now the Roman Catholic Church, which since the sixteenth century lives almost entirely on her past greatness, retains
much of the character under consideration, though no longer the
mistress of the world. She embraces all spheres of human life, attends it through all its stations from the cradle to the grave, per-
vades all conditions with her spirit, anoints all occupations with
her consecrating oil, and in this way exercises a much greater
power than Protestantism over the consciences and spirits of those
who stand in her communion. In the midst of the visible world,
remembrancers of the world unseen meet us on all sides, in
crosses, churches, images of saints, relics, and expressive symbols
of every kind. True we encounter in the same quarter also all
sorts of superstition, error, and abuse. These it is an easy thing
to assault with rude hand, and anathematize incontinently as the
work of the devil. Instead of this however it might be well if
more pains were taken to fathom and bring home to ourselves (as
could be done with great profit and no great difficulty, where
proper knowledge and feeling were combined in the inquiry) the
original truth, and the deep religious want, that lie at the ground
of almost every abuse and error, and impart to it its tough life.
"Prove all things, and hold fast that which is good."

Notwithstanding all now said however, one radical fault characterizes the relation of the Roman Church to the world. She does not sufficiently respect the world in its own divine rights, and seeks to subject it to herself in a violent, unnatural, premature way, without regard to the measure of her own development. Instead of waiting humbly, and following the course of tribulation prescribed by Christ, she would anticipate in a fleshly way the ideal state, when "the kingdom and dominion, and the greatness of the kingdom under the whole heaven, shall be given to the people of the saints of the Most High; whose kingdom is an everlasting kingdom" (Dan. 7:27), and when it shall be said that "salvation and strength, and the kingdom of our God, and the power of his Christ is come" (Rev. 12:10). Thus the heathen mythologies also were a fleshly prolepsis of the mystery of the incarnation.* The papacy in the Middle Ages conducted itself tyrannically toward the state and trampled on the rights of the nations; it did not permit science and inquiry to take their own course in a free way; it surrounded the arts with arbitrary bounds; in a word, it affected to swallow up the world at once in a wholesale way. The world, however, thus overwhelmed but not assimilated to the true life of the church, has reasserted its rights in the bosom of the church itself, and taken revenge upon it by impressing this with its own character, especially at the papal court. Romanism forms accordingly a secular state, at the expense of the free, quietly advancing, inward character of Christianity. Its worship has an outwardly pompous complexion; filling the senses; half heathenish. Even in doctrine, this remarkable dialectic process may be seen; particularly in the dogma of transubstantiation;

---

* A similar thought is uttered by J. P. Lange (*Vermischte Schriften,* Vol. IV, p. 84), when he says in his striking way: "The characteristic fault of the papacy is the show it makes of a perfect Christianity. In popery the Christian world renovation is exhibited in a premature, hypocritical, violent way—exhibited *a tout prix.* All that is human is sacrificed, all truth, all reality, development itself, to secure this dazzling show of Christian perfection. Popery is thus the impatience of shallow, unsound Christian feeling that cannot wait quietly for the end of the world, and so will have it before its time; through impatience settled, and by its settled character again impatient. All is *forced;* that which is a process must appear throughout an issue *(das Werden ein Gewordenes),* though the truth itself even should be lost, yea openly resisted, to secure the point.

according to which, on the one hand, the divine is revealed only through the annihilation of the natural substances, bread and wine, here representing the world, and this in virtue of the consecration of the priest, of course the act of a mere creature; while however, on the other hand, these transmuted elements, retaining still in fact their natural character, are made the object of divine worship, by which means a paganizing creature deification comes to prevail. Thus we find explained the seemingly inexplicable contradiction of the system, its contempt for the world in one direction and its undue regard for it in another. Monkish austerity and Pelagian secularity dwell harmoniously together in the same cell.

The powers of the world, under the legal discipline of the Middle Ages, became gradually mature. The church however, refusing to distinguish between different periods of life, and unwilling to put away the rod at the proper time, paid no respect to the change. The world then avenged itself on a large scale, by breaking away from the church entirely, and entering upon a new course of development for itself. This took place with the Reformation. It is accordingly in this respect also a process of emancipation, but as such here too not yet complete, requiring still a closing act to unite once more what has been disjoined.

The world since the sixteenth century has reached a measure of cultivation, such as it never possessed before. The Protestant states are incomparably superior to those which have been or are now under the staff of the Roman bishop; showing altogether more order, obedience, and contentment; whereas the pope has often enough preached insurrection against the temporal powers, released subjects from their oath of allegiance, and favored and sanctioned state conspiracy and the murder of kings. In place however of the former slavish dependence on the church, the opposite extreme has come to prevail. The Protestant states have either separated themselves entirely from the church (at least this is the case with our own), or in contradiction to the principles of the Reformation have subjected it more or less to their dominion, as in Germany, England, and Switzerland, so that out of church states have arisen state churches. For in these countries the governments have taken the supreme administration of the church into their own hands, and thus in practice at least make Caesar to be pope, which is no whit better than making the pope to be Caesar. It is true indeed that in a number of states the freedom of the Romish Church too is restrained by the secular authority, as in Austria, and still more recently in Russia, Spain, and Portugal. With inflexible consistency, however, she steadily protests against every such invasion, and always contrives in the end to make good again her pretensions; as is strikingly shown by the noted affair of Cologne, and recent events in Spain, as well as by the controversy on the subject of church instruction in France.

Protestant science, philosophy in particular, is so far from being the mere handmaid of theology and the church, that it appears just as often at least arrayed against them. Above all in Germany, philosophy is regarded commonly as the all-comprehending, absolute science of reason itself, of which theology is only a single branch. We cannot hesitate a moment to bestow the title Christian on the scholastic philosophers of the Middle Ages, an Anselm, a Peter Lombard, or a Thomas Aquinas; but there is no room for this, in the strict sense, in the case of Locke, Hume, Wolff, Kant, Fichte, and others, if for no other reason, for this alone that they show themselves destitute of humility and penitence, which are the ground of all piety. However, considered in the way of pure science only, the modern systems, internally united like the links of a chain from Leibnitz (a view to be sure but dimly apparent in this country, where the empiricism of Locke still sways its despotic scepter over the most republican spirits), exhibit a vastness, depth, and comprehensive variety that find no parallel in the Church of Rome, whose only approved philosophy, indeed may be said to be the scholastic Aristotelian. The advantage of all this to the Protestant theology is at least so much, that it has become more scientific.

A like aspect of things is presented to us in the sphere of the arts and polite literature. These too, since the Reformation, have emancipated themselves more or less from the church. If we except our sacred hymns and chorales, in the case of which certainly a wonderful productivity has appeared in the German Church, the Lutheran especially during the sixteenth and seventeenth centuries, we possess almost no works of church art that are fairly entitled to the name. All artistic ornament has been banished from the churches on principle; and our modern structures often bear more resemblance to a theater or a Grecian temple than to the true idea of a Christian house of worship.

Thorwaldsen[37] has indeed formed statues of Christ and the apostles; but they are by no means equal to his mythological representations. The painters since the Reformation (until very recently the Düsseldorf school—Overbeck,[38] Cornelius,[39] Kaulbach[40] in his "Destruction of Jerusalem"—and other masters, partly Catholic and partly Protestant, began to bring in a change again) have had recourse to the kingdom of nature and to profane history for their subjects, rather than to the Bible and the church. So with the Dutch painters in particular. The greatest modern composers, even such as are Catholic, as Mozart, Beethoven, and the Italian school, are not certainly to be counted church artists in the strict sense. The prayers and priest choirs of the *Magic Flute* and the Nemesis in *Don Juan,* as well as the *Requiem,* show only that the modern world is impregnated with Christian ideas and feelings, without surrendering still its natural character; and of Beethoven's incomparable symphonies it has been strikingly observed by one fully at home in the subject, that they are so many monologues of the absolute *me* of the present age, that with desperate struggle to stand upon itself, sinks into immeasurable grief and braves it again with saucy humor, bringing as it were all its resources together to sustain itself in the arduous task. Our poets of the first rank (among whom we cannot reckon the pious but tedious singers Milton and Klopstock), take them altogether, are forms that spring from nature only. Shakespeare belongs rather properly to the Middle Period, whose traditions have supplied him with almost all his poetic material. He is in a certain sense the completion of Dante, in whom is mirrored the religious glory of that time. Goethe has his bright and dark sides both in this, that he is all *nature,* in the largest and most comprehensive sense of the word. Where he introduces Christianity, it is exhibited (except perhaps in *Faust,* which however moves rather in the medieval elements) not at all as the universal life power by which the whole world is to be pervaded and renewed, but as being itself

simply a remarkable object in nature, *one* only among the countless phenomena in which the universal genius is required to feel
the same interest. Characteristic in this view is the episode style,
in which the confessions of a virtuous soul are presented in the
midst of gay actresses and amiable coquettes. Schiller's ideal is
abstract, moral nature; the gigantically struggling, stoic will.
The religious element with him, where it appears in objective
dramatic form, is Catholic, as in the *Maid of Orleans,* in *Maria
Stuart,* and in *Wallenstein;* and where it proceeds from his own
breast, a mere homesickness, an unsatisfied longing, as it flows
sorrowfully upon us, for instance, in the poem *"Ach aus dieses
Thales Gruenden."* Byron shows himself a stranger in full to the
peace-whispering accents of the gospel, and to all true humility.
His home is the howling storm of all wild passions. He is the
demoniacally inspired poet of despair.

Still who may refuse his admiration to the vast poetical powers
and resources, the natural greatness simply of these extraordinary
men; who persuade himself that God has introduced such colossal figures into our modern world without purpose, and allowed
them to exert so measureless an influence on the culture of millions for no end whatever? No, such a mass of thought and beauty
cannot possibly be lost for the kingdom of God. Rather it chal-
lenges the church to the high and solemn task of subduing this
gigantic life to the power of her own spirit, that so she may rise
above it, and attain thus to a higher position than any to which
she has yet come.

As regards, finally, the order of common social life, we may
say that Christianity no longer wears a distinguishing priestly
dress, but the ordinary citizen's coat. The almost universal ban-
ishment of the gown from the pulpit itself, in this country, is
characteristic in this view; a novelty at the same time which is
by no means to be approved, as savoring of an unhistorical spiritualism and a want of proper respect for what is sacred. The
abstract, extramundane character of religion has been laid aside,
and the claims of the present life are more fully appreciated.
Marriage is no longer depressed [as a lower grade of sanctity in
comparison to celibacy], but the minister is expected to let the
light of his example shine before his congregation, as a husband

and a father. Monkery is abolished, and men are directed to exercise their virtue in the natural employments of life, and while
standing and working in the world to keep themselves unspotted
from it. True, at the same time, purely material interests, traffic and trade, industry and steam, and along with all this utilitarianism and selfism, have acquired an importance to which they
are not entitled. For the spirit *ought* to reign over matter. But
still, in the hand of God, even steamships and railroads must
serve to extend more rapidly his kingdom.

This whole posture of the world toward the church carries
both a discouraging and a cheering aspect, as has already been
intimated in the notice of particulars. It is an unsound condition;
since all divinely constituted forms and spheres of life should
stand, and must in the end stand, in perfect harmony with one
another. It serves to show the weakness of the church, that she
has allowed these natural interests thus to overtop her in her
growth, instead of mastering them, and so directing them continually to the glorification of their Creator. It is crying ingrati-
tude besides on the part of the world, that luxuriating now in her
own prosperity, she affects to be independent of Christianity, yea,
even presumes to oppose it broadly; while yet she is indebted to
it for the best she has, and without an inward reconciliation to
the church, a full return to the element of religion, can never fulfill her own highest destiny. For the end or scope of all history is
this, that the world may resolve itself into the kingdom of God,
reason into revelation, morality into religion, and earth into
heaven. All sciences must be raised and refined into theosophy, all
government into theocracy, all art into divine worship, and the
whole of life into a joyful proclamation of the glory of God.

Since however this ultimate identification of the world with
Christianity may be apprehended also as an absolute molding of
the church into all the forms of the world, the full identification
of Christianity with nature, we must recognize again on the other
side an encouraging advance toward this end, in the present relation of the two systems. The Christian principle by means of
it has become more naturalized, more at home in the world. It
stands no longer in mere abstract opposition to the natural life;
has the world no longer under itself as a foreign element; but is

forming it into itself, much as this may be denied by the world in its present stage. The modern culture is not that of heathenism, but is carried throughout on the shoulders of Christianity, draws from this constantly its most substantial life, and must on this very account, however unwillingly, come into subjection to it in the end. In this respect also then, Protestantism is only an apparent regression; in truth it has carried the church materially forward. Roman Catholicism here has remained behind the time; and has either refused altogether, with willful bigotry, to admit the advance of modern cultivation; or has yielded to the force of it to a certain extent, only for the most part where it has stood in near contact with Protestantism, and always in consequence at least of its influence either direct or indirect. The more recent Catholic theology, for instance, springs from Germany, and is conditioned in its best productions by Protestant elements. Let anyone think only of Hug, Moehler, von Drey, Gehring, Hirscher, Staudenmaier, Papst, and Guenther.[41] The principal seats of Romanism—Italy, Spain, and Portugal—have done little or nothing in this sphere within the last centuries, and as regards the education of the people, are incredibly far back.

Thus in this case also our contemplations point us, not backward, but forward to a rich future for Protestantism, that will leave all the glory of the Catholic Church far in the rear. The better tendency of the time is indeed toward *objectivity;* not toward that of the Middle Ages however, that could be upheld only by violently crushing, or willfully restraining, the rights of the individual subject; but it seeks the objective rather in a higher form, *in which it shall be enriched and spiritualized by all that has been gained on the part of the subjective, the good fruits of the development of Protestantism through a period of three hundred years.* The day must come when all the forms of life which God has constituted in the world shall feel that they need a union with religion and the church to realize in full their own idea, and when they shall voluntarily return to the Lord, and lay their richest products upon his altar. That memorable word of Bacon, *Philosophia obiter libata abducit a Deo, penitus hausta reducit ad eundem,* may be applied with just as much force to art, politics, and social order, and must be fulfilled sooner or later in all.

That our hope of a new life for Protestantism to be secured through its full reconciliation with the objective idea of the church is no empty dream, many appearances of the present time, in part still incomplete indeed and solitary, serve to show. These now demand our attention, which will be directed again first to Germany, and then to America.

Germany is still far from having completed her part in the world's history. Such as are acquainted with the present state of the country, as regards science, morals, and religion, and viewed in comparison with what it was during the last century and the beginning of this, will understand the force of this remark. What a melancholy time was that, when English deism, French frivolity, and superficial German popular philosophy, were joined in common conspiracy against the church. Pietism indeed had still its representatives, for the most part however spiritual cripples, who placed the substance of Christianity in a few poor forms, and turned the fresh air of life into an uncomfortable, gloomy chamber of death. The Moravian Brethren, it is true, were not without influence; but it was exerted, apart from theology, in the stillness only of retired practical life. True again, supranaturalism, technically so called, the last scientific stand on the part of orthodoxy, mustered, in men like Reinhard[42] and Storr,[43] learned and venerable theologians in opposition to the rationalists; but its position was one-sided, in the way particularly of a too abstract conception of the formal principle of Protestantism, and it treated with the enemy so far, that in the end it fairly fell over to his side, as we see in the case of Schott,[44] Ammon,[45] and Bretschneider.[46] Its whole standpoint was outward and empirical; of the Holy Spirit in the church it had no sense whatever, and could not possibly therefore keep its ground. So dry and waste had the German Church then become that minds of the deeper, more earnest order, such as Stolberg,[47] Novalis, and Friedrich Schlegel,[48] were fain to take refuge in the bosom of Catholicism. And the revolutionary epoch was so shorn of all religious life and consciousness that Schleiermacher, in his masterly *Discourses on Religion,* of the year 1779, found it necessary to start from the beginning; taking his stand as it were in the court of the Gentiles, to teach his Wolffian, Kantian, and philanthropistic contemporaries the nature of religion first in general, that he might gain footing again for an intelligible representation of the Christian system.

And how does it now stand with German theology? [I am well aware indeed of the fearful episode that has broken in from the left side of the Hegelian philosophy upon the quiet course of its development, already ripening toward the best results—an episode like the storm of the July Revolution, which may be said to have brought up the rear of the political convulsions, through which France was carried with the close of the last century.[49]] Taking however a broad, general view, and looking especially to the most recent movements, we may say with full confidence that the theology which now has the floor of the age is not rationalism, but orthodoxy resuscitated with a higher life from its ruins. With the decision, power, and fervor of the old church faith, it unites that scientific freedom, disentanglement from prejudice, and full roundness of method, which have become possible only through the modern development of rationalism and philosophy.

Look now where we may, either in the widely extended school of Schleiermacher, with its numerous derivations, the most independent of which are presented to us in Neander,[50] Nitzsch[51] and J. Mueller[52]; or among those who are more or less ruled by the conservative elements of the *Hegelian* philosophy, in the writings especially of a Goeschel,[53] Rothe,[54] Dorner,[55] Martensen,[56] Hoffmann,[57] Hasse[58]; either to the productions of the orthodox *Unionist* tendency of a Hengstenberg[59] and his spiritual colleagues, or the *New Lutheran* theology of a Harless[60] and others; everywhere, it is true, we find much mixed disputation and hard conflict, the result however in part of mere misapprehension; but still everywhere also the spring-breath of a newly wakened faith, and the bursting germs of a new, bright, and fruitful era in theology. This must be rich and full, in proportion as the boundless range of history has been brought more fully and clearly into view, by the untiring, most learned and profound researches, *monumenta aere perenniora* of German scholarship and German diligence combined. What is most animating however is the genial union of free scientific interest and true church feeling that is showing itself in some of the theologians who have been named, and in many more especially who are now coming forward. This

church feeling shows itself moreover in the formation continually
more and more of ministerial associations, for conference on reigning defects and mutual encouragement in efforts after improvement; and particularly also in the concern now so general, which
is felt to have the church service renewed and enriched, by
thrusting aside all watery, rationalistic pretended improvements,
and falling back in a proper way to the incomparable treasures
of the old church songs and liturgies. Here again however the
new which is at hand will not be a mere repetition, but an enlargement and rectification of the old; inasmuch as by means of
the vast researches of science, in which rationalism itself has fulfilled an important part, the wealth of all centuries, as already
intimated, is now rendered accessible to such an extent as never
before. In short, the German Church and theology, in spite of all
difficulties and dangers, may be said to have a fair wind, and it
were disgraceful cowardice just now to draw in the sails, and
stand despairingly inactive with hands folded upon the bosom.
It is the period emphatically for hope and action.

And from what quarter has this favorable change proceeded?
Not wholly from theology and the church themselves, but in large
part, and indeed mainly, from the side of the secular life, involving thus to some extent already a verification of the idea that
all natural relations are to be pervaded in a new way by the
spirit of religion. This precisely is striking and peculiar in Germany, that the same foe, the same science in particular, which
inflicted such deep wounds upon its orthodoxy, has again turned
round of its own accord, and furnished the means for their cure.
For this very reason, however, the cure must prove vastly more
thorough than such soundness as may be maintained in other
lands, where all the attacks of philosophy and secular culture
against Christianity are repelled only with the rusty armor of the
old apologetic methods or simple proofless appeals to pious feeling. It is justly remarked by Tholuck,[61] in his learned and spirited
work against the *Leben Jesu* of Strauss, that the shallow race of
rationalistic illuminatists, at whose head Nicolai[62] of dull and tedious memory once stood, received its death blow first among the
*laity,* by the powerful wingstroke of the romantic writers, Tieck,[63]
Schlegel, and Novalis[64]; after which it was consumed to the bone

by the lixivium of ingenious satire, and so remanded again to its original nothing. The romantic school indeed fixed its view not so much upon the holiness of religion as its beauty, making it an object of esthetic enjoyment, which the ironic *me* saw *under* itself; but it helped mightily nevertheless to put an end to the reign of the mere bald understanding. The abstract separation of Christianity and art has since that time disappeared more and more from the consciousness of the cultivated in Germany. Art itself, in many of its most important representatives, has again become religious—in particular, painting and music and poetry. True, the poetry of despair and of sentimental world grief is still to be met with on all sides; but it has of late pronounced its own doom by plunging into politics and all sorts of projects for the world's amelioration, which contradict entirely the very idea of art.

A second powerful agent in the production of the change which has been mentioned is presented to us in the modern philosophy since the rise of Schelling. He freed German science, and with it theology also, from the bonds of Kant's standpoint of reflection and Fichte's subjective idealism, and led forth the spirit again into the objective world both of nature and history. Speak as men may against German transcendentalism, as the word passes here in a wholesale way, this at least no one acquainted with the subject can deny; that at the very time when the most celebrated theologians cast away the cardinal evangelical doctrine of the incarnation and atonement, as antiquated superstition, Schelling and Hegel stood forth in their defense, and claimed for them the character of the highest reason; and that while the reigning view saw in history only an aggregate of arbitrary opinions, a chaos of selfish passions, they taught the world to recognize in it the ever-opening sense of eternal thoughts, an always advancing rational development of the idea of humanity and its relations to God. Such a view must gradually overthrow the abrupt revolutionary and negative spirit which characterized the last century, restoring respect for the church and its history, and making room for the genuine power of the positive.* It is true indeed that one sec-

---

* Just after I had written this, the article of Professor Stowe, in the *Bib. Repos.*, Jan. 1845, entitled "Teutonic Metaphysics or Modern Transcendentalism," came to my sight; and as it has been already welcomed in several papers

tion of the Hegelian school (the so-called *left side*) has produced the latest and most dangerous form of rationalism, in which the doctrine of myths and pantheistic hero worship are made to play so large a part. But this tendency is diametrically opposed to the historical, objective element that clearly rules the spirit if not always the letter of the great philosopher's writings, and cannot be regarded therefore at all events as a complete application of his system to theology. And then again it must be considered that the movement in question is rendered so dangerous just because it has received into itself, pantheistically caricatured to be sure, so many truths of Christianity for which the old rationalism had no organ whatever, and because it is conducted also with so much more spirit and depth; which itself again is to be referred to a general advance, that may be easily remarked also in the form

------

as highly important and seasonable, I do not feel at liberty to pass it over in silence. I am truly sorry to find myself disappointed in Dr. Stowe.[65] In view only of his relations to my honored instructor and friend Dr. Dorner,[66] now counselor of consistory and professor of theology at Königsberg, I held him capable of understanding and appreciating the German philosophy and theology, much beyond what he has shown in this unfortunate article. It is not in my mind at all to undertake a wholesale defense of any system of German philosophy as such, for I prize too much the liberty of thought to be bound by any philosophical school, and yield my reason to be led only by the Bible. But men like Kant, Fichte, Schelling, and Hegel, who have devoted their whole life to the most laborious and profound inquiries, and who beyond all question belong to the greatest names in the history of the world, should be treated in different style by such a man as Stowe, in justice only to his own character. Instead of saying a word to us on the contents of the later positive system of Schelling, he informs us of his controversy with Dr. Paulus[67] of Heidelberg, which has nothing in the world to do with the matter in hand; and even takes the part of this wretched rationalist, who closed his career as a writer with a literary theft, against the great philosopher—not dreaming at all, as it would seem, that it is precisely the acknowledged merit of this last, to have overcome the standpoint of the abstract understanding, from which the old common rationalism made war upon all the deeper truths of Christianity. For this "common sense," entitled as it is to all respect in its own sphere, the region of the simply finite, will always hold the doctrines of the Trinity and incarnation for nonsense; since according to its shallow, empty way of reasoning, three cannot be one or one three, God cannot be man or man God. If then no higher principle be allowed to prevail in theology, it must be shorn of all its deeper import. Such a higher principle is the *reason* by which we apprehend the supersensuous, the infinite, the divine. But it is Schelling precisely who has successfully asserted the supremacy of this principle in science. To be convinced of this, let Dr. Stowe read Schelling's *Lectures on the Method of Academic Study*, particularly the fifth and sixth. He will find there a

of the later theology as more scientific than before. The very
latest speculation besides, in the person of the still-living founder
of the Identity System, Schelling himself, has taken a direction decidedly toward positive revelation; and it may be said now with
good certainty at least that the bloom period of the pantheistic
logic and purely negative antitheology is already over. Strauss
and his colleagues, by reason of the much greater weight of religious and church feeling they have been called to encounter,
have outlived themselves much sooner than their predecessors
Paulus, Wegscheider,[68] and others. Bruno Bauer,[69] the object now
of almost universal aversion, has been formally deprived of his
office—the sort of thing scarcely anybody would have dreamed
twenty years ago. Such as are acquainted with the state of things
in this quarter must allow that the latest critical and philosophical
opposers of Christianity have in a great measure, by their own

most masterly and powerful argument against the presumption of the mere
understanding, in thrusting itself with its poor surface-skimming nature into
the region of the higher sciences, which have to do with everlasting ideas—
making all flat by trying to make all clear. Hegel's works, Prof. Stowe tells us,
he has "waded through"—so long since however, or in such cursory style, that
he can no longer recollect of how many volumes they consist, missing the mark
entirely in his general guess (p. 86). No wonder that his memory should be
found still more at fault, as regards the actual contents of this exceedingly
difficult system. In fact he does not pretend to draw from the fountain itself,
but only from the *Conversations-Lexicon* of Brockhaus; an ass's bridge notoriously for superficial and lazy thinkers, used by shopkeepers' clerks, but by
no true German scholar, at least in so weighty a case. After giving us in this
way a most lean skeleton, translated as he himself says not *ad sensum,* but only
*ad verbum,* he informs us with all honesty that he cannot understand the philosopher at all. He cannot find out indeed "what the man means by anything
he says in all his writings," so far as examined. Yet he adds, "Let no one say I
have caricatured the system"—as if a translation of isolated fragments *ad verbum* only, could possibly in such a case be anything else than caricature!
What a man by his own confession does not comprehend, it might be as well
perhaps that he should not undertake to explain. Especially so, where as in
the present instance the explanation is expected to carry with it a sort of
"official authority" for the general public. Hegel has errors and sins enough
to answer for, no doubt. But this is no reason why he should be loaded with
misrepresentation, and made to appear little better than a fool at the bar of
the common understanding. It is always however sheer, gross misrepresentation, when his words or thoughts are violently sundered from their true historical life, and forced to stand by abstract translation in new connections and
relations entirely, in which inevitably all their original sense is transmuted,
for the popular mind especially, into bare nonsense.

contradictions and extravagance, destroyed themselves. Thus the leaders of the orthodox theology, after a brief interregnum, are again at the helm of the vessel under most encouraging auspices.

In Germany philosophy, as the spirit of the age exalted to scientific consciousness, exerts a controlling influence over all departments of higher knowledge. From the school of Schelling accordingly, in such men as Eschenmayer,[70] Steffens,[71] Schubart,[72] a decidedly religious tone has been imparted to investigations in the sphere of nature, by which this department has been effectually rescued from the hands of atheism and abstract deism. Steffens in particular has made it the great object of his life, in his scientific and poetic representations, to reconcile nature with religion, the cultivated world consciousness with the consciousness of Christianity. So also the greatest later historians, as Leo, Ranke, Haug,[73] show a special interest in religion and the church, as forming the central force and life pulse properly of the world's history; and bring them continually into the view of their readers, unfettered by the old spiritless pragmatism, with living reproduction, and that freedom from prejudice and love of justice peculiar to the German mind, by which every age is allowed to enjoy its own proper greatness unimpaired. Philology itself, both Oriental and classical, has come by its inward development to stand in a new relation to the holy Scriptures. The earlier rationalism imposed its own arbitrary hypotheses and neological dreams on the Old and New Testaments by a fearful grammatical recklessness and truly wheel-breaking exegesis; and even the supranaturalism of the same period, as exhibited by Storr[74] and others, lies open to censure in the same view. But before the bar of the later philology, this is no longer possible.

Professor Winer[75] of Leipzig, whose grammatical authority as free from all theological bias is universally acknowledged, says unreservedly, "Our exegetical controversies have led back usually to that sense as correct, which the Protestant Church held in the beginning."* Such a man as K. Fr. Aug. Fritzsche,[77] who

---

* *Leipziger Literatur Zeitung,* 1833. No. 44. Comp. the preface to the third edition of his *Grammar of N.T. Idioms,* p. iv ff., as well as the whole admirable work itself. A similar regeneration has been effected by Ewald and Hitzig[76] in the department of the Old Testament.

stands in no inward affinity with the spirit of the Bible, but who as it regards philological learning and accuracy (at times even pushed to excess), is fairly rivaled among recent interpreters only by Harless[78] and Bleek,[79] finds himself constrained, from the grammatico-historical standpoint alone, to prefer in the most important cases the interpretations of a Chrysostom, Augustine, Luther, Calvin, Beza, Bengel,[80] to those of the rationalistic school. Strauss himself has rendered good service to the cause of truth, in his *Leben Jesu*, by the overwhelming force with which he has employed the *reductio ad absurdum* upon the violent exegetical processes, made use of by the older rationalism in carrying out its so-called natural explanation of miracles. Unbelief is thus forced to look in the future for help in some different direction; it can no longer cover its nakedness with a philological mantle. The scientific study of language itself, by its own inward development and without any regard to Christianity, has led to the immensely important result that the church, orthodox Protestantism in particular, has understood the Bible in substance correctly, and must be allowed therefore to have all right against rationalism at the bar of science, if only the assumption of the divine inspiration of the Scriptures be securely established.

Finally, the political circumstances of Germany have also contributed much to the new impulse which has been given to religion. In the war for freedom particularly against the French Usurper, both princes and people were overpowered with an ever-memorable, sacred enthusiasm, when the Lord of hosts, after long-continued, well-deserved oppression, interposed so powerfully by the thunder of battle, and revealed himself so clearly in the direction of events. Since that time, too, the state has begun to change its posture materially toward the church. Formerly this was treated too generally as the mere creature of Caesar, being regarded simply as *one* among the several institutions by which the state was expected to serve its own purposes. Now however it is coming to be understood and felt that the church has a life of its own, and that the state consults its own welfare best, when this life is respected as an independent interest, and suffered to develop itself freely from its own nature. If anyone will compare the administration of the present kings of Prussia and Württem-

berg with that of their predecessors, particularly Frederick the
Great, he will at once admit the great change which has taken
place in this respect.

From the state moreover, under Frederick William III, proceeded in the first instance that *union* of the Lutheran and Reformed Churches, which has since become almost universal in
Germany, and must be regarded now as a great step gained toward the catholicity and unity necessarily involved in the idea of
the church itself. It is not good either that Christ's bride should
bear the name of a mere man, as Lutheran, and the like.* The
title Evangelical is much more catholic and appropriate; though
not in the sense to be sure which it is frequently made to carry
in our western states, when used as a mere cloak for rationalism
and indifferentism.[81] The stiff, absolute Old-Lutheranism of Prussia and Bavaria may be considered indeed a salutary reaction
against the indifference of many of the friends of the union to
doctrines; and in this view, we are glad to find its representatives
in this country also. But apart from this particular advantage, it
is certainly a crying, stubborn misapprehension of the wants of
our time, which reach far beyond its narrow horizon. It is truly
ridiculous indeed, thus to fancy the Formula of Concord the absolute perfection of theology, and to require virtually that not only
the Greek and Roman Churches, but the Reformed also with its
German, Low Dutch, French, English, Scotch, and American
branches, should make it their great business to subscribe it and
submit themselves to Lutheran baptism. The future belongs certainly to the union, and within its range precisely the most religious life is to be found at the present time. The most important

---

* The designations Presbyterian, Congregational, Protestant Episcopal are
also unsatisfactory, as referring only to government; which however is clearly
but a secondary element of the church, belonging not to its spirit but to its
outward form. Our title Reformed, coupled only if need be with the national
distinction, is plainly the best. For it implies no dependence whatever on any
particular man, and includes the view besides that we are no new body, but
the old Catholic Church itself, only regenerated and purified from human
additions. As however this term has acquired in Germany a definite historical
sense, in opposition to the idea of Lutheranism, it was altogether proper that
the title Evangelical should be preferred. Names in so weighty a case are not
mere smoke, but the impression of the idea; and it is known that Luther most
decidedly disapproved the designation of his followers after his own name.

and pious theologians of Germany, as Neander, Hengstenberg, Twesten, Marheinecke, Sartorius, Tholuck, Mueller, Hupfeld, Nitzsch, Sack, Bleek, Kling, Hasse, Hahn, Lange, Hoffmann, Luecke, Liebner, Ullmann, Rothe, Umbreit, Schmidt, Dorner, Landerer, go with it fully; though for themselves a number of them prefer, in a doctrinal respect at least, the Lutheran standpoint. To be sure the union, in its present form, is to be viewed merely as a beginning; and the closer adjustment of it, especially in the symbolical direction, creates just at this time no small difficulty. Nor can it be denied that the measures of the government to promote church improvement in Prussia labor under the defect of more or less irresolution. Goodwill is present, but there is a lack of fixed principles and talent for practical organization; for which at all events, the German, whose spiritual universalism is always multiplying possibilities and doubts before him, has never been particularly distinguished. The case however is in its own nature immensely difficult, and becomes still more so by the manifold spiritual tendencies and peculiarly diversified forms of culture that enter into the constitution of the Prussian State, enough to confound the most thorough practical skill that is not prepared to violate all the rights of history. And then it must not be forgotten that the whole Evangelical Church is at present in an interimistic state, involved in a process of fermentation and transition, which brings along with it necessarily a measure of uncertainty and experiment. In any case, this is something better however than to repose lazily on pillows worn out by use, or to dream with unbounded self-complacency and pretension of being in a condition already complete.

Let us leave however the king of Prussia, with his spiritual and secular counselors, to work out as they best may, under the favor of heaven, the problem they are called to solve, and turn our attention once more upon our own land. What prospect is there here in the way of encouragement for the church? May we hope to see our Protestant Zion conducted safely out of the Babylonish captivity of sectarism and faction, without being carried to old Rome or young Oxford?

We have no such deep scientific conflicts among us, as those we have just had in our view. The philosophical life questions

of Germany, the relation of the church to the arts and to the
state, with which the greatest minds there are exercised in the
severest way, bring no trouble whatever to the American. "*Cui
bono?*" he is ready to exclaim, in view of every speculation of the
sort; dubbing it perhaps with the convenient title transcendentalism or mysticism, to justify his contempt. What has it accomplished for the souls of men or their bodies? Can it fill an empty
pocket or an empty stomach? Has it ever manufactured a steam-
boat or so much even as a pin? Such is the style, in substance if
not in form, in which the interest of philosophical thinking is
too often undervalued in this country, in favor of what is practical and useful. With such a spirit, of course, I can feel no sympathy. It is greatly to be lamented that the German churches of
America in particular should be so sadly defective in theological
and philosophical culture, and without a single literary institution after the pattern of the German gymnasia or universities. The
result of this must be in the end that our congregations will lose
themselves in the English denominations, with the sacrifice of
their own proper character entirely, unless they can be brought
betimes into spiritual communication with the mother church in
Germany. On the other hand, if they might be led thus to participate with proper life in the later movements of German theology,
they would take a position peculiar to themselves, and must exercise gradually an important influence also on their English
sister churches. For these too need a vastly more thorough and
vigorous theology to carry them prosperously forward, and make
them superior to the foes that now threaten them from every
side. Theology is no less necessary for the regeneration of Protestantism now than it was for the accomplishment of the Reformation in the sixteenth century. To prevent misunderstanding, it
may be well to be a little more particular on the importance of
theology in its relation to practical church life.

Some take ground on principle against all theological training as injurious to the interests of living, practical piety. Such
are welcome to the illiterate declaimers in whom they choose to
take delight, with all their rant and noise and animal excitement;
men who trample underfoot the apostolic caution with regard
to this point (James 3:1) and in their wretched spiritual pride

deal forth the stale conceits and fantastic soap bubbles of their
own poor brain, for the inspirations of the Holy Spirit. Alas for
the congregations whose want of discernment leads them to accept such husks for bread. Show us then, you opposers of knowledge, which the apostle makes the element of eternal life, where
are the men whom a miraculous illumination of the Spirit has
constituted theologians with a single stroke; and no one will be
more ready to show them respect than ourselves. But you substitute your own fanatical feeling for the Holy Spirit. Pentecosts
are not common days in history; and according to the general rule
and order of God, which we are bound humbly to observe, even
our spiritual bread is to be earned by the sweat of our brow. Our
intellectual and moral faculties are given us, not to be buried
or left to rust, but to be put to use and made productive. We are
directed to search the Scriptures continually, and to grow in all
wisdom and knowledge. If the apostles themselves, after an intercourse of three years with the Master of all masters, needed
still an extraordinary furniture of divine gifts for their work, it
must certainly be considered no small presumption, when a little
religious experience merely—and this often in the most superficial form—together with some tolerable fluency of speech, is
held—as with many in this country at the present time—a sufficient preparation for the most important and difficult of all of-
fices. Let us hope that the age of such presumption may soon come
to an end. For nothing is more adapted to bring the ministry
into disrespect, to strip the pulpit of its true sacred dignity, and
to make the church itself in the end an object of general indifference and derision.

Others pronounce theology *useful* at least, and regard this as
quite a fine compliment paid to the science. These are your
utilitarians and materialists, who measure the value of all things
in heaven and upon earth by the interest they bring. While seeming to praise it, they sink the first of all sciences into the same
category with a bushel of potatoes; and indeed lower, since these
last may lay claim to a much more general and palpable utility.
Theology is neither useful nor harmful; it is raised immeasurably
above the poor category of serviceableness; it is no means with
which to procure something beyond itself, as we employ money

or a mechanical instrument; but an end in itself, and for anyone who will hold a prominent place in the church just as indispensable as the knowledge of law for a statesman or the knowledge of nature for a physician. It is absolutely *necessary* so that no well-ordered condition of the church is to be thought of where theology does not flourish.

The necessity for it does not spring from mere outward occasions, but from the inmost nature of the Christian faith itself. Our religion is not simply for feeling or for the will separately taken, but full as much for the faculty of knowledge also, the understanding and reason; it seeks to penetrate and pervade harmoniously all the powers of man's nature, and thus to refine and perfect him in the undivided totality of his person. It belongs to the inmost nature of faith that it should raise itself continually to clearer consciousness, attain always to a more distinct and full knowledge of its object, that is, of God as revealed in Christ. *Pistis* is in itself the fruitful germ of a true *gnosis,* and rests not till it becomes at last the vision of God face to face, which is at the same time also the conception of the full blessedness of heaven itself. If faith be true, it must allow this to be shown, so far as this may be possible in the present world. Christianity is not against reason, but only above reason.* Only superficial knowledge is irreligious; true, thorough knowledge stands in covenant with faith, and is not possible without it. But faith should be ever struggling to become knowledge; Christianity should enter always more and more into the comprehension of reason. "Negligentia mihi videtur, si postquam confirmati sumus in fide, non studemus quod credimus intelligere." Thus speaks the greatest theologian of the Middle Ages, one of the most eminently pious men at the same time belonging to the history of the church.† So Augustine, whose name is above all praise, and before whose powerful spirit both the Catholic and Protestant Churches bow with almost equal reverence, represents growth in theological knowledge to be a growth of God in the soul itself. "Crescat ergo Deus, qui semper perfectus est, crescat in te. Quanto enim magis

---

* Or, to speak with Pascal, "La foi dit bien ce que les sens ne disent pas, mais jamais le contraire. Elle est *au dessus,* non pas *contre.*"

† Anselm of Canterbury, in the beginning of his work *Cur Deus homo?*

intelligis Deum, et quanto magis capis, videtur in te crescere Deus. . . . Intelligebas heri modicum, intelligis hodie amplius, intelliges cras multo amplius: lumen ipsum Dei crescit in te. . . . Sic est et interior homo: proficit quidem in Deo, et Deus in illo videtur crescere; ipse tamen minuitur, ut a gloria sua decidat, et in gloriam Dei surgat."* Theology appears thus an indispensable organ in the life of the church—its head, its consciousness, and so its ornament and joy; theology of course in the sense of our Protestant ancestors, in whose production are joined *oratio, meditatio,* and *tentatio,* the *theologia regenitorum,* besides which indeed there is none that is entitled to the name.

Happy is he who has attained to this exalted view! A generation that crawls in the dust may style him, in pity or derision, an idealist, even perchance a man given to phantasy. But all this he counts an honor. For he knows that it is not gold or steam, but *ideas* that rule the world and constitute the soul, the heart's blood of history, producing in it all that is either true or abiding. For no price would he separate himself from the *regina scientiarum;* all the glory of the world, all the praise of men, are to him as nothing, in comparison with the excellency of the knowledge of God in Christ.

It follows then with logical necessity that the progress of the church moves hand in hand with the progress of theology. Where ignorance rules an age, where the diligent study of the Scriptures is neglected, there at the same time the whole Christian life grows sickly, and one form of error after another creeps into the sanctuary. On the contrary, where genuine piety flourishes, where the whole church is made to feel the life-giving presence of God's Spirit, there knowledge shows itself clear and fresh to the same extent. What is it we admire so much in the age of the apostles? The striking union of the deepest insight into the character and works of God, with the most vigorous activity; the full-toned harmony of all the powers of the soul, filled and governed by one and the same principle. Paul, who labored more than all the rest of the apostles, is also a master in the way of knowledge, to whom we are indebted for the fullest development of doctrine,

* In *Evang. Joann.,* c. 3, Tract 14. [Schaff alters the text of Augustine slightly.]

a wonderfully profound exhibition of Christian truth, and most powerful confutation of error at the same time. By his scriptural arguments and his keen logical combinations and conclusions, he so handled his adversaries, both heathen and Jewish, as to leave them ever after without excuse for their unbelief. John, the apostle of love, has been styled not without reason by the church, the "theologian" *per eminentiam.* For by the eagle flight of his believing speculation into the depths of God and his Word, made flesh for our salvation, as existing before the world, he may be said to have led the way to Christian theology in its bold and glorious course.* His love is only the strong will-force of knowledge; his knowledge, but the keen vision of love. The whole history of the church furnishes proof that the men who have exerted the greatest and happiest influence, the wakers of a new life, the pillars in the temple of God, have always been distinguished also above their contemporaries by a thorough scientific cultivation. It is sufficient to call up the names simply of such men as Irenaeus, Origen, Cyprian, Athanasius, the Cappadocian Gregory, Basil the Great, Augustine, Anselm, Thomas Aquinas, Luther, Melanchthon, Calvin, Beza, Johann Gerhard,[83] Spener, Bengel, Wesley, Edwards. Where a new religious movement is not rooted at the same time in a solid doctrinal ground—the case of our later awakenings too generally—it is found also to have no enduring force, or at all events cannot carry the church forward as a whole.

Shall now the general rule as established by the history of the church have no application to the time in which we ourselves live? There is an opinion indeed that the Reformers and theologians of the seventeenth century have accomplished in theology all that is to be done, so that we need now only to hold fast this Protestant tradition and hand it on mechanically to the next generation. This principle of stagnation is openly advocated by

---

* Hence the ancient hymn sings of him:

> Volat avis sine meta,
> Quo nec vates nec propheta
>     Evolavit altius.
> Tam implenda, quam impleta
> Numquam vidit tot secreta
>     Purus homo purius.[82]

one at least of the most influential theological journals of the
country, whose authority with a large portion of the American
church is counted well-nigh infallible. With all our respect however for the piety and standing of its conductors, we must protest decidedly against every such view. How inconsistent to admit
a perfectibility and actual progress, both of the individual and
of the race, in all departments of mind, in the natural sciences,
in jurisprudence, in the knowledge of history, in political development, in all material or outward interests, in morality and
piety, only *not* in philosophy and theology. Is then the Bible alone
a book so clear and plain that all its depths are already exhausted? Are then the powers of the human mind so abstractly
separate from one another that one may become absolutely complete without the rest? Have our Protestant ancestors perhaps
declared themselves to be infallible, requiring us to receive their
decisions as oracles; or have they not rather set us free from all
bondage to men? Did their work too, in its theoretic character
only, spring forth at once complete like Minerva from the head
of Jupiter; or was it not rather a gradual process in which they
were themselves led from one view and one measure of clearness
still onward to another? If Protestantism be indeed the blind
faith of authority, unthinking rehearsal of what has been handed
down, let us then confess at least that we have no reason to reproach popery on this score. But the case stands not thus. Protestantism is the principle of movement, of progress in the history
of the church; progress, not such as may go beyond the Bible and
Christianity, but such as consists in *an ever-extending knowledge*
of the Bible itself, and an *ever-deepening appropriation* of Christianity as the power of a divine life, which is destined to make *all*
things new. Our church should be always prepared to give an
account of her faith with joy and to contend manfully against all
human distortions of the truth, against every false and injurious
representation of the gospel. She dare not, unless she would renounce herself, stiffen into lifeless stability and suffer herself to
be left behind by her adversaries in the way of scientific movement. Rather she must explore still further and further the inexhaustible mines of God's word, and seek a fuller and freer representation continually of her own principle; remembering al-

ways that there is still beyond measure much to be learned, and that she can never become complete in herself, except as her knowledge also may be carried to the highest point.

But the proper home of Protestant theology is Germany, and hence we may say that those who refuse to take account of German theology, set themselves in fact against the progress of Protestantism. The land which gave birth to the Reformation stands pledged by that movement itself not to rest till the great work shall have been made complete, when the revelation of God in Christ shall be apprehended in full and the contents of faith shall be reduced to such form as to carry with them also the clearest evidence and most incontrovertible certainty in the way of knowledge. We wish not to depreciate in the least the merits acquired in former times, by the Dutch and the English in particular, in the way of biblical study—critical, exegetical, and antiquarian. The German is always disposed rather to put an undue value on what is foreign, and has long since appropriated the results of these investigations and worked them into the process of his own cultivation. But what is all this beside the gigantic creations of German theology! All its heresies cannot destroy my respect for it. In England and America one learns first to prize it according to its true worth. It must not be forgotten that even the German rationalism, worthy of all reprobation as it is, gives evidence, at least in its better forms, of an extraordinary scientific energy and a deep interest in the investigation of truth, from which we are authorized to draw a favorable conclusion on the opposite side. For only an archangel can become a devil. As England and America would not have been able at all to produce so fearful an enemy of Christianity as David Friedrich Strauss,[84] so must they have been much less able to meet him with a proper refutation; and I shudder at times to think of the desolation his writings must occasion, if they should come to be much read—which may God prevent—in this country.* It must be borne in

---

* I was informed by a friend, one of the Fellows of Baliol College in Oxford, that two prominent young clergymen of the English Church had fallen upon the *Life of Jesus* by Strauss and were so overpowered by it as absolutely to despair of all scientific help in opposition to it with the resources or from the standpoint of the English theology as it has stood thus far.

mind also on the other side that there is a species of orthodoxy, by no means rare, which rests upon the foundation of mere convenience or intellectual indolence, or the lowest motive possibly of self-interest, and is consequently no whit better, yea by reason of such hypocrisy in its constitution is even much worse, than open and honest unbelief.

If we look into church history, we shall be still less disturbed in our estimate of German theology by the heretical elements that belong to it, since they must appear to us only as negative conditions of a new doctrinal conquest. Thus the full determination and clear, close definition of the doctrines of the Trinity and of the relation of the two natures in Christ, as exhibited to us in the ecumenical councils, were conditioned throughout by a succession of heresies in the direction of these articles. The Pelagian error must serve, in the hand of God, to unfold and establish more profoundly, through Augustine, the doctrine of divine grace and human liberty. At the Reformation also heretical tendencies, Socinianism, Anabaptism, antinomianism, and so on, come into view; as in a period of such vast excitement was to be expected. They wrought with salutary force on the development of orthodox Protestantism, making it necessary for it to understand more clearly its own commission, to discriminate more closely its proper sphere, and to fortify itself against unauthorized consequences and various misapprehensions of its true character. So we may say that the later heresies of Germany are but the negative side of the process by which the theology of that country has been advancing toward higher and more solid ground than it occupied before. In this view, nothing can well be more unfair than to confound them with the idea of German theology itself. Those who do so only show their own ignorance of the actual posture of things in the German Church at the present time.

It is to be lamented indeed that the representations usually exhibited of German theology in this country, by those who pass for its friends as well as others, have been, and to a great extent still continue to be, borrowed from a period which has been fairly surmounted and left behind in Germany itself—the period of the older rationalism, in which the truth might be said to have become for a time so entangled in the folds of error as hardly to be distinguished from it, even in the writings of its most orthodox defenders. There is reason to believe that this *rationalistic* orthodoxy, as represented for instance by such men as Ernesti[85] and Morus,[86] has indeed been made the vehicle by which more or less of a truly pernicious neological spirit has been introduced into the American church in the name of German theology. Undoubtedly at least, rationalistic elements and tendencies are extensively involved in the religious thinking of the country, even under what are regarded often as its most orthodox forms. Elements and tendencies that need only to be carried out consistently to their proper consequences, to show themselves in their true light. Elements and tendencies, it may be added, which the orthodox German theology of the present day, all slandered as it is, would reject as heretical and false, no less decidedly than it rejects the entire standpoint of a Bretschneider[87] himself. Nothing, I repeat, can well be more unfair than to confound the true, positive theology of Germany, now so successfully asserting its spiritual independence, with the negative heretical entanglements of a former time, from which it has extricated itself in large part already and is in the way of extricating itself still more triumphantly, we may hope, in time to come.

It is not to be desired of course that the mighty struggles of German philosophy and theology should repeat themselves, in their whole compass, in this country. Rather it may be trusted that the victory achieved by believing science in Germany, over both the popular and speculative forms of rationalism, will redound to the general benefit of the entire Protestant Church. But what we wish is this, that the spirit of German theology in its better form, as now predominant, might be transplanted into our midst, and with proper modification of course and adjustment to our circumstances made to enter organically into our religious life. Here all must be more practical; science must go hand in hand with the proper activities of the Christian life. As we will have no order of priests specifically different from the laity, so we want no separate order of theologians, restricting to itself all sacred wisdom. Such a union of the German scientific and English practical tendencies would furnish a better form of existence than either of these separately taken, which it might seem to be the vocation of America in particular to realize, where German elements, in the middle and western states especially, are entering so largely, and with such vast increase every year, into the social mass. I regret not in the least the modification, which the science of Germany, and its theology in particular, must thus undergo, to be turned here to any good account. Rather I rejoice in it with all my heart. For decided foe as I am to the mere utilitarian principle, I am well aware that German science is but too prone to run to an extreme in the other direction, and thus to lose itself in unprofitable speculations and subtleties that come in the end to nothing.* Nor should it be forgotten that a large proportion of the German immigration has been, and still is, of such a character, that we must wish to see it brought under the force of the English nationality for its own sake, and have reason to bless God for the favorable change it has been made to undergo by this means in part already. But this is not enough. May we not trust that the time is at hand when the American Germany shall again rise from the ruins of its own nationality and language, purified and enriched with the advantages belonging to the English character, and so enter upon a new career of its own, that shall be fraught with lasting benefit to the whole country.

Altogether there seems to be reason to believe that the way is opening at least toward such an order of things as the wants of the time are found to demand. There are indications certainly which imply that our church relations are destined, before a great while, to assume a new form in one way or another. The system of thinking which has hitherto prevailed is coming to lose its authority at different points. Difficulties are causing themselves to be felt, where formerly they were not imagined to exist. Ideas of deep and far-reaching import are steadily working their way, where only a few years since perhaps hardly a trace of their presence was to be found.

---

* To which the well-known verse in Goethe's *Faust* may be applied in all its force:

   Ein Kerl, der speculirt,
  Ist wie ein Thier, auf duerrer Heide
   Von einem boesen Geist im Kreis herumgefuehrt,
   Und rings umher liegt schoene gruene Weide.

The absolute despotism of the metaphysics of Locke is in a measure broken. In spite of the earnest warnings of certain influential literary organs, the general unconditional confidence with which the system was formerly held has been seriously shaken, particularly, it would seem, in New England. Let us hear on this point Professor Stowe[88] of Lane Seminary, who will not at least be suspected of any improper leaning toward German transcendentalism. "The metaphysics of Locke," he tells us, "under various modifications, have prevailed over the English and French mind —the most effective mind in the civilized world—for more than a century, a long period certainly in an active and thinking age for any one system of mental science to maintain its dominion. This style of philosophizing did not long retain its ascendancy among the Germanic nations, but was there entirely overthrown more than sixty years ago; and for about twenty-five years past there has been a gradual but certain undermining of its influence in France, England, and the United States. *Almost all the ardent, youthful, investigating minds in these countries, now feel that the system of Locke, in all its modifications, is meager, unspiritual, and unsatisfying, and are anxiously looking for something better.*"* This change has been produced mainly by the writings, on the one hand, of the French eclectic Cousin,[89] who is known to have borrowed largely from the later German philosophy, and by the works of Coleridge and Thomas Carlyle, on the other—both of them thoroughly steeped in the element of German thought. Coleridge, a noble, fertile, half-poetic, half-philosophic spirit, proceeded from the school of Schelling, which is characterized by a tendency toward the objective and historical; whence it is not strange that his numerous disciples in England sympathize to a certain extent with the Puseyite movement, though not so as to yield themselves to it in a slavish way. One of the most able and interesting productions called forth in this connection is *The Kingdom of Christ* by F. D. Maurice[90] of London. Carlyle's mind is more of the negative, critical order, with a strong leaning to pantheism; as is seen particularly in his hero worship, which reaches even to Muhammad, and toward Goethe rises into extravagance

---

* *The Biblical Repository and Classical Review* (New York, January, 1845), p. 65.

itself. By the uncommon richness of his intellect, however, and his keen portraits, he exerts a kindling influence on youthful, excitable spirits, and at all events enlarges the field of their vision and opens before them new regions of thought. He sees the defects of our time indeed, and of our present Protestantism, only too well; but has no power to direct us to any positive remedy. Hence a certain character of gloomy dissatisfaction, not to say cynical despair, runs through all his writings. Still the knowledge of the disease must always precede its cure, and in this view the widely extended influence of this energetic writer is to be considered favorable, as leading beyond itself to something that may be better.

In theology itself, directly or indirectly, Germany is coming to be more and more widely felt. An almost absolute authority having been exercised for nearly a hundred years in church history by the learned chancellor of Göttingen, Mosheim[91]—long since thrown into the background in his own country by those who have come after him—the works of Neander[92] and Gieseler[93] have at length made their appearance here also in an English dress. These it is known are distinguished for the most conscientious study of original sources; to which must be added in the case of the first the genial presence of a deep religious spirit, that lovingly welcomes the manifestations of the divine life under all forms and causes them to live again upon the historic page with magic reproduction. We could wish only it were pervaded with deeper *church* feeling. *The History of the Reformation,* also, by Merle d'Aubigné,[94] which has had such an immense circulation in this country, is, properly speaking, in its main parts, a skillful working up of German material, particularly the *Geschichte der Reformation* by Marheinecke,[95] which still remains superior to it in the estimation of all competent judges.*

---

* The recent production of the celebrated Genevan doctor, translated for *The Biblical Repository and Classical Review* (Jan. 1845), under the title "Lutheranism and the Reform: Their Diversity Essential to Their Unity," can make still less pretension to originality. We hold this essay important on account of its catholic spirit and tendency, and for the acknowledgment it contains, that the question concerning the church has now become the first question, "the greatest, the all-engrossing subject." We have been really surprised, however, to see how Dr. Merle allows himself to plunder German

Still all this, as compared with the wealth of the German literature, is but a small beginning. It would be easy to name more
than a score of new works, of exegetical and dogmatic character
in particular, which are fully as worthy to be translated as those
which have been mentioned, and some of them much more so.
A special society has been formed in French Switzerland for trans-
planting the better theological literature of Germany into that
country, which has already entered upon its work with good success. Much more might we look for some institution of the sort
here, and that no such measure has been thought of only shows
how little interest the Germans of this country take in the monuments which reflect the greatest honor on their own race. They are
put to shame in this respect, even by the English themselves. The
best literary institutions of the land are coming to understand

---

authors. One idea is taken from the first volume of Twesten's *Dogmatik;*
three ideas are borrowed from Lange's academical inaugural address at
Zurich; all the rest are found in the well-known book of Goebel on the
*Union.* Here we meet the representation, for instance, that Lutheranism
places the material principle foremost; the Reformed Church, the formal;
that the first has proceeded on the maxim of holding fast all that is not expressly condemned by God's word; the second, on the maxim of rejecting all
for which no explicit authority is to be found in the Bible; that the work of
reformation with the first was carried on prevailingly in a doctrinal and theological way; while with the second, it took also a practico-moral and political
form; that the first was aristocratic and monarchial; the second, democratic
and republican; that the first showed itself exclusive and in the end hostile
to the Reformed Church; while the second was always disposed to a union
with Lutheranism, but perseveringly opposed to all peace with Rome; etc., etc.
Even the examples, pp. 139, 148, and 160, are copied from Goebel.

All this is mentioned, not to depreciate at all the Genevan theologian, but
only to show how ready the most distinguished French writers are to take
lessons in the school of German learning and to recommend their example
to imitation in this country. Why should we undervalue in German what we
are ready to laud as exhibited to us at second hand in French? What confidence is to be reposed in the judgment of those who undertake to proscribe
the entire theological literature of Germany as worthless and full of peril
only to the church, without having read perhaps a volume of it themselves,
while they suffer the same material to be smuggled in upon us in any quantity
from a different quarter, as profitable and wholesome in the highest degree?
The French theological literature, such as it is, owes nearly all its value to
the use of German helps; and when all is done, it may be pronounced immeasurably poor and meager, as compared with the theological literature of
Germany itself.

that no modern education can be complete which does not include some acquaintance with German learning, and think it necessary accordingly to make some provision for the cultivation of it in their academical course. The most distinguished theologians in the country, such as Stowe, Stuart,[96] Hodge,[97] and Robinson,[98] have bestowed their careful study on the theological literature of Germany and acknowledge themselves under lasting obligations to its help. This study ought not indeed to be confined simply to the critical, isagogical, and antiquarian departments, which some appear to consider most valuable and safe; though in fact they have been occupied to a great extent by rationalism. We need to have rather, in larger measure, the *spirit* and the *ideas* of the later German theology. We need to fortify ourselves in this way against errors and tendencies to err, to which we are already exposed. Against the rationalism of the abstract understanding we can have no better protection in the way of science than is here placed within our reach. In no other quarter have these false forms of thought been met and vanquished in the same thorough style. Germany has produced the most pious as well as the most godless philosophers and theologians; those whose influence has been the most salutary, as well as those who seem to have been born only to work mischief and death. The greatest demerit of the land and its highest glory are found here in close conjunction. So it was with Greece, where the Sophists appear in intimate connection with a Socrates, and along with the followers of Plato, the followers of Epicurus. One tendency is always naturally coupled with another, as its own opposite.

This then is one desideratum in our circumstances. A fresh, vigorous theology, in which the most decided faith might appear in union with the freest and most thorough scientific culture, could not fail to advance us to a new position, and to give us a triumphant advantage over infidelity and popery and semipopery in all their forms.

This however of itself is not of course enough. We need also a change in our practical church state, an antidote to the sect plague. What is first wanted in this direction is the conviction that the present distracted condition of Protestantism is contradictory to the idea of the church, whose normal character neces-

sarily includes catholicity and unity, as well as an earnest sacred
grief on this account. Nor have we any right to console ourselves
with the fancy of a vague spiritual unity in the case. It belongs
to the inward always, if it have life, to manifest itself in an outward way. The soul must form for itself a body as its appropriate
organ. Visibility lies necessarily in the conception of the church,
which is the Body of Christ; the mark of unity consequently must
also clothe itself in an outward form. The unity we are to seek
must be no dead sameness indeed, but such as is full of life, one
and endlessly manifold at the same time. Here again the case requires, not that we should go back to the old, but that we should
go forward rather with all that has been won by Protestantism, in
the way of developed subjectivity. Outward unity does not require *one* visible head, as the pope, who is called antichrist for this
very pretension. This place belongs to Christ alone, and he needs
no *vicarius,* since he is himself present in his own Body. In the
apostolic age, and long after, the unity of the church was maintained without any such human chief bishop. Even at the end
of the sixth century, Gregory the Great, it is known, wrote to the
patriarch of Constantinople*: "Certe Petrus Apostolorum primus,
membrum sanctae et universalis Ecclesiae, Paulus, Andreas, Ioannes, *quid aliud quam singularium sunt plebium capita, et tamen
sub uno capite omnes membra?*" And in another letter†: "Ego
autem fidenter dico, quia quisquis se universalem Sacerdotem
vocat, vel vocari desiderat, *in elatione sua Antichristum praecurrit,*
quia superbiendo se caeteris praeponit. Nec dispari superbia ad
errorem ducitur, quia sicut perversus ille Deus videri vult super
omnes homines; ita quisquis iste est, qui solus Sacerdos appel-
lari appetit, super reliquos Sacerdotes se extollit." Neither is a
single organization absolutely necessary, as the Puseyites dream.
The unity must proceed from within, from the deepest ground of
the religious life itself, and then it will provide for itself a suitable external form. What this will be, we are not prepared now
of course to say. In any case, however, a living outward intercom-
munication must come to hold among all Christian churches, such
as may furnish practical proof that they are not only one spirit

* Lib. V, Epist. 18.
† Ad Mauricium Aug., Lib. VII, Ep. 33.

but one body also, that is, the Body of our Lord Jesus Christ.

What cheering indications now, the guaranty of a better future in this direction, can the time be said to bring to our view? There, to be sure, in England and America, is the mighty movement of Puseyism. With this however we can make no common cause; if for no other reason, yet simply as nonepiscopal Protestants, whom it unchurches without ceremony altogether; on which account too it can never find much favor on the continent in Europe. It has been already shown, in the way of objection to the system, that it has no proper sense of the world-historical importance of Protestantism in its origin and later development. It leads backward rather than forward. Still it must be counted a salutary fermentation. It has served to bring up again, with powerful interest, the great questions of the church: catholicity and unity. These questions belong not exclusively to the Episcopal Church and there is no reason why they should be identified at all with the idea of episcopacy. They challenge the attention of the entire Christian communion. We may make room for them and yield ourselves to their power, without surrendering ourselves in so doing to the errors of the false tendency with which they stand connected in the Oxford Episcopal school. The force of them has already begun to be felt indeed, in some measure, in other denominations. The different sections of orthodox Protestantism have not by any means now the same quiet confidence in their own position, as the *ne plus ultra* of church perfection, the unimprovable absolute of Christianity itself, which they had only ten or fifteen years ago. It is coming to be felt that the present posture of things cannot be rested in, as permanent and ultimate, and along with this is waking the desire for something better. Single voices are heard here and there, from the bosom of the evangelical church, calling for a true union among all who belong to the household of faith, in spirit, soul, and body, and find a lively echo in many a breast. It is to me a source of great satisfaction and encouragement to find among these the man with whom I am called to labor as a colleague in the same institution; with whom altogether, notwithstanding the entirely independent and widely separate spheres of our previous history—God be praised—that I have been enabled, to my own no small surprise, so fully to sympathize in the most weighty points from the first moment of our acquaintance.*

True, appearances are not such at present as to encourage the idea that a general union will soon take place. The differences which prevail in doctrine, government, and worship, and the abstract view too generally taken of the relation of Christianity to the world, stand hopelessly in the way. Rather, division threatens to go still further, as the question of slavery—to say nothing of other difficulties—is fastening itself with resistless force upon the heart of the church. Episcopal Methodism is already rent by it into two great sections, which are not likely soon to be reconciled. Other denominations, it is to be feared, will be gradually involved in similar division. At this very time there are strong indications that the great Presbyterian body, of *both* schools, will very soon find it necessary to meet the question in its whole length and breadth; and already the most serious apprehensions are entertained of a new ecclesiastical rupture on its account.

In the Protestant Episcopal Church, on other grounds, as all know, there is still less show of peace. The mournful scandal of the Onderdonk trial[100] has brought the quarrel between the Puseyite and evangelical parties to its climax. The Puseyites are now in desperate plight, not only by reason of the moral wreck of their principal leader in the view of the public, but still more as they are drawn into collision with their own principles; since they declare the sentence of suspension which has taken place to be unjust, though passed by a decided majority of their own bishops, those anointed and inviolable bearers of the apostolical succession, wronging thus in heart at least the duty of canonical obedience. The appeal of Seabury[101] to the example of Fénelon[102] (*si parva licet componere magnis*), who himself read in his church the

------

* [A very long note occurs here in the German work, containing a special reference to the translator's sermon *Catholic Unity,* preached at the opening of the Convention of the Reformed Dutch and German Reformed Churches, Harrisburg, Aug. 8, 1844, with a series of extracts exhibiting its principal thoughts. For various reasons it has been considered best to attach the whole sermon to the present publication in the way of an appendix, to which of course it is enough at this place to refer. The original note closes with a notice also of the last chapter in particular of the second edition of *The Anxious Bench,* as unfolding the same general views.—TRANSLATOR][99]

papal bull directed against his own person, is here of no avail. For Fénelon submitted himself truly to the judgment of the church; acknowledged the faults charged upon his work *Explication des Maximes des Saintes;* forbade the reading of it in his diocese; and burned all the copies of it he could reach, in a court belonging to his archiepiscopal palace, with his own hand. This the Puseyites could not easily be brought to do in the case of their "Tracts for the Times"; and in the present instance they even proclaim the suspended Onderdonk openly to be their bishop still; so that even that outward subjection to the decision of the court of bishops, for which Seabury takes credit to himself in his noted sermon, amounts at last to nothing. Whether they will now go over in mass to Rome, or form a church of their own, remains to be seen. At all events the matter has gone so far that they must either bend or break.

Still all these storms that gather on the horizon will but serve fully to purify the atmosphere. The disease must pass through its last crisis before it can be thoroughly cured. The growth of division will cause the longing after Christian union to break forth at last with irrepressible force. The mighty advances of the Romish Church, stalking forward through the motley crowd of our sects, in proud confidence of victory, as a *single* man, though in very questionable alliance with the most rank political demagogism, must in the end compel the Protestants to take another position in order that they may save themselves. The conflict is waxing more earnest every day. Who would have thought twenty years ago that popery was ever to acquire importance in the land of freedom?\* Now according to the *Metropolitan Catholic Al-*

---

\* [I remember very well that when the venerable Dr. Alexander of Princeton, less than twenty years ago, solemnly warned the students under his care of the danger that was to be expected from this quarter, exhorting us to prepare for the conflict with Rome as the *great* controversy of the American church, his words to most were very much like empty wind. And yet how prophetical they have proved to be already! What a change in fact have not the last five years only produced in the posture of Romanism in this country relative to both church and state? The numerical increase of the body is no proper measure of its actual gain. By far the largest amount of progress is in the form of preparation for action that is expected to tell with wide effect hereafter. It is actually startling to find in what broad, comprehensive, and far-reaching style, the policy of the system is revealing itself on all sides; and *manac* for the year 1845, it embraces in the United States: a population of 800,000 souls; 21 episcopal dioceses with one apostolical vicarship; 675 churches, 709 priests; 28 male and 63 female seminaries; 94 orphan houses and other benevolent institutions; a multitude of convents and religious associations—as Jesuits, Redemptorists, Lazarists, Augustinians, Dominicans, Eudists, the Society of the Precious Blood, the Brethren of St. Joseph; also, Sisters of Charity, Carmelitesses, Nuns of the Visitation of Mary, Nuns of Loretto, Dominican Nuns, Ladies of the Good Shepherd, Sisters of Notre Dame, Sisters of Providence, Ursuline Nuns, Ladies of the Most Sacred Heart, etc. There appear among us, besides, *ten* weekly and *three* monthly Roman Catholic periodicals; to which must be added now the quarterly of Brownson,[103] a man of much reading and ready pen, whose accession to the Roman Church has recently been hailed with no small triumph. Romanism directs its eye mainly toward the West, well knowing that this must hereafter give law to the whole land. "Give us the West," says one of its bishops, "and we will soon take care of the East."

For the final issue of the conflict, we have no fear, since the Lord of hosts reigns supreme. Let all human work fall to pieces, that the work of God may have the more free scope. In the end all must advance the glory of his name and the welfare of his children. We will not be dismayed then at the gathering conflict. We will carry on the sacred war in word and in life, keeping always in view the honor of God and the interest of the church, for-

---

with how much quiet, unaffected confidence, it is pursuing a course that looks confessedly to nothing less than the spiritual conquest of the whole land. Within a very short time, the Catholic press has gained immensely in point of respectability and power; and there is reason to believe that the literary weight of the system will be made to press upon us, in the course of the next ten years, in a way of which few have begun to dream. Most assuredly the American church has need now to consider well the danger that is fast gathering upon her in this direction. But alas, how few seem to understand what the times require or to be prepared for the emergency which is at hand. How few show themselves qualified to go to the *ground* of the controversy and to deal with it in its principles. *Here* precisely is our greatest danger. For one who has only begun to comprehend something of the force of the *ideas* that are involved in the conflict, and who can feel at all the nature of the historical crisis to which we have come, it is truly alarming to consider the style in which the championship of Protestantism among us is too generally conducted.—TRANSLATOR] getting not our own faults in our zeal against those of others; not with the rough weapons of the flesh in the way of wild fanaticism, but with the weapons of the Spirit—the sword of God's word, the breastplate of faith, and the helmet of hope. Let it be a war of extermination against all error and division, but a conflict of prayer at the same time and love toward the souls of the blinded enemies of the church, to win them if possible to eternal life. Then shall we be soldiers in the sense of Paul, worthy followers of this spiritual hero. Then shall we too at last be adorned with the crown of righteousness, which the glorified apostle has long since received from the Judge, who holds life and death, heaven and hell, in his almighty hand.

As members of a particular division of the Church of Christ, we must be true to the patrimony of our fathers, conscientiously turn to profit the pound entrusted to our care, and advance with free, genuine historical progress as the wants of the time may require. To forsake the church communion in which we have been born naturally and spiritually, without urgent reason, is base perfidy. Let us labor then *within* our own denomination and *for* it, as knowing that God has given us here our own special commission to fulfill. We will manifest, in this very way, our church feeling and regard for history. Only, let all be subordinated to the interest of the general kingdom of God. If we have any right idea of the church as the communion of the redeemed transcending all limits of time and space, we shall feel that we cannot extend our view too far. We may not exclude the Romanists themselves. Let them go on to treat us as lost heretics; we must still return good for evil. We believe confidently that even for this church, which once thrust out our fathers with terrible ban from its bosom, the Lord has still great things in store. Why should we despair of another reformation as impossible in the case of its vast and powerful communion? This is wished and hoped for, by many even of its own best members.*

---

* [Who can say what vast results may not yet proceed from the agitation, which is going forward in the German Roman Catholic Church[104] at this very time, in connection with the case of priest Ronge, and the stirring example set by the congregation at Schneidemühl? All accounts concur in representing the excitement to be immense and not likely soon to subside. The idea of a

Protestantism cannot be consummated without Catholicism;
not in the way of falling back to the past, but as coming into reconciliation with it finally in a higher position, in which all past
errors shall be left behind whether Protestant or Catholic, and
the truth of both tendencies be actualized, as the power of one
and the same life, in the full revelation of the kingdom of God.
The consummation of both will be at the same time their union.
It is written, John 10:16, "There shall be one fold and one
shepherd"—a word that can be accomplished in its *full* and *absolute* sense only when all confessional antagonisms shall come to
an end.

It is an interesting and beautiful thought (to be felt indeed
only by those who have some sense for the *philosophy* of church
history) by which the three most conspicuous apostles—Peter,
Paul, and John—are made to stand as the representatives in character of three great stages of development, through which the
church is to be carried to its final consummation. We meet the

---

separation from the headship of Rome, with a general retention at the same
time of the Catholic system, is taking hold of many minds, in every direction,
with extraordinary power. Steps indeed have begun to be taken, it would
seem, toward the organization of churches on this plan in a number of the
most prominent places—Berlin, Leipzig, Breslau, Dresden, Elberfeld, etc. If
only the Catholic Church in Germany might be severed from Rome, what vast
bearings the event must have, at the present crisis, on the history of Christianity! Still, the whole movement as yet needs to be regarded and spoken of with
caution. We know too little of its moral constitution, its secret principles and
reigning spirit, to speak of it with much confidence. Let us hope that we shall
soon be permitted to look upon it through the medium of a proper critical
review on the part of the evangelical press in Germany itself. It is certainly
very precipitate, to say the least, for our religious papers, on the authority of
the notoriously rationalistic correspondence of the New York *Schnellpost*, to
glorify Johannes Ronge at once as a second Huss or Luther. His second letter
furnishes painful evidence that he stands in the element of a widely different
spirit. To say nothing of the air of self-reliance which runs through the whole
article, what must we think of the Christianity of a man, who can say,
"Humanity is the Church of God, and in it rules the Spirit; to this church I
am sworn"? Is not this the very cant of rationalism itself? The whole movement however is deeply interesting, in this view at least, that it serves to
show the force with which the spirit of the age, even in the Church of Rome
itself, is struggling toward a new order of life. In such a case it is not strange
that much should seem dark and chaotic. But the Spirit of God, we may trust,
is moving on the face of the deep.—TRANSLATOR]

idea even among some of the old theologians, particularly with the prophetic monk Joachim of Fiore[105] in the twelfth century.* Among the moderns, H. Steffens (*Four Norwegians*) and H. E. Schmieder (*Introduction to the Holy Scriptures*) again bring it into view. Very recently, however, it has been clothed with new poetically scientific interest by the greatest living philosopher, who in the evening of his days has again come forth like the sun from behind the clouds, and is now pouring the last splendid rays of his genius from Berlin, over the philosophical horizon of Germany. Schelling closes his *Philosophy of Revelation*, promised in vain for twenty years past as the complement and crown of the negative system published in his youth, with a section on the great periods of the church. So far as I can recollect from his lectures, this is the amount of his view. The Lord chose three favorite disciples, who are to be regarded as types at the same time of as many stages of development for the church. Peter, the apostle of the Father, the New Testament Moses, or the representative of the principle of authority and law, answers in his personality and form of doctrine to the first stage of church history, the period of Catholicism, flowing over in the end to popery itself. Paul, the apostle of the Son, the New Testament Elias, the representative of the principle of movement and of the free justifying power of faith, is the type of Protestantism. Both stages, separately taken, are one-sided and incomplete. The principles of authority and freedom, law and gospel, hope and faith, must at last become united. The Roman Catholic Church, it is true, has like Peter denied her Lord by a threefold gradation in the way of apostasy; but she will one day yet go out and weep bitterly. Then will the Lord turn toward her with a look of compassion, and restore her again to confidence and trust. This will be, at the same time, the epoch of the final reconciliation of both communions. So united, they will form the ideal church, whose type is exhibited to us in the disciple that lay on Jesus' bosom, the apostle of the Holy Spirit, the apostle of that love which shall never fail, the law of freedom made perfect and complete in the gospel. To him corresponds, under the old economy, John the Baptist, in whose

---

* Compare on him, Neander's *Kirchengeschichte,* Band V, Abth. 1, pp. 291 ff.

person the rigor of the law and consolation of prophecy are united. As he immediately preceded the first appearance of Christ, like the dawn of morning, so also the revivification of the spirit of John the evangelist, in the church, will open the way directly for his second coming, to establish the church absolute and triumphant, in which law and freedom shall both be perfect in one and the results of all previous development appear conserved as the constituent elements of a higher and more glorious state. To this refers the mystical sense of Christ's word (John 21:22), where he speaks enigmatically of John's tarrying till his second coming.

Such is an outline of this prophetical speculation of Schelling. We mean not of course to endorse it as correct, though it is certainly ingenious and beautiful. But putting out of view all that may seem to be simply fancy, it still turns at least upon a great and most consoling truth as regards the church, to which, though in quite different form, the faith and hope of thousands upon thousands of Christians have been directed.*

May the nineteenth century, by a magnificent union, consummate the ever memorable Reformation of the sixteenth! May the New World, enwombing the life spirit of almost every nation of the Old, prove the birth soil of this new era for the church! As the distractions of Protestantism have been most painfully experienced here, so here also may the glorious work of bringing all the scattered members of Christ's Body into true catholic union be carried forward with the greatest zeal and soonest crowned with the great festival of reconciliation, transmitting its blessings in grateful love to the world we honor and love as our general fatherland.

---

* The reader is referred to substantially the same thought, presented by the celebrated church historian, Neander, at the close of the third edition of his *History of the Planting of the Christian Church.*

# . 6 .

## General Summary:
## Theses for the Time

THE FOLLOWING THESES have been added by the author, not for the purpose of presenting any new matter, but simply to furnish a clear synopsis of the leading thoughts exhibited in the treatise itself. Of course, to be fully understood, each proposition must be examined in the light of the connections in which it comes forward in the general work. If any should choose to disregard this admonition and undertake to hold up single propositions to reproach, according to the sound simply which they may carry to the ear of popular prejudice, in their separate form, it will be quite easy to fix upon the author the charge of heresy, in the most opposite directions. This low polemic trick can be practiced here without even the small amount of cleverness it calls for in ordinary cases. The author has himself furnished to its hand in these theses all the opportunity it could wish to do him wrong in this way. Can the trick itself, however, in such circumstances, cease to be either dishonorable or immoral?—TRANSLATOR

### INTRODUCTION

1. Every period of the church and of theology has its particular problem to solve; and every doctrine, in a measure every book also of the Bible, has its classic age in which it first comes to be

219

fully understood and appropriated by the consciousness of the Christian world.

2. The main question of *our* time concerns the nature of the church itself in its relation to the world and to single Christians.

### THE CHURCH IN GENERAL

3. The church is the Body of Jesus Christ. This expresses her communion with her Head, and also the relation of her members to one another.

4. In the first respect, she is an institution founded by Christ, proceeding from his loins and animated by his Spirit, for the glory of God and the salvation of man; through which alone, as its necessary organ, the revelation of God in Christ becomes effective in the history of the world. Hence out of the church, as there is no Christianity, there can be no salvation.

5. In the second respect, she is, like every other body, a living unity of different members; a communion in faith and love, visible as well as invisible, external as well as internal, of the most manifold individualities, gifts, and powers, pervaded with the same Spirit and serving the same end.

6. The definition implies further that as the life of the parents flows forward in the child, so the church also is the depository and continuation of the earthly human life of the Redeemer, in his threefold office of prophet, priest, and king.

7. Hence she possesses, like her Founder, a divine and human, an ideal and a real, a heavenly and an earthly nature; only with this difference, that in her militant stage, freedom from sin and error cannot be predicated of her in the same sense as of Christ; that is, she possesses the principle of holiness and the full truth, mixed however still with sin and error.

8. To the church belong, in the wider sense, all baptized persons, even though they may have fallen back to the world; in the narrower sense, however, such only as believe in Jesus Christ.

9. The relation of the church to the world, with its different spheres of science, art, government, and social life, is neither one of destruction on her part nor one of indifference; but the

object of it is that she should transfuse the world with the purifying power of her own divine life, and thus bring it at last to its
true and proper perfection.

10. The ultimate scope of history accordingly is this, that Christianity may become completely the same with nature, and the
world be formally organized as the kingdom of Christ; which
must involve the absolute identity of church and state, theology
and philosophy, worship and art, religion and morality; the state
of the renovated earth, in which God will be All in all.

11. In relation to single Christians, the church is the mother
from which they derive their religious life and to which they owe
therefore constant fidelity, gratitude, and obedience; she is the
power of the objective and general to which the subjective and
single should ever be subordinate.

12. Only in such regular and rational subordination can the
individual Christian be truly free; and his personal piety can as
little come to perfection apart from an inward and outward
communion with the life of the church, as a limb separated from
the body or a branch torn from the vine.

13. Christianity in itself is the *absolute* religion, and in this
view unsusceptible to improvement.

14. We must not confound with this, however, the *apprehension* and *appropriation* of Christianity in the consciousness of
mankind. This is a progressive process of development that will
reach its close only with the second coming of the Lord.

15. All historical progress then, in the case of the church, consists, not in going beyond Christianity itself, which could only be
to fall back to heathenism and Judaism, but in entering always
more and more (materially as well as formally) into the life
and doctrine of the Redeemer and in throwing off by this means,
always more and more, the elements of sin and error still remaining from the state of nature.

16. It is possible for the church to be in possession of a truth
and to live upon it, before it has come to be discerned in her
consciousness. So it was, for instance, with the doctrine of the
Trinity before the time of Athanasius, with the doctrine of divine grace and human freedom before Augustine, and with the
evangelical doctrine of justification during the Middle Ages.

Thus the child eats and drinks long before it has the knowledge of food, and walks before it is aware of the fact, much less *how* it walks.

17. The idea, unfolded in comprehensive and profound style particularly by the later German philosophy, that history involves a continual progress toward something better, by means of dialectic contrapositions (*Gegensaetze*), is substantially true and correct.

18. It must not be forgotten however, in connection with this, that there is a corresponding movement also on the part of evil toward that which is worse. Light and darkness, the wheat and the tares, grow together till their development shall become complete.

19. We must distinguish in the church accordingly between idea and manifestation. As to her idea, or as comprehended in Christ, she is already complete; in the way of manifestation, however, she passes—like every one of her members—outwardly and inwardly, through different stages of life, until the ideal enclosed in Christ shall be fully actualized in humanity and his body appear thus in the ripeness of complete manhood.

20. Such a process of growth is attended necessarily with certain diseases and crises, as well theoretical, in the form of heresies; as practical, in the form of schisms.

21. These diseases are to be referred partly to the remaining force of sin and error in the regenerate themselves, and partly to the unavoidable connection of the church with the still unchristian world, by means of which the corrupt elements of this last are always forcing their way into her communion.

22. They can never overthrow however the existence of the church. The church may fall down, sore wounded, divided and torn, without ceasing for this reason to be the Body of Christ. Through her humiliation gleams evermore the unwasting glory of her divine nature.

23. In the wise providence of God, all heresies and schisms serve only to bring the church to a clearer consciousness of her true vocation, a deeper apprehension of her faith, and a purer revelation of the power included in her life.

24. But the presence of disease in the body requires to the

same extent a remedial or curative process, that is, a reformation.

25. Protestantism consequently, in the true sense, belongs indispensably to the life of the church; being the reaction simply of her proper vitality, depressed but not destroyed, in opposition to the workings of disease in her system.

## THE REFORMATION

26. Protestantism runs through the entire history of the church, and will not cease till she is purged completely from all ungodly elements. So, for instance, Paul protested against Jewish legalism and pagan licentiousness as found insidiously at work in the first Christian communities; the Catholic Church of the first centuries, against the heresies and schisms of Ebionitism, Gnosticism, Montanism, Arianism, Pelagianism, Donatism, etc.

27. The grandest and most widely influential exhibition of Protestantism is presented to us under the formal constitution of a special church, in the Reformation of the sixteenth century, as originated, and in its deepest inward, and truly apostolic form, carried out and consummated by the German nation.

28. It is a jejune and narrow conception of this event, to look upon it as a restoration simply of the original state of the church, or a renewal of Augustinianism against the Pelagian system by which it had been supplanted.

29. Such a view proceeds on the fundamentally erroneous supposition that the religious life revealed in the person of Christ primarily, and by derivation from him in his apostles, has been fully actualized also from the beginning in the general mass of the church.

30. Rather, the Reformation must be viewed as an actual advance of the religious life and consciousness of the church, by means of a deeper apprehension of God's word, beyond all previous attainments of Christendom.

31. As little is the Reformation to be regarded as a revolutionary separation from the Catholic Church, holding connection at best perhaps with some fractionary sect of the Middle Ages, and only through this and the help of certain desperate historical leaps besides, reaching back to the age of the apostles.

32. This contracted view of Protestantism is not only unhistorical and unchurchly altogether, but conscious or unconscious treason at the same time to the Lord's promise that he would build his church upon a rock, and that the gates of hell should not prevail against it; as well as to his engagement: "Lo I am with you always even to the end of the world"; and to the apostolic word: "The church is the pillar and ground of the truth."

33. Rather, the Reformation is the greatest act of the Catholic Church itself, the full ripe fruit of all its better tendencies, particularly of the deep spiritual law conflicts of the Middle Period, which were as a schoolmaster toward the Protestant doctrine of justification.

34. The separation was produced, not by the will of the Reformers, but by the stiff-necked papacy, which like Judaism at the time of Christ, identifying itself in a fleshly way with the idea of the absolute church, refused to admit the onward movement.

35. Thus apprehended, Protestantism has as large an interest in the vast historical treasures of the previous period, as can be claimed rightfully by the Church of Rome. Hence the arguments drawn by Romanists from this quarter, and particularly from the Middle Ages—the proper cradle of the Reformation—have no application against our standpoint.

36. Equally false finally is the view, whether popular or philosophical, by which the Reformation is made to consist in the absolute emancipation of the Christian life subjectively considered from all church authority, and the exaltation of private judgment to the papal throne.

37. This view confounds with the Reformation itself the foul excrescences that revealed themselves along with it in the beginning, and the one-sided character of its development since.

38. On the contrary, it is quite clear from history that the Reformers aimed only at such liberty of faith and conscience and such independence of private judgment, as should involve a humble subjection of the natural will, which they held to be incapable of all good, to God's grace, and of the human reason to God's word. Indeed their opposition to the Roman traditions was

itself based on the conviction that they were the product of such reason sundered from the divine word.

39. The material or life principle of Protestantism is the doctrine of justification by grace alone, through the merits of Jesus Christ, by means of living faith; that is, the personal appropriation of Christ in the totality of the inner man.

40. This does not overthrow good works; rather they are rightly called for and made possible only in this way—with dependence however on faith, as being its necessary fruit, the subjective impression of the life of Christ, in opposition to Pelagianism which places works parallel with faith, or even above it.

41. The formal or knowledge principle of Protestantism is the sufficiency and unerring certainty of the holy Scriptures as the only norm of all-saving knowledge.

42. This does not overthrow the idea of church tradition, but simply makes it dependent on the written word, as the stream is upon the fountain—the necessary, ever-deepening onward flow of the sense of scripture itself, as it is carried forward in the consciousness of the Christian world; contrary to the Romanish dogma by which tradition, as the bearer of different contents altogether, is made coordinate with the Bible or even exalted above it.

43. These two principles, rightly apprehended, are only different, mutually supplementary sides of one and the same principle, and their living interpenetration forms the criterion of orthodox Protestantism.

44. Opposition to the Roman Catholic extreme, according to the general law of historical progress, led the Reformers to place the strongest emphasis on justification and faith, scripture and preaching; whence the possibility of a one-sided development in which holiness and love, tradition and sacrament, might not be allowed to come to their full rights.

45. Respect for the Reformation as a divine work in no way forbids the admission that it included some mixture of error and sin; as where God builds a church, the devil erects a chapel by its side.

46. In any view moreover the Reformation must be regarded as still incomplete. It needs yet its concluding act to unite what

has fallen asunder, to bring the subjective to a reconciliation with the objective.

47. Puritanism may be considered a sort of second reformation, called forth by the reappearance of Romanizing elements in the Anglican Church, and as such forms the basis to a great extent of American Protestantism, particularly in New England.

48. Its highest recommendation, bearing clearly a divine signature, is presented in its deep practical earnestness as it regards religion, and its zeal for personal piety, by which it has been more successful perhaps than any other section of the church, for a time, in the work of saving individual souls.

49. However, it falls far behind the German Reformation by its revolutionary, unhistorical, and consequently unchurchly character, and carries in itself no protection whatever against an indefinite subdivision of the church into separate atomistic sects. For having no conception at all of a historical development of Christianity, and with its negative attitude of blind irrational zeal toward its own past, it may be said to have armed its children with the same right and the same tendency, too, to treat its own authority with equal independence and contempt.

## THE PRESENT STATE OF THE CHURCH

50. Protestantism has formed the starting point and center of almost all important world movements in the history of the last three centuries, and constitutes now also the main interest of the time.

51. The history of Protestantism in the spheres of religion, science, art, and government, especially since the commencement of the eighteenth century, may be regarded as the development of the principle of *subjectivity,* the consciousness of *freedom.*

52. In this development, however, it has gradually become estranged to a great extent from its own original nature, and fallen over dialectically into its opposite, according to the general course of history.

53. Its grand maladies at this time are *rationalism* and *sectarism.*

54. Rationalism is one-sided *theoretic religious subjectivism* and its fullest and most perfect exhibition has taken place accordingly in Germany—the land of theory and science—and in the bosom of the Lutheran Church.

55. Sectarism is one-sided *practical religious subjectivism* and has found its classic ground within the territory of the Reformed Church, in the predominantly practical countries, England and America.

56. These two maladies of Protestantism stand in a relation to it similar to that of the papacy to Catholicism in the Middle Ages; that is, they have a conditional historical necessity and an outward connection with the system to which they adhere, but contradict nevertheless and caricature its inmost nature.

57. The secular interests—science, art, government, and social life—have become since the Reformation always more and more dissociated from the church, in whose service they stood though with unfree subjugation in the Middle Ages, and in this separate form are advanced to a high state of perfection.

58. This is a false position, since the idea of the kingdom of God requires that all divinely constituted forms and spheres of life should be brought to serve him in the most intimate alliance with religion, that God may be All in all.

59. The orthodox Protestantism of our day, with all its different character in other respects, is distinguished in common with rationalism and sectarism, particularly in this country, by the quality of one-sided subjectivity; only with the advantage of course of a large amount of personal piety.

60. Its great defect is the want of an adequate conception of the nature of the church and of its relation to the individual Christian on the one hand, and the general life of man on the other.

61. Hence proceeds, first, indifference toward sectarian, or at least denominational divisions, which are at war with the idea of the church as the Body of Christ.

62. Second, a want of respect for history, by which it is affected to fall back immediately and wholly upon the Scriptures without regard to the development of their contents in the life of the church as it has stood from the beginning.

63. Third, an undervaluation of the sacraments as objective institutions of the Lord, independent of individual views and states.

64. Fourth, a disproportionate esteem for the service of preaching, with a corresponding sacrifice in the case of the liturgy, the standing objective part of divine worship, in which the *whole congregation* is called to pour forth its religious life to God.

65. Fifth, a circumscribed conception of the all-pervading leaven-like nature of the gospel, involving an abstract separation of religion from the divinely established order of the world in other spheres.

66. To this must be added in the case of a number of denominations the fancy of their own perfection, an idea that *their* particular traditional style of religion can never be improved into anything better; which is a rejection of the Protestant principle of mobility and progress, and a virtual relapse accordingly into the ground error of the Romish Church.

67. From all this it is clear that the standpoint, and with it the wants of our time, is wholly different from that of the sixteenth century.

68. Our most immediate and most threatening danger is not now from the Church of Rome, but from the in part heterodox and antichristian, in part orthodox and pious, but always one-sided and false subjectivism, by which the rights of the church are wronged in our own midst; which however must itself be considered again as indirectly the most alarming aspect of the danger that does in fact threaten us on the side of Rome, since one extreme serves always to facilitate the triumph of another.

69. The redeeming tendency of the age therefore is not such as looks directly to the emancipation of the individual and subjective from the bonds of authority, as at the time of the Reformation, but it is that rather which regards the claims of the objective in the true idea of the church.

70. Not until Protestantism shall have repented of its own faults and healed its own wounds, may it expect to prevail finally over the Church of Rome.

71. As this duty has been thus far in a great measure neglected,

it is to be taken as a divine judgment in the case that popery has been enabled to make such formidable advances lately, especially in England and the United States.

72. Puseyism (with which of course we must not confound the spurious afterbirth of fantastic, hollow-hearted affectation, always to be expected in such a case) may be considered in its original intention and best tendency a well-meant, but insufficient and unsuccessful attempt to correct the ultra subjectivity of Protestantism.

73. In this view we have reason to rejoice in its appearance, as indicating on the part of the Protestant world a waking consciousness of the malady under which it labors in this direction, and serving also to promote right church feeling.

74. By its reverence for church antiquity it exerts a salutary influence against what may be viewed, as the reigning error of our time, a wild revolutionary zeal for liberty, coupled with a profane scorn of all that is holy in the experience of the past.

75. So also its stress laid upon forms exhibits a wholesome reaction against the irrational hyperspiritualism so common among even the best Protestants; which the doctrine of the resurrection alone, as taught in the Bible, is enough to prove fallacious.

76. Church forms serve two general purposes: first, they are for the lower stages of religious development conductors over into the life of the spirit; second, they are for the church at large the necessary utterance or corporealization of the spirit, in the view in which Oetinger's remark holds good: "Corporeity is the scope of God's ways."

77. All turns simply on this that the form be answerable to the contents and be actuated by the spirit. A formless spiritualism is no whit better than a spiritless formalism. The only right condition is a sound spirit within a sound body.

78. The grand defect of Puseyism, however, is its unprotestant character in not recognizing the importance of the Reformation and the idea of progress in the life of the church since.

79. It is for this reason only half-historical and half-catholic, since its sympathy and respect for the past life of the church stop short with the sixteenth century.

80. Its view of the church altogether is outward and mechani-

cal, excluding the conception of a living development through the successive periods of its history.

81.   This character appears particularly in its theory of episcopal succession, which is only a new form of the old pharisaic Judaism, and moreover makes the apostolicity of the church dependent on a historical inquiry (in the case of which besides no absolute certainty is possible), resting it thus on a wholly precarious human foundation.

82.   Puseyism is to be viewed then as nothing more than a simple reaction, which has served to bring to light the evils of ultra pseudo-Protestant individualism, but offers no remedy for it save the perilous alternative of falling back to a standpoint already surmounted in the way of religious progress.

83.   The true standpoint, all necessary for the wants of the time, is that of *Protestant Catholicism,* or genuine historical progress.

84.   This holds equally remote from unchurchly subjectivity and all Romanizing churchism, though it acknowledges and seeks to unite in itself the truth which lies at the ground of both these extremes.

85.   Occupying this conservative historical standpoint, from which the moving of God's Spirit is discerned in all periods of the church, we may not in the first place surrender anything essential of the positive acquisition secured by the Reformation, whether Lutheran or Reformed.

86.   Neither may we again absolutely negate the later development of Protestantism, not even rationalism and sectarism themselves, but must appropriate to ourselves rather the element of truth they contain, rejecting only the vast alloy of error from which it is to be extracted.

87.   Rationalism and sectarism possess historical right, so far as the principle of subjectivity, individuality, singleness, and independence can be said to be possessed of right; that is, so far as this comes not in contradiction to the principle of objectivity, generality, the church, authority, and law, so far then as it continues subordinate to these forces.

88.   Rationalism was a necessary schoolmaster for orthodox theology, destroying its groundless prejudices and compelling it

both to accept a more scientific form in general, and also in particular to allow the human, the earthly, the historical, in the the-anthropic nature of Christ and the church, to come more fully to its rights.

89. While however the earlier historico-critical rationalism has promoted a right understanding of the natural and historical in Christianity, this understanding in its case remains still but *half* true, since it has no organ for *ideas,* the inward life of which history after all is but the body.

90. The later speculative rationalism, or pantheistic mythologism, or the "Hegelingians" as they have been deridingly styled (Strauss and his colleagues), which from the Ebionitic standpoint of the old system has swung over to the opposite extreme of docetic Gnostic idealism, fails to apprehend the idea of Christianity in its full truth and vitality, and substitutes for it a phantom or mere shadow, since it has no organ for historical *reality,* the outward life without which after all the idea must perish.

91. As in the first centuries, the theology of the Catholic Church gradually developed itself through scientific struggles with the two ground heresies—Ebionism or christianizing Judaism, and Gnosticism or christianizing heathenism—so now also we are to look for a higher orthodoxy, overmastering inwardly both forms of Protestant rationalism, which shall bring the real and the ideal into the most intimate union and recognize in full as well as the eternal spirit of Christianity as its historical body.

92. The germs of all this are at hand in the later movements and achievements of the believing German theology, and need only a further development to issue at last in a full dogmatical reformation.

93. Separation, where it is characterized by religious life, springs almost always from some real evil in the state of the church, and hence sectarism is to be regarded as a necessary disciplinarian and reformer of the church in its practical life.

94. Almost every sect represents in strong relief some single particular aspect of piety, and contributes to the fuller evolution of individual religious activity.

95. Since however the truths of the gospel form an inseparable unity, and the single member can become complete only along

with the whole body of which it is a part, it follows that no sect can ever do justice fully even to the single interest to which it is one-sidedly devoted.

96. Sects then owe it to themselves, as soon as they have fulfilled their historical vocation, to fall back to the general church communion from which they have seceded, as in no other way can their spiritual acquisitions be either completed or secured, and they must themselves otherwise stiffen into monumental petrifactions, never to be revisited with the warm life pulse of the one universal church.

97. It is a cheering sign of the time that in the most different Protestant lands, and particularly in the bosom of the Reformed Church, in which religious individualism both in the good and in the bad sense has been most fully developed, it is coming to be felt more and more that the existing divisions of the church are wrong, and with this is waking more and more an earnest longing after a true union of all believers, in no communication whatever with the errors either of Oxford or Rome.

98. Finally, also, the liberation of the secular spheres of life from the church since the Reformation, though not the ultimate normal order, forms—notwithstanding as compared with the previous vassalage of the world to a despotic hierarchy—an advance in the naturalization process of Christianity.

99. The luxuriant separate growth of these interests, as unfolded in the Protestant states, sciences, arts, and social culture, lays the church under obligation to appropriate these advances to herself, and impress upon them a religious character.

100. The signs of the time, then, and the teachings of history point us not backward, but forward to a new era of the church that may be expected to evolve itself gradually from the present process of fermentation, enriched with the entire positive gain of Protestantism.

101. As the movement of history in the church is like that of the sun from east to west, it is possible that America, into whose broad majestic bosom the most various elements of character and education are poured from the Old World, may prove the theater of this unitive reformation.

102. Thus far, if we put out of view the rise of a few insignificant sects and the separation of church and state, which to be sure has very momentous bearings, American church history has produced nothing original, no new *fact* in the history of the church as a whole.

103. Nowhere else however is there at present the same favorable room for further development, since in no country of the Old World does the church enjoy such entire freedom, or the same power to renovate itself from within according to its own pleasure.

104. The historical progress of the church is always conditioned by the national elements, which form its physical basis.

105. The two leading nationalities, which are continually coming into contact in this country, and flowing into one another with reciprocal action, are the English and the German.

106. The further advancement of the American church, consequently, must proceed mainly from a special combination of German depth and *Gemuetlichkeit* with the force of character and active practical talent, for which the English are distinguished.

107. It would be a rich offering then to the service of this approaching reformation, on the part of the German Churches in America, to transplant hither in proper measure the rich wealth of the better German theology, improving it into such form as our peculiar relations might require.

108. This their proper vocation however they have thus far almost entirely overlooked, seeking their salvation for the most part in a characterless surrender of their own nationality.

109. In view of the particular constitution of a large part of the German immigration, this subjection to the power of a foreign life may be regarded indeed as salutary.

110. But the time has now come, when our churches should again rise out of the ashes of the old German Adam, enriched and refined with the advantages of the English nationality.

111. What we most need now is, theoretically, a thorough, intellectual theology, scientifically free as well as decidedly believing, together with a genuine sense for history; and practically, a determination to hold fast the patrimony of our fathers and to go forward joyfully at the same time in the way in which God's Spirit

by providential signs may lead, with a proper humble subordination of all we do for our own denomination to the general interest of the one universal church.

112. The ultimate, sure scope of the church, toward which the inmost wish and most earnest prayer of all her true friends continually tend, is that perfect and glorious unity, the desire of which may be said to constitute the burden of our Lord's last, memorable, intercessory prayer.

Editors' Notes

---

## EDITORS' PREFACE

1. *The Acts and Proceedings of the Synod of the German Reformed Church* at Allentown, Lehigh Co., Pa., 1844 (Chambersburg, 1844), p. 5.

2. Schaff's manuscripts prepared in Germany prior to his arrival in America illustrate that he spelled his name inconsistently as "Schaff," and "Schaf."

Philip Schaff (1819-1893) was born in the town of Chur, Switzerland, of humble parentage. He was educated in Germany at the universities of Tübingen, Halle, and Berlin. At the age of twenty-five, he was elected professor of biblical literature and ecclesiastical history in the Theological Seminary of the German Reformed Church, Mercersburg, Pa. During the Civil War, Mercersburg, situated just a few miles north of the Mason-Dixon line, suffered raids by Confederate cavalry and the Seminary was temporarily closed in 1863. Schaff then moved to New York City to become secretary of the Sabbath Committee. In 1870 he was elected a professor at Union Theological Seminary, and held the chair of church history until his death. See David S. Schaff, *The Life of Philip Schaff* (New York: Scribner, 1897).

3. *The Acts and Proceedings, op. cit.,* p. 26.

4. The Seminary of the German Reformed Church was founded

in 1825 on the campus of Dickinson College, Carlisle, Pa. Because of "incompatibility of temperament" between the two schools, the Seminary moved to York, Pa. in 1829, and a high school or preparatory classical department was added to the curriculum. The preparatory school moved to Mercersburg, Pa. in 1835 and the following year was chartered as Marshall College by the State of Pennsylvania. Since the charter of the Seminary stated that it was to be permanently located in York, the removal of that institution to Mercersburg was delayed until the fall of 1837. After the merger of Franklin College (Lancaster, Pa.) and Marshall College to form Franklin and Marshall College on the Lancaster campus in 1853, the Seminary remained in Mercersburg until 1871, when it also moved to Lancaster.

The corporate name of the institution at the present time is "The Lancaster Theological Seminary of the United Church of Christ." See George W. Richards, *History of the Theological Seminary of the Evangelical and Reformed Church at Lancaster, Pennsylvania* (Lancaster, 1952), pp. 129 ff.

5. *Weekly Messenger,* Nov. 20, 1844, p. 1913.

6. See *The Acts and Proceedings of the Synod of the German Reformed Church* at Greencastle, Pa., October 1840 (Chambersburg, 1840), pp. 25-26.

7. B. C. Wolff, *A Sermon Delivered at the Opening of the Synod of the German Reformed Church at Reading, Pa.,* October 21, 1841 (Chambersburg, 1841), pp. 4-12. (Appended to *The Acts and Proceedings* of 1841.)

8. John Williamson Nevin (1803-1886) was born on a farm near Shippensburg, Cumberland County, Pennsylvania, in a staid Scotch-Irish Presbyterian settlement. Educated at Union College and Princeton Theological Seminary, he became professor of Hebrew and biblical literature at Western Theological Seminary (Presbyterian), Pittsburgh, Pa. in 1829. He was called to the Theological Seminary of the German Reformed Church, Mercersburg, Pa. in 1840. He became the honored colleague of Philip Schaff at that institution and one of the founders of the Mercersburg theology. His writings have been called "one of the first significant American contributions to the history of theology." See James Hastings Nichols, *Romanticism in American Theology: Nevin and Schaff at Mercersburg* (Chicago: University of Chicago Press, 1961); Theodore Appel, *The Life and Work of John Williamson Nevin* (Philadelphia: Reformed Church Publication House, 1889).

9. *Addresses Delivered at the Inauguration of Rev. J. W. Nevin,*

*D.D.*, Mercersburg, Pa., May 20, 1840 (Chambersburg, 1840), p. 24.

10. *The Acts and Proceedings of the Synod of the German Reformed Church* at Allentown, Lehigh Co., Pa., 1844 (Chambersburg, 1844), p. 34.

11. *The Acts and Proceedings of the Synod of the German Reformed Church* at Greencastle, Pa., October 1840 (Chambersburg, 1840), pp. 75-83.

12. *Ibid.*, pp. 77-78.

13. Nevin's important articles on the Heidelberg Catechism were carried by the *Weekly Messenger*, beginning Dec. 9, 1840 (p. 1085), and extending to Aug. 10, 1842.

14. Judging mainly from the Mayer Liturgy. See *Liturgy for the Use of the Congregations of the German Reformed Church in the United States of North America.* Approved by the Synod of said Church (Chambersburg, 1841), pp. 52-71.

15. *The Constitution of the German Reformed Church in the United States of North America,* adopted by the Synod in 1846 (Chambersburg: Kieffer, 1850), p. 44. ("The Sacrament of the Lord's Supper shall be administered in every congregation where it is practicable twice a year and oftener.")

16. See Bard Thompson, "The Catechism and the Mercersburg Theology," *Essays on the Heidelberg Catechism* (Philadelphia: United Church Press, 1963), pp. 53-74.

17. *The Acts and Proceedings of the Synod of the German Reformed Church* at Allentown, Lehigh Co., Pa., 1844 (Chambersburg, 1844), p. 28.

18. "A true revival" was certainly the ideal of Nevin in his first edition of *The Anxious Bench* (1843).

19. The text of the Church Order is given in: Wilhelm Niesel (ed.), *Bekenntnisschriften und Kirchenordnungen der nach Gottes Wort reformierten Kirche* (Zollikon—Zurich: Evangelischer Verlag, 1938), pp. 136-218.

20. J. P. Perrin, *Histoire des Vaudois* (Geneva, 1619); translated into English as *History of the Old Waldensians* (New York: Mason, 1843).

21. *Weekly Messenger,* Feb. 2, 1842, p. 1324.

22. See the *Weekly Messenger,* Jan. 27, 1841; Nov. 11, 1840; Sept. 15, 1841. Note the Zwinglian character of the Mayer Liturgy.

23. *A Sermon Delivered at the Opening of the Synod* (1841), p. 10.

24. See "Does the Roman Catholic Church Constitute Any Part of the Church of Christ?" *Weekly Messenger,* Jan. 12, Feb. 2, 16, 1842, pp. 1315, 1324, 1334. See James Hastings Nichols, *Romanticism in American Theology: Nevin and Schaff at Mercersburg* (Chicago: University of Chicago Press, 1961), pp. 169 ff.

25. *Weekly Messenger,* Nov. 25, 1840, p. 1079.

26. Joseph F. Berg, *The Old Paths* (Philadelphia, 1846), p. viii.

27. See *The Principle of Protestantism,* thesis 31.

28. See *The Principle of Protestantism,* p. 73.

29. Philip Schaff, *What Is Church History?* (Philadelphia: Lippincott, 1846), pp. 80 ff.

30. *Ibid.,* pp. 75-77.

31. *The Acts and Proceedings of the Synod of the German Reformed Church* at York, York Co., Pa., October 1845 (Chambersburg, 1845), pp. 72-91.

## INTRODUCTION: JOHN W. NEVIN

1. Development, evolution.

2. Schaff was ordained on April 12, 1844 in the Reformed Church at Elberfeld, at which the distinguished Friedrich Wilhelm Krummacher (1796-1868) preached. Following Dr. Krummacher's remarks in which he admonished the young scholar to go to America "as the bearer of a pure German national spirit" to rescue the Germans in that land from "the many-headed monster of pantheism and atheism, issuing from the sphere of German speculation," Schaff preached a sermon on "The Macedonian Call," Acts 16:9. In the sermon he pictured the deplorable religious condition of the Germans in America, a view held generally by the leaders of the German Church. Printed copies of the sermon reached America about the same time that Schaff did, and brought down upon him immediately virulent attacks from the German-American press. The tenor of the sermon can be seen from the following quotation from the English translation:

> Fix your attention . . . closely on yonder man [the German Christian in the United States] and give earnest heed to his words. He is well prepared to support his plea, *Come over and help us,* with such reasons as ye cannot disregard, if ye be Christians, German Evangelical Christians. He tells you of a threefold abyss, on the verge of which he stands giddy, and into which he is likely to fall, without your timely help. Heathenism, Romanism, Sectarism— these are the three foes that press upon him from every quarter and

that will assuredly swallow up his life, if ye place not arms in his hands, and skillful soldiers at his side, without delay.

See David S. Schaff, *The Life of Philip Schaff* (New York: Scribner, 1897) , pp. 79 ff.; "Ordination of Professor Schaf," an article in the *Weekly Messenger,* Wednesday, September 4, 1844, p. 1869, translated from Krummacher's *Palmblaetter.* See the bibliography of this book, No. 29.

3. See *Weekly Messenger,* Wednesday, September 4, 1844, p. 1869.

4. See John W. Nevin, *The Mystical Presence* (Philadelphia: Lippincott, 1846) , Ch. 2, Sec. 4.

5. See J. H. S. Burleigh, *A Church History of Scotland* (Oxford: Oxford University Press, 1960) , pp. 281 ff.

6. George Bush (1796-1859) , esteemed Hebrew scholar and orientalist, onetime instructor in Union Theological Seminary, New York (1836-37) . In 1845 Bush associated himself with the Swedenborgians. His *Anastasis* (New York and London: Wiley & Putnam, 1845) repudiated the traditional doctrine of the resurrection of the body. In *The Soul* (New York: Redfield, 1845) , he wrote: "We hope to show that . . . the soul is the real man, and that he begins to live at once after death in the full integrity of his true manhood" (p. 19) . See *The New Schaff-Herzog Encyclopedia of Religious Knowledge* (1908 ed.) , II, 318.

7. See note 6 above.

8. Christoph Friedrich von Ammon (1766-1850) , German rationalistic theologian, accomplished scholar in many fields, and influential official in church and state. See *The New Schaff-Herzog Encyclopedia of Religious Knowledge* (1908 ed.) , I, 155.

9. Both Nevin and Schaff were influenced by the distinguished German church historian Johann August Wilhelm Neander (1789-1850) . Schaff, who studied under Neander at the University of Berlin, called him the father of modern church history. In a reply to a letter sent to Schaff by the theological faculty of the University of Berlin on the occasion of the fiftieth anniversary of his academic teaching, he wrote:

Dr. Neander—that Christian Israelite without guile, who was led by Moses and Plato to Jesus the Messiah—attracted me still more by his original personality, his childlike simplicity, his evangelical catholicity, and his deep spiritual insight into the religious and moral forces of history. He wrote in my album the Pauline motto: **"Theologica crucis, non gloriae."**

See David S. Schaff, *The Life of Philip Schaff* (New York: Scribner, 1897), pp. 164 ff.; *Berlin 1842-New York 1892, the Semi-Centennial of Philip Schaff* (New York: Privately printed, 1893), p. 16. See also the bibliography of this book, Nos. 52, 53, 86, 87, 91.

10. See the Editors' Preface to this book.


## PART ONE

1. Schaff is probably referring to Mechtildis of Magdeburg (ca. 1212-1280) who belonged to the famous school of mystics at the convent of Helfta in Saxony.

2. Schaff is not referring to the theologian Arminius, but to Arminius (18 B.C.-A.D. 17), chief of the Cherusci, who thwarted the Roman conquest of Germany. See Tacitus, *Ann.* 1-2.

3. German humanist, nationalist (1488-1523), literary champion of German nationalism in the early Lutheran Reformation. See E. G. Schwiebert, *Luther and His Times* (St. Louis: Concordia, 1950), pp. 550 ff.

4. Noted German Lutheran poet of Nuremberg (1494-1576). See *The New Schaff-Herzog Encyclopedia of Religious Knowledge* (1908 ed.), X, 138-39.

5. Franz von Sickingen (1481-1523), German Knight and would-be protector of Luther; leader of the Knights' Uprising in 1522-23. See E. G. Schwiebert, *Luther and His Times* (St. Louis: Concordia, 1950), pp. 550 ff.

6. Florentine scholar (1433-1499), member of the celebrated Platonic Academy of Florence. See E. Cassirer, P. O. Kristeller, J. H. Randall, Jr. (eds.), *The Renaissance Philosophy of Man* (University of Chicago Press, 1948), pp. 185-92.

7. The Albigensians, Bogomiles, and Cathari were Manichaean sects of the Middle Ages. See "The New Manicheans," *The New Schaff-Herzog Religious Encyclopedia* (1908 ed.), VIII, 143-47. The Beguines and Beghards designate respectively male and female communities, semimonastic in nature, which arose apparently in the twelfth century and represented the general mendicant piety of the era. They were persecuted as heretics, owing largely to their association (supposed and real) with unconventional parties in the church.

8. Preacher of "apostolic poverty" who was executed in 1155 for his repeated attacks upon the riches and temporal power of the church.

9. Paris theologian (d. 1204); his intellectual development led

him finally to pantheism, of which he was forced to recant by Innocent III.

10. French theologian (d. after 1215); his pantheistic system was condemned by provincial council, Paris, 1210.

11. I.e., Brethren of the Common Life.

12. See B. J. Kidd, *The Counter-Reformation* (London: SPCK, 1933), pp. 11 ff.

13. Perhaps better known as *Theologia Germanica*. See the edition by Joseph Bernard (New York: Pantheon, 1949). For Luther's interest in this book, see J. MacKinnon, *Luther and the Reformation* (New York: Longmans, Green, & Co., 1925), I, 212-35.

14. French theologian and ecclesiastical statesman (1367-1437), colleague of d'Ailly and Gerson, author of numerous treatises dealing with the errors and conceptions of the church.

15. French theologian (1350-1420), chancellor of the University of Paris, later bishop of Cambrai and cardinal; his conciliar views are treated by M. Spinka in *Advocates of Reform: Library of Christian Classics*, XIV, 91-105.

16. Better known perhaps as Wessel Gansfort. See E. W. Miller and J. W. Scudder, *Wessel Gansfort: Life and Writings* (2 vols.; New York/London, 1917).

17. In English: Carl Ullmann, *Reformers Before the Reformation* (2 vols., 4th ed.; Edinburgh: Clark, 1872-74).

18. See G. H. Williams, *The Radical Reformation* (Philadelphia: Westminster, 1962), Chs. 22-29.

19. Roman Catholic theologians and teachers of the early nineteenth century with strong evangelical and reforming tendencies. Consult appropriate volumes in *The New Schaff-Herzog Encyclopedia of Religious Knowledge* (1908 ed.).

20. Bruno Bauer (1809-1882), biblical critic; his radical application of Hegelian principles led to his dismissal from Bonn in 1842. See *The New Schaff-Herzog Religious Encyclopedia* (1908 ed.), II, 5.

21. Schaff apparently refers to the dogmatic constitution "Unigenitus" of September 1713. It was directed against Jansenism in general, and the errors of Paschasius Quesnel in particular. Cf. Carl Mirbt, *Quellen zur Geschichte des Papsttums und des Römischen Katholizismus* (4th ed.; Tübingen: Mohr, 1924), pp. 395-99.

22. Johann Baptist Hirscher (1788-1865), Roman Catholic theologian, professor of pastoral theology at Freiburg, 1834-63.

23. The editors have not been able to verify this specific passage. A comparable statement is found in Melanchthon's *Loci praecipui*

*theologici* of 1559, under the heading "De vocabulo fidei." See *Melanchthons Werke in Auswahl,* II/2 (Gütersloh: Bertelsmann, 1953) , 371.

24. Paolo Sarpi in his *History of the Council of Trent* (London, 1619; Eng. trans., 1676) .

25. Ernst Wilhelm Christian Sartorius (1797-1859) , German Lutheran theologian who defended the doctrine of the Augsburg Confession against both German rationalism and Roman Catholicism.

26. See Luther's *Church Postil;* Gospel for the 20th Sunday After Trinity.

27. Preface to the Wittenberg edition of *Luthers Werke* (1545) ; Weimar Ausgabe, LIV, 185 f.

28. Martin Chemnitz (1522-1586) , Lutheran theologian and controversialist. His *Examinis Concilii Tridentini* (1565-73) was one of the most formidable attacks upon Roman claims. For his part in the Formula of Concord, see Philip Schaff, *Creeds of Christendom,* Vol. I, Sec. 45.

29. Albertus Pighius (1490-1542) , Roman Catholic controversialist. In his principal work, *Hierarchiae ecclesiasticae assertio,* he gave a comprehensive defense of the papal system, and openly asserted the authority of tradition alongside of scripture.

30. William Damasus Lindanus (1525-1588) , Roman Catholic bishop and inquisitor of the Low Countries. The writing referred to is *De optimo scripturas interpretandi genere* (Cologne, 1558) .

31. Leander van Ess (1772-1847) . See *The New Schaff-Herzog Religious Encyclopedia* (1908 ed.) , IV, 178.

32. Council of Toulouse, 1229. See J. D. Mansi, *Sacrorum Conciliorum nova et amplissima collectio* (Florence, 1759-98) , XXIII, 197.

33. Council of Tarragona, 1234. See J. D. Mansi, *Sacrorum Conciliorum nova et amplissima collectio* (Florence, 1759-98) , XXIII, 329.

34.    Johann Adam Moehler (1796-1838) , Roman Catholic historian, professor in Tübingen, and then in Munich; author of the noted *Symbolik oder Darstellung der dogmatischen Gegensätze der Katholiken und Protestanten* (1832) .

35. Vincent of Lérins (flourished ca. 450) . The quotation ("which is believed everywhere, always, and by all") is from Vincent's *Commonitorium.*

36. The illustrations following are discussed briefly, but with further documentation, in B. J. Kidd, *The Counter-Reformation* (London: SPCK, 1933, 1937) , pp. 59 ff.

37. Council of Constantinople; held in 754 at the insistence of the

Emperor Constantine Copronymos; consisted of 338 oriental bishops; no patriarch was present, nor any delegates from the great sees of Rome, Alexandria, Antioch, and Jerusalem; assumed the title ecumenical, but the Council of Nicaea II (787) is usually accorded "Ecumenical VII." See Schaff, *History of the Christian Church* (New York: Scribner, 1891) IV, 454-64.

38. These references are to the Formula of Concord. The pages noted correspond to Carolus Augustus Hase, *Libri Symbolici* (Leipzig, 1837).

39. I.e., Karl Daub (1765-1836), professor of theology at Heidelberg.

40. See note 28 above.

41. *Examinis Concilii Tridentini* (Francofurti, 1606), Part I, p. 135, lines 37 f.

42. Council of Trent, Session 4: Decretum de editione et usu sacrorum librorum. See Carl Mirbt, *Quellen zur Geschichte des Papsttums und des Römischen Katholizismus* (4th ed.; Tübingen: Mohr, 1924), p. 292.

43. I.e., Johann Gerhard (1582-1637), Lutheran dogmatician.

44. See note 34 above.

45. *Against Heresies*, V, xxxiii, 4.

46. Spanish Dominican (1500-1563), Catholic controversialist, writer of compendia and catechisms, professor of theology in Oxford during the reign of Mary Tudor, active participant in later sessions of the Council of Trent.

47. See *Luthers Werke*. Weimar Ausgabe XXX:3, 547 f.

48. Johannes Andreas Quenstedt (1617-1688), Lutheran dogmatician. See Robert Preus, *The Inspiration of Scripture: A Study of the Seventeenth Century Lutheran Dogmaticians* (Mankato, Minn.: Lutheran Synod Book Co., 1955); bibliography, pp. 212-16.

49. Karl Immanuel Nitzsch (1787-1868), German Protestant, prominent representative of the mediating theology.

50. Followers of Astemon or Artemas (ca. 235?), hence adoptionists or dynamic monarchians.

51. The teachings of Georg Hermes (1775-1831), German Catholic theologian, who taught, in prejudice to the Catholic view of authority, that "a man can believe only that which he has recognized as true from evidence furnished by his reason." His teachings were condemned by a papal brief of 1835. See *The New Schaff-Herzog Religious Encyclopedia* (1908 ed.), V, 242-43.

PART TWO

1. Johann Adam Moehler (1796-1838), Roman Catholic historian, professor in Tübingen, and then in Munich; author of the noted *Symbolik, oder, Darstellung der dogmatischen Gegensätze der Katholiken und Protestanten* (1832).

2. Johann Josef von Goerres (1776-1848), political essayist, authority in German literature. Associated with J. J. I. Doellinger and J. A. Moehler at Munich.

3. Schaff is apparently referring to the works of Jakob Boehme (1575-1624) and Johann Arndt (1555-1621).

4. See Robert Preus, *The Inspiration of Scripture: A Study of the Seventeenth Century Lutheran Dogmaticians* (Mankato, Minn.: Lutheran Synod Book Co., 1955); bibliography, pp. 212-16.

5. On this point, see Philip Schaff, *Creeds of Christendom*, Vol. I, Sec. 45.

6. I.e., German Pietism, the teachings of Philip Jakob Spener. See John T. McNeill, *Modern Christian Movements* (Philadelphia: Westminster, 1954), Ch. 2.

7. In the German text *Das Princip des Protestantism*, Schaff uses the term "Brüdergemeinde." He is apparently referring, not to the American sect United Brethren, but to the Moravian Brethren.

8. Johann Albrecht Bengel (1687-1752), a leading figure of the liberal Pietism of Württemberg, whose major work was done in New Testament study, text and exegesis; his *Apparatus Criticus* became the starting point for modern textual criticism of the New Testament. See J. C. F. Burk, *A Memoir of the Life and Writings of John Bengel;* trans. by R. F. Walker (London, 1837).

9. Johann Salomo Semler (1725-1791), professor of theology at Halle (1752), a pioneer in biblical criticism. See Carl Mirbt, "Semler," *The New Schaff-Herzog Encyclopedia of Religious Knowledge* (1908 ed.), X, 354-55.

10. Christian Wolff (1679-1754), German philosopher, founder of the influential Wolffian School, professor at Halle until he was driven away in 1723 by pietistic opponents; in 1740 Frederick the Great called him back to Halle with honor and he taught there until his death. On his philosophical and theological views, see W. Windelband, *A History of Philosophy* (New York: Macmillan, 1950), pp. 460 ff.

11. Bruno Bauer (1809-1882), biblical critic; his radical application of Hegelian principles led to his dismissal from Bonn in 1842.

See *The New Schaff-Herzog Encyclopedia of Religious Knowledge* (1908 ed.), II, 5.

12. Johann Friedrich Roehr (1777-1848), German Lutheran theologian of the rationalistic school, chief pastor at Weimar (1820).

13. Julius August Ludwig Wegscheider (1771-1849), German rationalistic theologian, professor of theology in Halle (1810).

14. See note 1 above.

15. Dionysius Petavius (Denis Pétau: 1583-1652), French Jesuit, professor of theology at Paris (1621-44). One of his major works was avowedly antischolastic: *De theologicis dogmaticis* (5 vols.; Paris, 1644-50).

16. Richard Simon (1638-1712), French Roman Catholic biblical scholar. Eberhard Nestle has referred to Simon as "the real founder of biblical criticism." See *The New Schaff-Herzog Encyclopedia of Religious Knowledge* (1908 ed.), X, 422.

17. Karl Friedrich Bahrdt (1741-1792), a brilliant, dissolute assailant of all belief in revealed religion. His *System der moralischen Religion* (Berlin, 1787) advocates open naturalism.

18. Johann Christian Edelmann (1698-1767), German rationalist who denied the Bible as revelation, repudiated all formal religious bodies, and tried to base religion on nature and human thought.

19. *Der Licht-Freund,* a semimonthly German newspaper founded in Cincinnati, Ohio, in 1840, by Eduard Muehl and Karl Strehly. The editors moved it to Hermann, Mo., in 1843 and changed its name to *Freimanner Wochenblatt* in 1845. It carried a subtitle *Organ des Freisinnigen Deutschthums* and also organ of *Verein Freier Männer.* An incomplete file is held by the Concordia Historical Institute, St. Louis. See Karl J. R. Arndt and May E. Olson, *German-American Newspapers and Periodicals, 1732-1955* (Heidelberg: Quelle & Meyer, 1961), p. 240.

20. *Die Fackel* was published continually from 1843 to 1869. The place of publication varied. The periodical was a highly personal journal of the editor, Samuel Ludvigh, a noted, radical rationalist. He traveled extensively as a tireless missionary of free thought and anticlericalism. *Die Fackel* was read all over the nation and abroad by a select group of followers. A nearly complete file can be found among the holdings of the following libraries in Baltimore: Enoch Pratt Free Library, Society for the History of Germans in Maryland, Archives of Zion's Church. See Karl J. R. Arndt and May E. Olson, *German-American Newspapers and Periodicals, 1732-1955* (Heidelberg: Quelle & Meyer, 1961), p. 189.

21. Jakob Boehme (1575-1624), German Protestant mystic, a Görlitz shoemaker by trade.

22. John Kepler (1571-1630), German scientist, one of the founders of modern astronomy.

23. For a brief review, see John T. McNeill, *Modern Christian Movements* (Philadelphia: Westminster, 1954), Ch. 4, "The Tractarianism and Anglo-Catholicism" (bibliography, pp. 183-85). Cf. J. W. Nevin, "The Anglican Crisis," *Mercersburg Review* (1851), III, 359-98.

24. Benjamin Treadwell Onderdonk (1791-1861), Protestant Episcopal bishop of New York, supporter of the Tractarian movement in the American church, who prescribed the ordination of Arthur Carey in 1843, although an examining board had refused him ordination because of his Romish views. See E. Clowes Chorley, *Men and Movements in the American Episcopal Church* (New York: Scribner, 1946), pp. 207 ff.

25. See note 24 above.

26. Smith and Anthon were members of a special examining committee in the Carey affair. They reported their views in the pamphlet, Drs. [Hugh] Smith and [Henry] Anthon, *The True Issue for the True Churchman: A Statement of Facts in Relation to the Recent Ordination in St. Stephen's Church, New York* (New York: Harper & Brothers, 1843).

27. Lutheran dogmatician (1612-1686), professor at Wittenburg. His *Systema locorum theologicorum* (12 vols., 1655-77), based on the Formula of Concord, was one of the important dogmatic productions of the seventeenth century.

28. Lutheran theologian (1673-1749), superintendent at Dresden (1709). Loescher became leader of the orthodox party in the Lutheran Church, as opposed to its pietistic and naturalistic factions.

29. Heinrich Eberhard Gottlob Paulus (1761-1851), professor of biblical exegesis at Heidelberg (1811-44).

30. Fra Angelico (1387-1455), Dominican friar and Florentine painter.

31. Baccio della Porta, called Fra Bartolomeo di San Marco (1469-1517); celebrated Italian painter.

32. Pietro Perugino (1446-1524), Italian painter immediately preceding the era of Leonardo da Vinci and Raphael.

33. Erwin of Steinbach (d. 1318), architect of Strasbourg Cathedral.

34. Bramante or Bramante Lazzari (1444-1514), celebrated Italian

architect who was commissioned by Pope Julius II to make the design for St. Peter's Basilica.

35. Distinguished German men of letters: Johann Gottfried von Herder (1744-1803), a contemporary of Lessing; Christopher Martin Wieland (1733-1813); Ludwig Tieck (1773-1853), a conspicuous figure in the German romantic school; Friedrich von Hardenberg (1772-1801), better known as Novalis, a poet and philosopher, often called "the prophet of the romantic school"; August Wilhelm von Schlegel (1767-1845), German poet, translator, critic; and his brother, Karl Wilhelm Friedrich von Schlegel (1772-1829), historian of literature. Both Schlegels were leaders of the rising romantic school.

36. Justus Moeser (1720-1794), German historian and economist; Johann von Mueller (1752-1809), eminent Swiss historian; Heinrich Leo (1799-1878), German historian whose interests extended to politics and literature.

37. Bertel Thorwaldsen (1770-1844), Danish sculptor who made the colossal statues of Christ and the apostles which are now in the Fruenkirche in Copenhagen.

38. Johann Friedrich Overbeck (1789-1869), German painter, prominent figure in the nineteenth-century revival of Christian art.

39. Peter von Cornelius (1784-1867), German painter, leader of German art revival in the nineteenth century, by whom the academy at Düsseldorf was reorganized.

40. Wilhelm von Kaulbach (1805-1874), German painter, associated mainly with the city of Munich; celebrated for his murals.

41. Roman Catholic scholars in Germany. The editors have been able to identify the following: Johann Leonhard Hug (1765-1846), biblical scholar at Freiburg. Johann Adam Moehler (1796-1838), distinguished church historian at Tübingen (1823-35). Johann Sebastian von Drey (1777-1853), professor of theology at Tübingen (1817-46); his principal work was in apologetics. Johann Baptist Hirscher (1788-1865), professor of moral and pastoral theology at Tübingen (1817-34) and Freiburg (1834-63). Franz Anton Staudenmaier (1800-1856), professor of theology at Giessen (1830), author of *Die Christliche Dogmatik* in 4 vols. (1844-52). Anton Guenther (1783-1863), Jesuit theologian and philosopher.

42. Franz Volkmar Reinhard (1753-1812), German Lutheran theologian and preacher, a leader of the supernaturalistic school.

43. Gottlob Christian Storr (1746-1805), founder of the so-called older Tübingen school—a tradition characterized by "biblical supernaturalism."

44. Probably Heinrich August Schott (1780-1835), German Lutheran theologian, at Jena after 1812.

45. Christoph Friedrich von Ammon (1766-1850), German theologian of varied career and vacillating opinions with decided rationalistic leanings.

46. Karl Gottlieb Bretschneider (1776-1848), German theologian whose standpoint was the so-called rational supernaturalism, founder of the *Corpus Reformatorum*.

47. Frederick Leopold Stolberg (1750-1819), German poet, a convert to the Roman Church in 1800.

48. On Novalis and Schlegel, see note 35 above.

49. Nevin's translation is neither lucid nor literal. The original reads: Zwar ich kenne die furchtbare Episode wohl, welche von der linken Seite der Hegelschen Philosophie aus in der ruhigen Gang der bereits im besten Zuge begriffenen Entwicklung hineingekommen ist, gleich dem Sturm der Julirevolution, diesem Nachzügler der französischen Staatsumwälzung der neunziger Jahre.

50. Johann August Wilhelm Neander (1789-1850), eminent German church historian, among whose disciples Schaff counted himself. For Schaff's appraisal of Neander, see his *History of the Apostolic Church* (New York: Scribner, 1853), pp. 95-107. For a general article on Neander, see *The New Schaff-Herzog Encyclopedia of Religious Knowledge* (1908 ed.), VIII, 95-96.

51. Karl Immanuel Nitzsch (1787-1868), German Protestant theologian, professor of theology at Berlin (1847), distinguished representative of the mediating theology.

52. Julius Mueller (1801-1878), German Lutheran theologian, professor of theology at Halle (1839), closely associated with Neander and Nitzsch. He was in favor of the union of the confessional churches.

53. Karl Friedrich Goeschel (1784-1861), German jurist and philosopher. His chief concern was the reconciliation of Christianity with modern culture, of which he saw Hegel to be the chief philosophical representative; and Goethe, the chief poetical representative.

54. Richard Rothe (1799-1867), German theologian, professor at the Wittenberg seminary, at Heidelberg and Bonn. His conception of church history and his speculative theology are discussed by F. Sieffert in "Rothe," *The New Schaff-Herzog Encyclopedia of Religious Knowledge* (1908 ed.), X, 100-3.

55. Isaac August Dorner (1809-1884), an eminent German Lutheran theologian of the mediating school; served in a number of German universities and closed his career at Berlin (1862). See P. Schaff, *Ger-*

*many: Its Universities, Theology, and Religion* (Philadelphia: Lindsay & Blakiston, 1857), pp. 376-80; P. Schaff, "Dorner," *The New
Schaff-Herzog Encyclopedia of Religious Knowledge* (1908 ed.), III,
492-93.

56. Hans Lassen Martensen (1808-1884), Danish bishop and theologian. While he professed to be a confessional Lutheran, Martensen
was a speculative thinker, influenced by Hegelian idealism, the theosophy of Franz von Baader, and the mysticism of Jakob Boehme.

57. Schaff probably means Johann Christian Konrad Hofmann
(1810-1877), German theologian and exegete, professor at Rostock
(1842) and Erlangen (1845). On his theology, see Joh. Hausleiten,
*Grundlinien der Theologie von Hofmanns in seiner eigenen Darstel-
lung* (1910). See also A. Hauck, "Hofmann," *The New Schaff-Herzog
Encyclopedia of Religious Knowledge* (1908 ed.), V, 312-13.

58. Friedrich Rudolf Hasse (1808-1862), German theologian, professor of church history at Bonn (1841).

59. Ernst Wilhelm Hengstenberg (1802-1869), German Lutheran
theologian and biblical scholar, professor in Berlin for four decades,
founder and editor of the influential *Evangelische Kirchenzeitung*, an
earnest critic of the rationalistic spirit.

60. Gottlieb Christoph Adolf von Harless (1806-1879); German
Lutheran theologian, who came lately to appreciate the Lutheran
symbols and defended them, at several important posts, against the
opposition of rationalism.

61. Friedrich August Gottreu Tholuck (1799-1877), German theologian and preacher, professor of theology at Halle (1826). He turned
Halle away from rationalism to the evangelicalism which characterized
it in the nineteenth century. See P. Schaff, "Tholuck," *The New
Schaff-Herzog Encyclopedia of Religious Knowledge* (1908 ed.), XI,
420-21.

62. Schaff probably refers to Christoph Friedrich Nicholai (1733-
1811), German author and bookseller. Nicholai edited several periodicals which characteristically assailed authority in religion, as well as
certain supposed extravagances in German literature. He misunderstood and misrepresented the new movement of ideas set forth by
Herder, Gothe, Schiller, Kant, and Fichte.

63. Ludwig Tieck (1773-1853), one of the most conspicuous figures
of the German romantic school of literature.

64. On Schlegel and Novalis, see note 35 above.

65. Calvin Ellis Stowe (1802-1886), Congregationalist theologian,
professor of biblical literature at Lane Theological Seminary (1833-
50).

66. On Dorner, see note 55 above.

67. Heinrich Eberhard Gottlob Paulus (1761-1851), German theologian, professor at Heidelberg (1811-44), a leading representative of the *Aufklärungs-Theologie*.

68. Julius August Ludwig Wegscheider (1771-1849), German rationalistic theologian, professor of theology at Halle (1810). After Tholuck's inauguration at Halle (1826), Wegscheider's popularity declined.

69. Bruno Bauer (1809-1882), Hegelian, biblical critic of extreme radicalism; dismissed from his academic post at Bonn in 1842.

70. Karl von Eschenmayer (1770?-1852?), German philosopher and physicist; in many particulars his views were identical to those of Schelling.

71. Henrik Steffens (1773-1845), Norse writer who introduced Schelling's ideas to Danish literary circles.

72. Schaff probably refers to Christian Friedrich Daniel Schubart (1739-1791), German poet and publicist.

73. Heinrich Leo (1799-1878), German historian, professor at Halle (1828). See *Die Religion in Geschichte und Gegenwart* (2d ed.), III, 1583. Leopold von Ranke (1795-1886), influential German historian. For critique and bibliography, see W. Koehler, "Ranke," *Die Religion in Geschichte und Gegenwart* (2d ed.), IV, 1699-1700. The other historian, whom Schaff mentions, is probably Martin Haug (1827-1876), orientalist, professor at Munich (1868-76).

74. On Storr, see note 43 above. See "Tuebingen School," *The New Schaff-Herzog Encyclopedia of Religious Knowledge* (1908 ed.), XII, 34-37.

75. Johann Georg Benedikt Winer (1789-1858), orientalist and New Testament grammarian, professor at Erlangen and Leipzig.

76. George Heinrich August Ewald (1803-1875), German orientalist, Hebraist and biblical critic, popularizer of the Development Hypothesis of Old Testament growth. Ferdinand Hitzig (1807-1875), German exegete and Old Testament critic, professor at Zurich (1833-61) and Heidelberg (1861).

77. Karl Friedrich August Fritzche (1801-1846), German exegetical scholar, professor at Leipzig, Rostock, Giessen. Fritzsche was one of the most industrious contributors to the grammatical method of Bible study introduced by Winer.

78. On Harless, see note 60 above.

79. Friedrich Bleek (1793-1859), German theologian and biblical scholar, professor at Berlin and Bonn.

80. On Bengel, see note 8 above.

81. For the midwestern use of "evangelical," see David Dunn (ed.), *A History of the Evangelical and Reformed Church* (Philadelphia: Christian Education Press, 1961), Ch. 6.

82. For the complete text of the hymn, see R. C. Trench, *Sacred Latin Poetry* (London: Macmillan, 1864), pp. 75-79.

83. Johann Gerhard (1582-1637), German Lutheran dogmatician and one of the foremost exponents of Lutheran orthodoxy in the seventeenth century. See note 4 above. On Bengel, see note 8.

84. See H. R. Mackintosh, *Types of Modern Theology* (London: Nisbet, 1937), pp. 117 ff. See Schaff, *History of the Apostolic Church* (New York: Scribner, 1853), pp. 111 f.

85. Johann August Ernesti (1707-1781), professor of theology at Leipzig who persisted in the older confessional orthodoxy, yet insisted that biblical philological interpretation, as such, deserved independent status in theology.

86. Samuel Friedrich Nathanael Morus (1756-1792), pupil of Ernesti, professor of theology at Leipzig.

87. Karl Gottlieb Bretschneider (1776-1848), German theologian whose standpoint was rational supernaturalism.

88. On Calvin Ellis Stowe, see note 65 above.

89. Victor Cousin (1792-1867).

90. Frederick Denison Maurice (1805-1872), theologian of the Church of England, professor of moral theology and philosophy at Cambridge, 1866 ff. The full title of the book is *The Kingdom of Christ, or, Hints to a Quaker Respecting the Principle, Constitution, and Ordinances of the Catholic Church.*

91. Johann Lorentz von Mosheim (1694?-1755); German Lutheran church historian, who conceived of Christian doctrine as a fixed, unalterable, apostolic system. Church history in America tended to be governed by Mosheim's ideas and books. For Schaff's appraisal of Mosheim as historian see his *What Is Church History?* pp. 42 ff., 56.

92. Johann August Wilhelm Neander (1789-1850); German church historian, to whom Schaff ascribed particular indebtedness, and called "the father of modern church history." See Schaff, *History of the Apostolic Church* (New York: Scribner, 1853), pp. 95-107. See also *The New Schaff-Herzog Encyclopedia of Religious Knowledge* (1908 ed.), VIII, 95-96.

93. J. C. L. Gieseler (1792-1854); professor of church history in Göttingen; contemporary of Neander, with whom he maintained a friendly rivalry. Schaff noted a rationalistic tendency in his historical

scholarship. See *History of Apostolic Christianity* (Edinburgh: Clark, 1893) , I, 42-43.

94. J. H. Merle d'Aubigné (1794-1872) . The man's name is Merle; "d'Aubigné" is merely an assumed byname. French Reformed church historian; author of *Histoire de la Réformation du 16 siècle* (5 vols.; Paris, 1835) , widely circulated in Britain and America.

95. Philipp Konrad Marheinecke (1780-1846) , German Protestant theologian and historian. See *The New Schaff-Herzog Encyclopedia of Religious Knowledge* (1908 ed.) , VII, 179-80.

96. Moses Stuart (1780-1852) , professor of sacred literature in Andover Theological Seminary (1810-48) ; brought American theology abreast of biblical scholarship in Germany.

97. Charles Hodge (1797-1878) , professor in Princeton Theological Seminary (1822) , advocate of old-school Calvinist orthodoxy, opponent of Schaff's colleague, Nevin, in the dispute over the Lord's Supper (1846-50) .

98. Edward Robinson (1794-1863) , professor of biblical literature in Union Theological Seminary, N. Y. (1837) . Schaff called him "probably the most distinguished biblical scholar whom America has produced, indeed, one of the most distinguished of the nineteenth century."

99. Nevin's sermon *Catholic Unity,* which was in fact appended to the English edition of *The Principle of Protestantism,* will be published in the second volume of this series, under the title *Early Writings of John W. Nevin.*

100. As a postlude to the Carey case (see note 24 above) the Evangelical party in the Episcopal Church brought charges of drunkenness and improper familiarities with women against a leading high churchman, Bishop B. T. Onderdonk of New York. He was found guilty and suspended. His brother, Bishop Henry Onderdonk of Pennsylvania, was also charged with drunkenness by the Evangelicals but resigned before being brought to trial. Both incidents were the result of conflict between Evangelicals and High Churchmen. See William Wilson Manross, *A History of the American Episcopal Church* (New York: Morehouse-Gorham, 1950) , pp. 266 ff.

101. Samuel Seabury (1801-1872) , editor of *The Churchman,* and one of the leaders of the High Church movement. He defended the suspended Bishop Onderdonk in the press. See Charles C. Tiffany, *A History of the Protestant Episcopal Church in the United States of America* (New York: Christian Literature Co., 1895) , pp. 478-79.

102. Francois Fénelon (1651-1751) ; French prelate and curate of

souls; associated with French mysticism of the 17th century; became involved, with Mme. Guyon, in the Quietist controversy. On his condemnation, see Pierre Pourrat, *Christian Spirituality* (Westminster, Md.: Newman, 1955), IV, 205-32.

103. Orestes Augustus Brownson (1803-1876), Roman Catholic convert in 1844 after a varied career as orthodox Presbyterian, Universalist minister, socialist politician, independent preacher, Unitarian clergyman, etc. He published an influential and somewhat independent Catholic journal, *Brownson's Quarterly Review,* 1844-64 and 1873-75.

104. "Deutschkatholicismus" is the technical name of a reform movement in the Roman Catholic Church of Germany, which was prompted by the protest of the priest, Johannes Ronge, ca. 1844. See "German Catholicism," *The New Schaff-Herzog Encyclopedia of Religious Knowledge* (1908 ed.), IV, 466-68.

105. Joachim of Fiore (Latin *Floris;* 1145?-1202), abbot of San Giovanni in Fiore. On Joachim's vision of three "ages," see R. C. Petry, *A History of Christianity: Readings in the History of the Early and Medieval Church* (Englewood Cliffs, N. J.: Prentice-Hall, 1962), pp. 470 ff.

Bibliography

PRIMARY SOURCES

*Principal Works by Philip Schaff*
*in the Mercersburg Period*

GERMAN WORKS

1. *Das Princip des Protestantismus.* (Inaugural address as professor of biblical literature and church history in the Theological Seminary of the German Reformed Church, Mercersburg, Pa.) Chambersburg: In der Druckerei der Hochdeutsch-Reformirten Kirche, 1845.

2. *Der Anglogermanismus.* Eine Rede gehalten den 10ten März, 1846, vor der Schillergesellshaft des Marshall Collegiums. Chambersburg, 1846.

3. *Geschichte der Christlichen Kirche, von ihrer Gründung bis auf die Gegenwart.* Vol. I, *Die apostolische Kirche.* (Dedicated to Neander. This was, in fact, the commencement of Schaff's monumental history of the church. It was also his first effort to treat the history of the apostolic church.) Mercersburg: Selbst-verlag des Verfassers, 1851.

4. *Geschichte der apostolischen Kirche, nebst einer allgemeinen Einleitung in der Kirchengeschichte.* (Second edition of 3, above.) Leipzig: Holtze, 1854.

255

5. *Amerika: Die politischen, socialen, und kirchlich-religiösen Zu-stände der Vereinigten Staaten von Nord-Amerika mit besonderer Rücksicht auf die Deutschen, aus eigener Anschauung dargestellt.* Berlin: Wiegandt & Grieben, 1854. Second edition, enlarged: 1858. Third edition, enlarged: 1865.

6. *Deutschland und Amerika.* (An address delivered to the German Evangelical Church Diet at Frankfurt am Main.) 1854.

7. *Der Heilige Augustinus.* Sein Leben und Wirken. Berlin: Hertz, 1854.

8. *Christlicher Katechismus mit Bibelsprüchen für Schule und Haus.* (The "Grosse Ausgabe" of Schaff's catechism.) Chambersburg: Kieffer, 1861. Second edition, enlarged, Philadelphia: Kohler, 1863.

9. *Katechismus für Sonntags-Schulen.* In zwei und fünfzig Lectionen mit Bibelsprüchen und Andeutungen für Lehrer. (The "Kleine Ausgabe" of Schaff's catechism.) Chambersburg: Kieffer, 1861. Second edition, enlarged, Chambersburg: Kieffer, 1863; and Philadelphia: Kohler, 1863.

10. *Der Heidelberger Katechismus.* Nach der Ausgabe von 1563 revi-dirt und mit kritischen Anmerkungen, sowie einer Geschichte und Charakteristik des Katechismus versehen. Ein Beitrag zur Drei-hundertjährigen Jubelfeier im Jahre, 1863. Philadelphia: Kohler, and Chambersburg: Kieffer, 1863. Second edition, revised: 1866.

11. *Der Bürgerkrieg und das christliche Leben in Nord Amerika.* Vor-träge gehalten in Berlin und mehreren Städten Deutschlands und der Schweiz. Berlin: Wiegandt & Grieben, 1865. Third edition: 1866.


ENGLISH WORKS

12. *The Principle of Protestantism as Related to the Present State of the Church.* Translated from the German, with an Introduction, by John W. Nevin, D.D. (A translation of 1, above.) Chambers-burg: Publication Office of the German Reformed Church, 1845.

13. *Anglo-Germanism, or, The Significance of the German Nationality in the United States.* An address delivered March 10, 1846, before the Schiller Society of Marshall College. Translated by J. S. Er-mentrout. (A translation of 2, above.) Chambersburg, 1846.

14. *What Is Church History?* Vindication of the Idea of Historical Development. Translated from the German by John W. Nevin. Philadelphia: Lippincott, 1846.

15. *History of the Apostolic Church,* with a General Introduction to Church History. Translated by Edward D. Yeomans. (A translation of 3, above. Includes Schaff's important Introduction to Church History, pp. 1-134.) New York: Scribner, 1853. An edition in 2 vols. was also published by T. & T. Clark, Edinburgh, 1854.

16. *The Life and Labors of St. Augustine.* Translated by T. C. Porter. (A translation of 7, above.) New York: Riker, and London: Bagster, 1854.

17. *America: A Sketch of the Political, Social, and Religious Character of the United States of North America.* Translated by Edward D. Yeomans. (A translation of 5, above.) New York: Scribner, 1855.

18. *American Nationality.* An address delivered before the Irving Society of the College of St. James, Md., June 11, 1856. Chambersburg: Kieffer, 1856.

19. *Germany: Its Universities, Theology, and Religion.* With sketches of Neander, Tholuck, Olshausen, Hengstenberg, Twesten, Nitzsche, Mueller, Ullmann, Rothe, Dorner, Lange, Ebrard, Wichern, and other distinguished German divines of the age. Philadelphia: Lindsay & Blakiston, 1857.

20. *The Moral Character of Christ, or, The Perfection of Christ's Humanity, a Proof of His Divinity.* A Theological Tract for the People. Chambersburg: Kieffer, 1861.

21. *Slavery and the Bible: A Tract for the Times.* Chambersburg: Kieffer, 1861.

22. *A Catechism for Sunday Schools and Families.* In Fifty-two Lessons. (Large edition, 167 pages; small edition, 74 pages.) Philadelphia: Lindsay & Blakiston, and Chambersburg: Kieffer, 1862.

WORKS EDITED

23. *Der Deutsche Kirchenfreund.* Organ für die gemeinsamen Interessen der amerikanisch-deutschen Kirchen. Mercersburg, 1848-53; Philadelphia, 1854-59. A monthly periodical; first American theological journal in the German language. Schaff was editor, 1848-53. After that, the editorship was taken up by Professor William Julius Mann of the Lutheran Theological Seminary in Philadelphia, who continued to publish the paper six years longer.

24. *A Liturgy, or, Order of Christian Worship.* Prepared and Published by the Direction and for the Use of the German Reformed

Church in the United States of America. (Called "the Provisional
Liturgy.") Philadelphia: Lindsay & Blakiston, 1858.

25. *Deutsches Gesangbuch.* Eine Auswahl geistlichen Lieder aus allen
Zeiten der christlichen Kirche. Nach den besten hymnologischen
Quellen bearbeitet und mit erläuternden Bemerkungen über die
Verfasser, den Inhalt und die Geschichte der Lieder versehen.
Philadelphia: Lindsay & Blakiston, and Berlin: Wiegandt & Grie-
ben, 1859. Second edition, Philadelphia and Chambersburg, 1860.
Enlarged edition, Philadelphia: Kohler, 1874. This hymnal was
prepared for, and adopted by, the German Reformed Church in
the United States.

26. *Evangelische Zeugnisse aus den Deutschen Kirchen in Amerika.*
Eine homiletische Monatsschrift. 3 Jahrgänge. Philadelphia: Kohler, 1863-66.

27. *Gedenkbuch der Dreihundertjährigen Jubelfeier des Heidelberger
Katechismus in der Deutsch-Reformirten Kirche der Vereinigten
Staaten.* Under the direction of the General Convention of the
Tercentenary Jubilee. Chambersburg: Kieffer, and Philadelphia:
Kohler, 1863. Published in English as *Tercentenary Monument:
In Commemoration of the Three Hundredth Anniversary of the
Heidelberg Catechism* (see 57, below).

28. *Gesangbuch für Deutsche Sonntagsschulen.* Sammt einem Anhang
ausgewählter Englischer Lieder. Philadelphia: Kohler, and New
York: Radde, 1864.


WORKS UNPUBLISHED

(Items 29 to 33 are found in the Library of the Historical Society of the Evangelical and Reformed Church, Lancaster, Pa. Titles, here, are sometimes descriptive, rather than exact. German titles appear in English translation.)

29. *Studenten-Arbeiten, Tübingen, Halle, Berlin, 1837-41.* Notebooks
and manuscripts in German script. Box 1 includes Schaff's disputation for the Licentiate of Theology: *De nexu Vetus Testam.
cum Novo T. cohaereat recte definiendo* (Halis, 1839). Box 2 includes two series of Schaff's sermons: (a) sermons preached in
Germany, thirty-two signatures,* including his ordination sermon
at Elberfeld, April 12, 1844; (b) sermons preached at Mercersburg, fifteen signatures.

---

* The word signature is used to describe several sheets of copy paper sewn
together. They are of various sizes.

30. Lecture Notes taken by Philip Schaff:

"Logic by Prof. George Schmid." German script. Stuttgart, 1836/37.

"Philosophy by H. Prof. [Georg] Schmid." German script. Stuttgart, 1836/37.

"Philosophy and Christian Ethics by Prof. [Georg] Schmid." German script. 1836/37.

"Harmony of the Gospels by Prof. Dr. [F. H.] Kern." German script. Tübingen, 1837/38.

"Lectures on Practical Philosophy by Prof. C. Ph. Fisher" [Karl Philipp Fischer]. German script. Tübingen, 1837/38.

"Lectures on Hegelian Philosophy delivered by Dr. Visher" [F. Theo. Vischer]. German script. Tübingen, 1838.

"Lectures on the Pentateuch by Dr. [G. H. A.] Ewald (the celebrated orientalist)." German script. Tübingen, 1838.

"History of Doctrine by Prof. Dr. Christian Ferdinand Baur" [Ferdinand Christian Baur]. German script. Tübingen, 1838/39.

"Lectures on Anthropology by Prof. K. Ph. Fischer." German script. Tübingen, 1838/39.

"Lectures of Prof. Dr. [D. F.] Schmid on N. Test. Theology." German script. Tübingen, 1839.

"Lectures on the Epistle to the Hebrews by Dr. [Gustav Friedrich von] Oehler." German script. Tübingen, 1839.

"Lectures on the Theology of the O. Test. by Dr. [Gustav Friedrich von] Oehler of Tübingen." German script. 1839.

"History of Philosophy from the Beginning of Christianity to the Fifth Century by Prof. [J. E.] Erdmann." German script. Halle, 1839/40.

"Evangelical Copy Book for Theology, Philosophy, Sacred Literature, and Philology." German script. Commenced in Halle, June 20, 1840.

"Lectures of Dr. [E.] W. Hengstenberg on the Epistle to the Romans." German script. Berlin, 1840.

"Lectures of Dr. [Ernst Wilhelm] Hengstenberg in Berlin on the Introduction to the Old Testament." German script. 1841.

"Lectures on Jurisprudence [Deutsche staats- und privatfürstenrecht] by [Prof. Friedrich Julius] Stahl." German script. Berlin, 1854/55. [These notes were apparently taken by Schaff during his sabbatical leave from Mercersburg in 1854.]

"Philosophy." Lecture notes in German script, otherwise unidentified.

31. Correspondence, 1840-79. A collection of 136 letters to Schaff or by him. The correspondents include I. A. Dorner, August Ebrard, E. W. Hengstenberg, Julius Mueller, Friedrich August Tholuck, as well as representative American theologians.

32. Manuscripts of Lectures, Books, and Pamphlets prepared by Schaff at Mercersburg:

"Explanation of the Epistle of Paul to the Romans." One signature. German script. Mercersburg, 1845.

"Historical-critical Introduction into the New Testament." One signature. German script. Mercersburg, 1845/46.

"Commentary on the Gospel of Matthew." Four signatures plus two extraneous signatures also on Matthew. German script. Mercersburg, 1846.

"History of the Church in the United States of North America." Four signatures. German script. Mercersburg, 1846.

"Commentary on the Epistle of Paul to the Philippians." One signature. German script. Mercersburg, 1846/47.

"General History of Poetical Literature." Five signatures. German script. 1846/47.

"Lectures on Dogmatic Theology." Nine signatures. German script. Mercersburg, 1847.

"History of German Literature." One signature. German script. Mercersburg, 1848.

"Commentary on the Acts of the Apostles." One signature marked *Einleitung*. German script. Mercersburg, 1849.

"History of German Poetry from the Reformation to the Present." One signature. German script. Marshall College, 1849.

"Commentary on the Epistle to the Hebrews." Five signatures. German script. Mercersburg, 1850/51.

"Lectures on the Epistle to the Romans." Five signatures plus one signature marked *Einleitung*. German script. "Commenced 1852."

"Commentary on the Acts of the Apostles." One signature. German script. Mercersburg, 1853.

"Lectures on Christian Dogmatics." Two signatures. English. Mercersburg, May, 1853.

"St. Paul's Epistle to the Romans, translated by Phil. Schaff, on the basis of the common English Version." One signature. English. Mercersburg, 1853.

"Christian Symbolics and Polemics: An Exposition of the Doctrinal Differences of the Various Christian Denominations." One signature. English. Mercersburg, November, 1855.

"The Acts of the Apostles, translated from the Greek." One signature, incomplete. English. "Commenced Oct. 1857."

"The Epistle to the Galatians, translated and explained." Two signatures. German and English. "Commenced May 5, 1857."

"Commentary on Ep. to the Galatians. Begun at Mercersburg 1860, completed in N. York —." Assorted signatures, the first of which is actually dated 1857. English.

"Commentary on the Epistles of the Apostle John: First Epistle." One signature. German script. Mercersburg, 1860/61.

"Revised Translation of the First Epistle of St. John." One signature. English. Mercersburg, 1860/61.

"History of the English Reformation." Five signatures. German script. No date.

"Lectures on the Middle Ages." Nine signatures, more or less. German script. Mercersburg, no date.

"M.S. on the History of the Reformation, written in Mercersburg, partly in German, partly in English. Superseded. Used for Vols. VI and VII" [of Schaff's later work, *History of the Christian Church*]. No date.

"The Reaction and Counter-Reformation of Romanism." Marked as the "Seventh Chapter" of "History of the Reformation Period." One signature. English. No date.

"The Reformation in England." One signature. English. No date.

"The Reformation in Scotland." One signature. German script. No date.

"St. Paul's Epistle to the Romans. Translated and explained for the general reader." One signature. English. No date.

"Symbolics: The Greek Catholic Church and the Oriental Sects or Schismatics." One signature. English. No date.

Sundry Commentaries on the Gospel of John. Three signatures. German script. No date.

33. Notes on Schaff's Lectures, taken by his students at Mercersburg. Twelve bound volumes, covering the years 1844-63.

Selected Works of Critical Bearing
on Schaff's The Principle of Protestantism

BOOKS AND PAMPHLETS

34. BAUR, FERDINAND CHRISTIAN. *Das Christenthum und die christliche Kirke der drei ersten jahrhunderte.* Tübingen: Fues, 1853. Translated by Allan Menzies as *Church History of the First Three Centuries.* 2 vols. London: Williams & Norgate, 1878-79.

35. ———. *Die christliche Kirche vom Anfang des vierten bis zum Ende des sechsten Jahrhunderts in den Hauptmomenten ihrer Entwicklung.* Tübingen: Fues, 1859.

36. ———. *Die christliche Kirche des Mittelalters in den Hauptmomenten ihrer Entwicklung.* Leipzig, 1861.

37. ———. *Kirchengeschichte des neunzehnten Jahrhunderts.* Tübingen: Feus, 1862.

38. ———. *Kirchengeschichte der neueren Zeit von der Reformation bis zum Ende des 18. Jahrhunderts.* Leipzig, 1863.

39. BERG, JOSEPH F. *Lectures on Romanism.* Philadelphia: Weidner, 1840.

40. ———.*The Great Apostacy, Identical with Papal Rome, or, An Exposition of the Mystery of Iniquity and the Marks and Doom of Antichrist.* Philadelphia: Lippincott, 1842.

41. ———. *The Old Paths, or, A Sketch of the Order and Discipline of the Reformed Church Before the Reformation, as Maintained by the Waldenses Prior to That Epoch, and by the Church of the Palatinate in the 16th Century.* Philadelphia: Lippincott, 1845.

42. ———. *Jehovah-Nissi. Farewell Words to the First German Church, Philadelphia.* Philadelphia, 1852. Also reported in the *Weekly Messenger,* XVII (April 28, 1851) , 3662.

43. ———. *A Vindication of the Farewell Words to the German Reformed Church.* Philadelphia: Young, 1852.

44. DORNER, I. A. *Entwicklungsgeschichte der Lehre von der Person Christi.* 2 vols. Berlin: Schlawitz, 1851-53. Translated by W. L. Alexander as *History of the Development of the Doctrine of the Person of Christ.* 5 vols. Edinburgh: Clark, 1882-84.

45. ———. *Geschichte der protestantischen Theologie, besonders in Deutschland.* Munich: J. G. Cotta'schen Buchhandlung, 1867. Translated by George Robson and Sophia Taylor as *History of Protestant Theology, Particularly in Germany.* 2 vols. Edinburgh: Clark, 1871.

46. HEGEL, GEORGE WILHELM FRIEDRICH. *Early Theological Writings.* Translated by T. M. Knox and Richard Kroner. Chicago: University of Chicago Press, 1948.

47. HELFENSTEIN, JACOB. *A Perverted Gospel, or, The Romanizing Tendency of the Mercersburg Theology.* Philadelphia: Young, 1853.

48. MAURICE, F. D. *The Kingdom of Christ, or, Hints Respecting the Principles, Constitution, and Ordinances of the Catholic Church.* New York: Appleton, 1843.

49. MAURICE, FREDERICK (ed.). *The Life of Frederick Denison Maurice, Chiefly Told in His Own Letters.* 2 vols. New York: Scribner, 1884.

50. MOEHLER, JOHANN ADAM. *Symbolik oder, Darstellung der dogmatischen Gegensätze der Katholiken und Protestanten.* Mainz: Kupferberg, 1838. Translated as *Symbolism, or, Exposition of the Doctrinal Differences Between Catholics and Protestants.* New York: Catholic Publication House, 1843.

51. MUELLER, JULIUS. *Die christliche Lehre von der Sünde.* Fifth edition, 2 vols. in 1. Breslau: Max, 1867. Translated by William Pulsford as *The Christian Doctrine of Sin.* 2 vols. Edinburgh: Clark, 1852-53.

52. NEANDER, JOHANN AUGUST WILHELM. *Allgemeine Geschichte der christliche Religion und Kirche.* 6 vols. in 11. Hamburg: Perthes, 1825-52. Translated by Joseph Torrey as *General History of the Christian Religion and Church.* Eleventh American edition, 5 vols. Boston: Crocker & Brewster, 1872.

53. ———. *Das Leben Jesu Christi in seinem geschichtlichen Zusammenhange und seiner geschichtlichen Entwickelung.* Hamburg: Perthes, 1837.

54. NEVIN, JOHN W. *Antichrist, or, The Spirit of Sect and Schism.* New York: Taylor, 1848.

55. NEWMAN, JOHN HENRY. *Essay on the Development of Christian Doctrine.* New York: Toovey, 1845.

56. SCHNECK, B. S. *Mercersburg Theology Inconsistent with Protestant and Reformed Doctrine.* Philadelphia: Lippincott, 1874.

57. *Tercentenary Monument: In Commemoration of the Three Hundredth Anniversary of the Heidelberg Catechism.* Chambersburg: Kieffer, 1863.

ARTICLES

NOTE: For a review of the periodical literature (ca. 1844-64) that pertained to the Mercersburg theology, see James H. Nichols, *Romanticism in American Theology: Nevin and Schaff at Mercersburg* (Chicago: University of Chicago Press, 1961), pp. 313-14.

58. BERG, JOSEPH F. "Mercersburg Theology," *The Protestant Quarterly Review,* III (1846), 75-87.

59. BROWNSON, ORESTES. "Newman's Development of Christian Doctrine," *Brownson's Quarterly Review,* III (1846), 342-68.

60. "History of the Apostolic Age" [review], *The Church Review and Ecclesiastical Register,* VI (1853-54), 607-8.

61. "History of the Christian Church" [review], *The American Theological Review,* 1/2 (1859), 318-26.

62. HODGE, CHARLES [?]. "Principle of Protestantism" [review], *The Biblical Repertory and Princeton Review,* XVII (1845), 626-36.

63. J. W. "Schaff on Protestantism" [review of *The Principle of Protestantism*], *Christian Examiner,* XXXIX (1845), 220-25.

64. LEWIS, TAYLER. "The Church Question" [a review of Schaff's *Principle* taken from *The Biblical Repository and Classical Review,* II, Jan., 1846], *Weekly Messenger,* XI (Jan. 21, 28, Feb. 5, 1846), 2153, 2157, 2161.

65. NEVIN, JOHN W. "Catholicism," *Mercersburg Review,* III (1851), 1-26.

66. ———. "Dr. Berg's Last Words," *Mercersburg Review,* IV (1852), 283-304.

67. ———. "False Protestantism," *Mercersburg Review,* I (1849), 194-97.

68. ———. "Historical Development," *Mercersburg Review,* I (1849), 512-14.

69. ———. "Pseudo-Protestantism," *Weekly Messenger,* X (Aug. 13, 20, 27, 1845).

70. ———. "Schaff's Church History," *Mercersburg Review,* III (1851), 296-304.

71. ———. "The Sect System," *Mercersburg Review,* I (1849), 482-507, 521-39.

72. ———. "True and False Protestantism," *Mercersburg Review,* I (1849), 83-104.

73. "Principle of Protestantism" [review], *Lutheran Observer,* XI (Apr. 11, 1845), 59.

74. PROUDFIT, JOHN W. "Dr. Schaff as a Church Historian," *New Brunswick Review*, I (1854-55), 278-325.

75. ———. "Dr. Schaff's Works on Church History," *New Brunswick Review*, I (1854-55), 1-63.

76. S. R. "The Protestantism of Mercersburg, as Contrasted with the Protestantism of the Bible and the German Reformed Church," *Weekly Messenger*, XI (Oct. 15, 1845), 2096.

77. SCHAFF, PHILIP. "Betrachtungen über das deutsche Kirchenwesen in Amerika," *Der Deutsche Kirchenfreund*, IV (1851), 177-80, 209-15, 241-52, 321-35, 433-43.

78. ———. "Christianity in America," *Mercersburg Review*, IX (1857), 493-539.

79. ———. "Dr. Berg's Austritt aus der deutsch reformirten Kirche," *Der Deutsche Kirchenfreund*, V (1852), 233-37.

80. ———. "Geschichte der Deutschen Kirche in Amerika," *Der Deutsche Kirchenfreund*, II (1849), 1-21, 129-48, 161-86.

81. ———. "Der Irvingismus und die Kirchenfrage," *Der Deutsche Kirchenfreund*, III (1850), 49-57, 81-87, 161-68, 223-33.

82. ———. "Katholizismus und Protestantismus," *Literarische Zeitung* (Berlin), October 31, Dec. 16, 1843.

83. ———. "The Mission of the German Reformed Church in America," *Tercentenary Monument* (see 57, above), pp. xxxvi-xxxix.

84. ———. "Neander as a Church Historian," *Mercersburg Review*, IV (1852), 564-77. See "Neander als Kirchenhistoriker," *Der Deutsche Kirchenfreund*, V (1852), 401-13.

85. ———. "Neanders Jugendjahre," *Der Deutsche Kirchenfreund*, IV (1851), 283-97.

86. ———. "The New Liturgy," *Mercersburg Review*, X (1858), 199-227.

87. ———. "Ordination of Professor Schaff" [sermon preached by Schaff at his ordination; see 29, above], *Weekly Messenger*, Sept. 4, 1844.

88. ———. "Prolegomena zur Kirchengeschichte der Vereinigten Staaten," *Der Deutsche Kirchenfreund*, I (1848), 257-64, 321-24, 353-61.

89. ———. "Recollections of Neander," *Mercersburg Review*, III (1851), 73-90.

90. SCHAFF, PHILIP [?]. "Gallerie der bedeutendsten jetzt lebenden Universitätstheologen Deutschlands," *Der Deutsche Kirchenfreund*, V, (1852), 129-39, 161-78, 241-55, 289-306, 321-38.

91. SCHAFF, PHILIP [?]. "German Theology and the Church Question,"

*Mercersburg Review,* V (1583), 124-44. See *Der Deutsche Kirchen-freund,* V (1852), 338-53.

92. "Schaff's Church History" [review], *Christian Examiner,* LXVI (1859), 438-41.

93. "Schaff's History and Mercersburg Theology," *The Church Review and Ecclesiastical Register,* XII (1859), 369-86.

MINUTES OF EASTERN SYNOD

94. *Acts and Proceedings of the Synod of the German Reformed Church in the United States of America,*
      Winchester, Frederick Co., Va., Oct., 1843.*
      Allentown, Lehigh Co., Pa., Oct., 1844.*
      York, York Co., Pa., Oct., 1845.*
      Carlisle, Cumberland Co., Pa., Oct., 1846.*
      Lancaster, Pa., Oct., 1847.*
      Hagerstown, Md., Oct., 1848.*
      Norristown, Pa., Oct., 1849.†
      Harrisburg, Dauphin Co., Pa., Jan., 1850.†
      Lancaster, Pa., Oct., 1851.†
      Baltimore, Md., Oct., 1852.†
      Philadelphia, Pa., 1853.†
      Lewisburg, Union Co., Pa., Oct., 1854.†
      Chambersburg, Franklin Co., Pa., Oct., 1855.†
      Reading, Berks Co., Pa., Oct., 1856.†
      Allentown, Lehigh Co., Pa., Oct., 1857.†
      Frederick City, Md., Oct., 1858.†
      Harrisburg, Dauphin Co., Pa., Oct., 1859.†
      Lebanon, Pa., Oct., 1860.†
      Easton, Pa., Sept. and Oct., 1861.†
      Chambersburg, Pa., Oct., 1862.†
      Carlisle, Pa., Oct., 1863.†

---

* Chambersburg: Publication Office of the German Reformed Church
† Chambersburg: M. Kieffer & Co.

## SELECTED SECONDARY SOURCES

95. APPEL, THEODORE. *The Life and Work of John Williamson Nevin.* Philadelphia: Reformed Church Publication House, 1889.

96. ———. *Recollections of College Life at Marshall College, Mercersburg, Pa., from 1839 to 1845: A Narrative, with Reflections.* Reading: Miller, 1886.

97. BINKLEY, LUTHER J. "The German Theological Antecedents of the Mercersburg Theology," *Bulletin*. Lancaster: Theological Seminary of the German Reformed Church, XXI (1950), 120-48.

98. ———. *The Mercersburg Theology*. Lancaster: Franklin and Marshall College, 1953.

99. GERHART, EMANUEL V. "Mercersburg Theology," *The New Schaff-Herzog Encyclopedia of Religious Knowledge*, VII (New York, 1910), 311-12.

100. GOOD, JAMES I. *History of the Reformed Church in the U.S. in the Nineteenth Century*. New York: The Board of Publication of the Reformed Church in America, 1911.

101. HERMAN, THEODORE F. "The Principle of Protestantism," *Bulletin*. Lancaster: Theological Seminary of the Evangelical and Reformed Church, XV (1944), 190-209.

102. JACOBS, H. E. "Dr. Schaff and the Lutheran Church," *Papers of the American Society of Church History*, VII (New York, 1894), 13-19.

103. JEDELE, E. *Die Kirchenpolitischen Anschauungen des Ernst Ludwig von Gerlach*. Ansbach: Bruegel, 1910.

104. KLEIN, H. M. J. *The History of the Eastern Synod of the Reformed Church in the United States*. Lancaster: Eastern Synod, 1943.

105. NICHOLS, JAMES H. *Romanticism in American Theology: Nevin and Schaff at Mercersburg*. Chicago: University of Chicago Press, 1961.

106. *The Reverend John H. A. Bomberger*. Centenary volume published by Ursinus College. Philadelphia: Publication Board of the Reformed Church in the U.S., 1917.

107. RICHARDS, GEORGE W., "A Forgotten Theology," *Church History*, IX (1940), 3-19.

108. ———. *History of the Theological Seminary of the German Reformed Church in the United States, 1825-1934* [and the] *Evangelical and Reformed Church, 1934-1952*. Lancaster: Rudisill, 1952.

109. ———. "The Life and Work of Philip Schaff," *Bulletin*. Lancaster: Theological Seminary of the Evangelical and Reformed Church, XV (1944), 155-72.

110. ———. "The Mercersburg Theology," *Church History*, XX (1951), 42-55.

111. ———. "Philip Schaff—Prophet of Church Union," *Christendom*, X (1945), 463-71.

112. SCHAFF, DAVID S. *The Life of Philip Schaff*. New York: Scribner, 1897.

113. *The Semi-Centennial of Philip Schaff*. New York: privately printed, 1893. Appendix: Chronological List of Dr. Schaff's Writings, pp. 57-66.

114. SHAW, P. E. *The Catholic Apostolic Church* (sometimes called *Irvingite*). New York: King's Crown Press, 1946.

115. SHRIVER, GEORGE H., JR. "Philip Schaff's Concept of Organic Historiography," interpreted in relation to the realization of an "evangelical Catholicism" within the Christian community. Ph.D. dissertation, Duke University, 1961.

116. THOMPSON, BARD. "The Catechism and the Mercersburg Theology," *Essays on the Heidelberg Catechism* (Philadelphia: United Church Press, 1963), Chap. 3.

117. TROST, THEODORE L. "Philip Schaff's Concept of the Church," with Special Reference to His Role in the Mercersburg Movement, 1844-1864. Ph.D. dissertation, Edinburgh University, 1958.

118. YODER, DONALD H. "Church Union Efforts of the Reformed Church in the United States to 1934." Ph.D. dissertation, University of Chicago, 1947.